HOW TO BE A LEADER

ANCIENT WISDOM FOR MODERN READERS

■ ■ ■ ■

HOW TO BE A LEADER

■ ■ ■ ■ ■

An Ancient Guide to Wise Leadership

Plutarch

Selected, translated, and introduced
by Jeffrey Beneker

PRINCETON UNIVERSITY PRESS
PRINCETON AND OXFORD

Published by Princeton University Press
41 William Street, Princeton, New Jersey 08540
6 Oxford Street, Woodstock, Oxfordshire OX20 1TR

press.princeton.edu

Library of Congress Cataloging-in-Publication Data

Names: Plutarch, author. | Beneker, Jeffrey, editor, translator, writer
of introduction. | Plutarch. Moralia. Selections. | Plutarch. Moralia.
Selections. English.
Title: How to be a leader : an ancient guide to wise leadership / Plutarch ;
edited, translated, and introduced by Jeffrey Beneker.
Description: Princeton : Princeton University Press, [2019] | Series:
Ancient wisdom for modern readers | In Ancient Greek with parallel
English translations on facing pages.
Identifiers: LCCN 2019019549 | ISBN 9780691192116 (hardcover)
Subjects: LCSH: Plutarch—Translations into English. | Leadership—
Early works to 1800.
Classification: LCC PA4368 .A23 2019 | DDC 873/.01—dc23
LC record available at https://lccn.loc.gov/2019019549

British Library Cataloging-in-Publication Data is available

Editorial: Rob Tempio and Matt Rohal
Production Editorial: Ali Parrington
Text and Jacket Design: Pamela L. Schnitter
Production: Merli Guerra and Brigid Ackerman
Publicity: Jodi Price, Amy Stewart, and Alyssa Sanford

Jacket/Cover Credit: The Athena Giustiniani, or Giustiniani Minerva.
Parian marble. Antonine Roman copy, 2nd century. Detail. Prisma
Archivo / Alamy Stock Photo

This book has been composed in Stemple Garamond LT,
Futura and Brill

Printed on acid-free paper. ∞

Printed in the United States of America

3 5 7 9 10 8 6 4 2

FOR HELEN AND LUIS

CONTENTS

INTRODUCTION

If you were a builder or stonecutter in the year 100 CE and happened to live near Chaeronea, a small city in central Greece, you might have been hired by Plutarch for a public works project. He would have been in his mid-fifties, too old to perform any heavy lifting himself, but eager to represent the people of Chaeronea and to supervise your work. And if you asked him why he—a learned and prolific writer who had studied in Athens, lectured in Rome, and made connections among the highest ranks of imperial society—bothered with such mundane local matters, like the installation of roofing tiles and the pouring of cement, he would have said, "I'm not building these things for myself, but for my native city." "City before self," in fact, might have been a motto that you heard him repeat quite often. It was certainly the basic principle of his political thought, especially as that thought is expressed in the three essays included in this collection: *To an Uneducated Leader*, *How to Be a Good Leader*, and *Should an Old Man Engage in Politics?*

For centuries leading up to Plutarch's time, the city had been the fundamental political unit of the Greek world. Often referred to as city-states, Greek cities before the advent of the Roman Empire were independent entities, with their own armies, foreign policy, trade, and political systems. Under Roman control, and so in Plutarch's day, they remained semi-independent, no longer involved directly in wars or foreign affairs, but still responsible for managing their internal matters, such as sponsoring festivals, raising funds, deciding legal disputes between citizens, and, of course, building public works. The city, then, was the environment in which Greek politicians operated. The English word "politics" is in fact borrowed from Greek and derived from *polis*, the word for city.

An underlying assumption of Plutarch's essays is that all who wished to become civic leaders first had to gain the confidence of their constituents, that is, of their fellow citizens. They practiced politics, and so built their reputations, by speaking in court, holding elected office, and performing benefactions and voluntary service. The rostrum, or speaker's platform, is especially important in Plutarch's view of political life. There politicians had their greatest visibility, as they attempted to persuade (and sometimes to trick) their fellow citizens into supporting their programs through legislation, decrees, and the allocation of funds. Leaders could expect to win prestige when the city prospered, and to be blamed when it did not. The accumulation of prestige (and the avoidance of blame) might lead in turn not only to election to more important offices, but also to civic honors and high-profile assignments, such as an embassy to a Roman official or an appointment to a prominent council or priesthood. It is important to note that these politicians were not professionals. They were elite men whose wealth allowed them the leisure for public service, and whose status could be established or enhanced through civic leadership. They would even be expected to use their fortunes to benefit their cities, by funding building projects, for example, or sponsoring festivals. Thus, politics was a place for aristocrats to perform the obligations of their rank and to compete against one another.

The political arena, in fact, was quite similar to the athletic arena, and Plutarch frequently employs the language of athletics—speaking of contests and competitors—to describe the interaction of politicians. As in sports, so in politics there were races to be won, which produced its own problems. Civic leaders might become focused on their own success rather than on the welfare of the state, conceiving of elections, for example, as competitions to be won mainly for the sake of winning, and interpreting electoral victory as proof of their general superiority. In such an environment, Plutarch's putative motto, "city before self," could easily be inverted, as politicians sought not only to enhance their reputations, but also to promote their friends and to enrich themselves at the public's expense. Their fellow citizens could become tired of all the winning, however, even when the winners had the city's best interests at heart, and so rather than praising successful politicians, the people might begin to envy them. Envy, in turn, often inspired attempts to derail a politician's ascendant career by means of factional opposition and personal attacks. None of this was good for a city's well-being.

In the three essays presented here, Plutarch seeks above all to emphasize that political leaders must subordinate their own interests to those of the state. Or, rather, he argues in various ways that the welfare of the individual and the welfare of the state are one and the same thing. Thus, he expects the successful political career to be established first and foremost upon an individual's character and personal integrity. The better the person, the better the leader; and the better the leader, the better the state. He makes this argument directly in *To an Uneducated Leader*, where it takes a theoretical form. In the other two essays, however, Plutarch grounds his advice and arguments in the lived experiences of great (and sometimes failed) leaders of the past. His essays are in that sense a roll call of the most famous political and military leaders of Greco-Roman history. He is aware, however, that times have changed, and that the leaders of the past commanded large armies and governed powerful cities, while those of his day operated in a more restricted sphere: Rome lurks ever in the background, furnishing peace and

political stability, but also ready to crush
the overly ambitious leader who reaches
too far. Plutarch is careful, therefore, to
distill from his examples the essence of
wise political leadership rather than simply to promote greatness. We read, for
example, how Themistocles and Aristides
set aside their partisan rivalry whenever
they were representing Athens abroad;
how Cato the Elder dedicated his life to
serving Rome but refused any and all material honors; how Theopompus, king of
Sparta, surrendered some of his power in
order to make the monarchy more stable;
and how Epaminondas of Thebes took the
same pride in overseeing the streets as he
did in leading the army. Relying on the
experiences of these and dozens of other
historical figures, Plutarch makes examples
from the past relevant to his contemporary

audience, and in the process, he has made them relevant to a modern audience as well.

Plutarch was uniquely suited to write these theoretical and practical essays. Both a native of Greece and a citizen of Rome, he lived during the first and early second centuries of the modern era. Though he called Chaeronea home, he traveled widely, made friends among the Roman elite, and held a priesthood at Delphi. His vast knowledge of politics, philosophy, and history gave him a unique ability not only to observe and evaluate his own time, the period when the Roman Empire was at its height, but also to reflect on both the Greek and the Roman past. His most ambitious literary project was the *Parallel Lives*, a series of biographies that pair the life of a Greek statesman with that of a Roman in a single book. He also wrote many essays, collectively known as the *Moralia*, on diverse topics, including politics, ethics, philosophy, and religion. The essays in this book come from that collection.

Both the *Parallel Lives* and the *Moralia* were read widely for more than a millennium after Plutarch's lifetime, especially in the Greek-speaking realm of the Byzantine Empire. They were first translated into French and English during the sixteenth century, when they began to influence political thinkers and authors, most famously Shakespeare. In the eighteenth century, the *Parallel Lives* in particular were read for their insight into leadership and government by some of the American founding fathers, who might well have imagined themselves as modern-day Greeks and Romans. Thus, they probably found men like Pericles and Cato to be inspiring role

models. Times have changed again, however, and so has the profile of the modern
leader. Although Plutarch imagined a male
politician, his focus on general principles
of leadership make his essays accessible to
anyone involved in democratic politics, not
just in their native city, but at the state and
national levels as well.

NOTES ON THE TRANSLATION
AND GREEK TEXT

Because Plutarch read so widely in Greek literature, he often expressed his thoughts by quoting from literary texts. In the essays collected here, Plutarch frequently invokes the words of Homer, Pindar, Sophocles, and Euripides, among others. When he does so, I have provided the specific references in the notes. At times he quotes from literature that has been lost to us and for which we lack even the names of the authors and the titles of the works. In those cases, I have put the words or phrases in quotation marks but have not included any reference.

Plutarch also names many historical figures and sometimes employs technical terms, especially when referring to offices in the Roman political system. For some of these people and terms, the essays themselves explain their meaning, or a simple note is sufficient. For the others, especially those that appear frequently, I have provided very brief biographies and definitions in an appendix.

As mentioned in the introduction, Plutarch's essays emphasize general principles of leadership that apply to everyone. Even so, he assumed a male readership and that anyone practicing politics would also be male. In places where he expresses this assumption by using masculine pronouns, I have taken the liberty of broadening his view by making the translation gender neutral. Even so, he sometimes uses examples that will strike the modern reader as archaic: the Persian king should be master of his wife, for instance, or managing the household is women's work. These are artifacts of Plutarch's world, and I have let them stand in translation.

The Greek text published here comes from Plutarch, *Moralia Volume X* (Harvard University Press, 1936) in the Loeb Classical Library, with only minor changes. The three essays in this volume have the following titles in the Loeb edition: *To an Uneducated Ruler* (*Ad principem ineruditum*), *Precepts of Statecraft* (*Praecepta gerendae reipublicae*), and *Whether an Old Man Should Engage in Public Affairs* (*An seni respublica gerenda sit*).

HOW TO BE A LEADER

TO AN UNEDUCATED LEADER

In this brief essay, Plutarch refutes the notion that the benefit of holding office is merely the opportunity to exercise power. This is the myopic stance of uneducated leaders, whom he portrays as insecure and afraid of the people they govern. Educated leaders, conversely, are primarily concerned with the welfare of their constituents, even at the expense of their own power or safety. A leader becomes educated, in Plutarch's view, by exposure to philosophy, and in particular to moral philosophy. The greatest benefit to be derived from this sort of education is the development of the *Logos*, or Reason, which is essential to controlling one's emotions and impulses. Leaders who allow themselves to be governed by Reason will in turn govern their cities benevolently. The uneducated leader, on the other hand, is plagued by greed, paranoia, and a false sense of grandeur.

Plutarch holds out god in this essay as the ideal to which leaders should compare and assimilate themselves. This god, however, is not one of the deities of the polytheistic Greek religion, but rather a philosophical concept that Plutarch has borrowed from Plato. It represents a pure Reason and the perfection of moral virtue. Plutarch conceives of this deity as existing in the heavens, where the sun becomes its physical manifestation. And just as the sun in the sky represents the perfection of the deity, so the leader who is governed by Reason exhibits an example of virtue to the citizens of a city, and, even more, this virtuous leader may in turn make the citizens virtuous. Thus, good political leadership depends not on formulating and executing particular policies, but on the moral development of the leaders themselves.

■ ■ ■

ΠΡΟΣ ΗΓΕΜΟΝΑ ΑΠΑΙΔΕΥΤΟΝ

1. Πλάτωνα Κυρηναῖοι παρεκάλουν νόμους τε
γραψάμενον αὐτοῖς ἀπολιπεῖν καὶ διακοσμῆσαι
τὴν πολιτείαν, ὁ δὲ παρῃτήσατο φήσας
χαλεπὸν εἶναι Κυρηναίοις νομοθετεῖν οὕτως
εὐτυχοῦσιν· "οὐδὲν γὰρ οὕτω γαῦρον" καὶ
τραχὺ καὶ δύσαρκτον "ὡς ἀνὴρ ἔφυ" εὐπραγίας
δοκούσης ἐπιλαμβανόμενος. διὸ τοῖς ἄρχουσι
χαλεπόν ἐστι σύμβουλον περὶ ἀρχῆς γενέσθαι·
τὸν γὰρ λόγον ὥσπερ ἄρχοντα παραδέξασθαι
φοβοῦνται, μὴ τῆς ἐξουσίας αὐτῶν τἀγαθὸν
κολούσῃ τῷ καθήκοντι δουλωσάμενος. οὐ
γὰρ ἴσασι τὰ Θεοπόμπου τοῦ Σπαρτιατῶν
βασιλέως, ὃς πρῶτος ἐν Σπάρτῃ τοῖς
βασιλεύουσι καταμίξας τοὺς Ἐφόρους, εἶτ'
ὀνειδιζόμενος ὑπὸ τῆς γυναικός, εἰ τοῖς παισὶν

1. The people of Cyrene were entreating Plato to write laws for them and to reorganize their constitution, but he declined, claiming that it would be difficult to establish laws for the Cyreneans because they were so well off. "For nothing is so naturally haughty" and harsh and hard to govern "as a man" who has acquired a reputation for success.[1] For the same reason, it is difficult to act as an advisor about governing to those who hold office, because they are afraid to accept Reason as their own governor, for fear that it will make them subservient to the obligations of their office and so reduce the benefit of their power. These people

ἐλάττονα παραδώσει τὴν ἀρχὴν ἧς παρέλαβε,
"μείζονα μὲν οὖν," εἶπεν, "ὅσῳ καὶ βεβαιοτέραν."
τὸ γὰρ σφοδρὸν ἀνεὶς καὶ ἄκρατον αὐτῆς
ἅμα τῷ φθόνῳ διέφυγε τὸν κίνδυνον. καίτοι
Θεόπομπος μὲν εἰς ἑτέρους τὸ τῆς ἀρχῆς
ὥσπερ ῥεύματος μεγάλου παροχετευσάμενος,
ὅσον ἄλλοις ἔδωκεν, αὑτοῦ περιέκοψεν· ὁ δ᾽ ἐκ
φιλοσοφίας τῷ ἄρχοντι πάρεδρος καὶ φύλαξ
ἐγκατοικισθεὶς λόγος, ὥσπερ εὐεξίας τῆς
δυνάμεως τὸ ἐπισφαλὲς ἀφαιρῶν, ἀπολείπει τὸ
ὑγιαῖνον.

do not know the example of Theopompus, king of the Spartans, who was the first in Sparta to involve the ephors in the affairs of the kings. When his wife reproached him with the complaint that he would leave to his children an office that was weaker than the one he had received, he replied, "Actually it will be stronger, to the same degree that it is more stable." For by letting go of the excessive and absolute character of his office, he escaped envy and so avoided danger. And yet, when Theopompus diverted royal power to the ephors, which was like diverting the current of a great stream, he deprived himself of whatever power he granted to them. Reason that has been conditioned by philosophy, however, once it has been established as a counselor and protector of the one who governs, removes the unstable element of power and leaves

2. Ἀλλὰ νοῦν οὐκ ἔχοντες οἱ πολλοὶ τῶν
βασιλέων καὶ ἀρχόντων μιμοῦνται τοὺς
ἀτέχνους ἀνδριαντοποιούς, οἳ νομίζουσι
μεγάλους καὶ ἁδροὺς φαίνεσθαι τοὺς
κολοσσούς, ἂν διαβεβηκότας σφόδρα καὶ
διατεταμένους καὶ κεχηνότας πλάσωσι· καὶ
γὰρ οὗτοι βαρύτητι φωνῆς καὶ βλέμματος
τραχύτητι καὶ δυσκολίᾳ τρόπων καὶ ἀμιξίᾳ
διαίτης ὄγκον ἡγεμονίας καὶ σεμνότητα
μιμεῖσθαι δοκοῦσιν, οὐδ᾽ ὁτιοῦν τῶν
κολοσσικῶν διαφέροντες ἀνδριάντων, οἳ
τὴν ἔξωθεν ἡρωικὴν καὶ θεοπρεπῆ μορφὴν
ἔχοντες ἐντός εἰσι γῆς μεστοὶ καὶ λίθου καὶ
μολίβδου· πλὴν ὅτι τῶν μὲν ἀνδριάντων ταῦτα
τὰ βάρη τὴν ὀρθότητα μόνιμον καὶ ἀκλινῆ
διαφυλάττει, οἱ δ᾽ ἀπαίδευτοι στρατηγοὶ

behind what is sound, just as happens when we apply Reason to the maintenance of our health.

2. Most kings and leaders, however, lack sense, and so they imitate the unskilled sculptors who believe that their colossal statues appear great and strong when they fashion their figures with a mighty stride, a straining body, and a gaping mouth. These kings and leaders, because they speak with a low-pitched voice, cast a harsh gaze, affect a cantankerous manner, and hold themselves aloof in their daily lives, suppose that they are imitating the dignity and solemnity of leadership. In fact, they are not at all different from those colossal statues, which on the exterior possess a heroic and divine facade but inside are filled with earth and stone and lead.[2] In the case of the statues,

καὶ ἡγεμόνες ὑπὸ τῆς ἐντὸς ἀγνωμοσύνης
πολλάκις σαλεύονται καὶ περιτρέπονται·
βάσει γὰρ οὐ κειμένῃ πρὸς ὀρθὰς ἐξουσίαν
ἐποικοδομοῦντες ὑψηλὴν συναπονεύουσι.
δεῖ δέ, ὥσπερ ὁ κανὼν αὐτός, ἀστραβὴς
γενόμενος καὶ ἀδιάστροφος, οὕτως ἀπευθύνει
τὰ λοιπὰ τῇ πρὸς αὐτὸν ἐφαρμογῇ καὶ
παραθέσει συνεξομοιῶν, παραπλησίως τὸν
ἄρχοντα πρῶτον τὴν ἀρχὴν κτησάμενον
ἐν ἑαυτῷ καὶ κατευθύναντα τὴν ψυχὴν καὶ
καταστησάμενον τὸ ἦθος οὕτω συναρμόττειν
τὸ ὑπήκοον· οὔτε γὰρ πίπτοντός ἐστιν ὀρθοῦν
οὔτε διδάσκειν ἀγνοοῦντος οὔτε κοσμεῖν
ἀκοσμοῦντος ἢ τάττειν ἀτακτοῦντος ἢ
ἄρχειν μὴ ἀρχομένου· ἀλλ᾽ οἱ πολλοὶ κακῶς
φρονοῦντες οἴονται πρῶτον ἐν τῷ ἄρχειν
ἀγαθὸν εἶναι τὸ μὴ ἄρχεσθαι, καὶ ὅ γε Περσῶν
βασιλεὺς πάντας ἡγεῖτο δούλους πλὴν
τῆς αὑτοῦ γυναικός, ἧς μάλιστα δεσπότης
ὤφειλεν εἶναι.

however, this weight keeps their upright posture stable and steady, while uneducated generals and leaders are oftentimes tripped up and toppled over by their innate foolishness. For they establish their lofty power upon a pedestal that has not been leveled, and so it cannot stand upright. Moreover, just as a builder's rule is first established straight and unbending, and then is used to correct the alignment of everything else through adjustments and juxtapositions with respect to it, in the very same way those who govern must first achieve governance of themselves, straighten out their souls, and set their character aright, and then they should assimilate their subjects to themselves. For the one who is tipping over cannot straighten up someone else, nor can the ignorant person teach, the disorderly establish order, the disorganized organize,

3. Τίς οὖν ἄρξει τοῦ ἄρχοντος; ὁ "νόμος ὁ
πάντων βασιλεὺς θνατῶν τε καὶ ἀθανάτων,"
ὡς ἔφη Πίνδαρος, οὐκ ἐν βιβλίοις ἔξω
γεγραμμένος οὐδέ τισι ξύλοις, ἀλλ᾽ ἔμψυχος
ὢν ἐν αὐτῷ λόγος, ἀεὶ συνοικῶν καὶ
παραφυλάττων καὶ μηδέποτε τὴν ψυχὴν
ἐῶν ἔρημον ἡγεμονίας. ὁ μὲν γὰρ Περσῶν
βασιλεὺς ἕνα τῶν κατευναστῶν εἶχε πρὸς
τοῦτο τεταγμένον, ὥσθ᾽ ἕωθεν εἰσιόντα
λέγειν πρὸς αὐτὸν "ἀνάστα, ὦ βασιλεῦ, καὶ
φρόντιζε πραγμάτων, ὧν σε φροντίζειν ὁ μέγας

the ungoverned govern. But most leaders misunderstand this, thinking instead that the greatest benefit in governing is the freedom from being governed themselves. Take the king of the Persians for instance: He believed that everyone was his slave except for his wife, over whom he ought especially to have been the master.

3. Who, then, will govern the governor? "The law, which is king of everyone, both mortals and immortals," as Pindar says. But I am not referring to a law that has been written in books or on any wooden tablets to be read, but I mean Reason, which exists within those who govern, always accompanying and guarding their souls, and never allowing them to lack guidance. Now, the Persian king assigned to one of his attendants this task: to come to him at dawn and

Ὡρομάσδης ἠθέλησε"· τοῦ δὲ πεπαιδευμένου
καὶ σωφρονοῦντος ἄρχοντος ἐντός ἐστιν ὁ
τοῦτο φθεγγόμενος ἀεὶ καὶ παρακελευόμενος.
Πολέμων γὰρ ἔλεγε τὸν ἔρωτα εἶναι "θεῶν
ὑπηρεσίαν εἰς νέων ἐπιμέλειαν καὶ σωτηρίαν"·
ἀληθέστερον δ᾽ ἄν τις εἴποι τοὺς ἄρχοντας
ὑπηρετεῖν θεῷ πρὸς ἀνθρώπων ἐπιμέλειαν καὶ
σωτηρίαν, ὅπως ὧν θεὸς δίδωσιν ἀνθρώποις
καλῶν καὶ ἀγαθῶν τὰ μὲν νέμωσι τὰ δὲ
φυλάττωσιν.

Ὁρᾷς τὸν ὑψοῦ τόνδ᾽ ἄπειρον αἰθέρα,
    καὶ γῆν πέριξ ἔχονθ᾽ ὑγραῖς ἐν ἀγκάλαις;

ὁ μὲν καθίησιν ἀρχὰς σπερμάτων προσηκόντων
γῆ δ᾽ ἀναδίδωσιν, αὔξεται δὲ τὰ μὲν ὄμβροις
τὰ δ᾽ ἀνέμοις τὰ δ᾽ ἄστροις ἐπιθαλπόμενα καὶ
σελήνῃ, κοσμεῖ δ᾽ ἥλιος ἅπαντα καὶ πᾶσι τοῦτο
δὴ τὸ παρ᾽ αὐτοῦ φίλτρον ἐγκεράννυσιν. ἀλλὰ
τῶν τοιούτων καὶ τηλικούτων ἃ θεοὶ χαρίζονται

to say, "Arise, O king, and attend to the matters that the great Ahuramazda wants you to attend to."[3] But this voice is always present within educated and self-controlled leaders, speaking out and exhorting them. Polemon used to say that erotic love was "a service of the gods intended for the care and well-being of young people." One might more truly say that those who govern serve god for the care and well-being of their fellow humans, with the aim of disbursing some of the noble and good gifts that god grants, and protecting the rest.

"Do you see this boundless sky, up on high and enfolding the earth in its soft embrace?"[4] The sky sends down the beginnings of the necessary seeds, while the earth yields them up. Some will grow from rain, others from wind, and others when warmed on their surface by the stars and

δώρων καὶ ἀγαθῶν οὐκ ἔστιν ἀπόλαυσις
οὐδὲ χρῆσις ὀρθὴ δίχα νόμου καὶ δίκης καὶ
ἄρχοντος. δίκη μὲν οὖν νόμου τέλος ἐστί,
νόμος δ᾽ ἄρχοντος ἔργον, ἄρχων δ᾽ εἰκὼν θεοῦ
τοῦ πάντα κοσμοῦντος, οὐ Φειδίου δεόμενος
πλάττοντος οὐδὲ Πολυκλείτου καὶ Μύρωνος,
ἀλλ᾽ αὐτὸς αὑτὸν εἰς ὁμοιότητα θεῷ δι᾽ ἀρετῆς
καθιστὰς καὶ δημιουργῶν ἀγαλμάτων τὸ
ἥδιστον ὀφθῆναι καὶ θεοπρεπέστατον.
    Οἷον δ᾽ ἥλιον ἐν οὐρανῷ περικαλλὲς
εἴδωλον ἑαυτοῦ καὶ σελήνην ὁ θεὸς ἐνίδρυσε,
τοιοῦτον ἐν πόλεσι μίμημα καὶ φέγγος ἄρχων
"ὅστε θεουδὴς εὐδικίας ἀνέχῃσι," τουτέστι
θεοῦ λόγον ἔχων, διάνοιαν, οὐ σκῆπτρον οὐδὲ
κεραυνὸν οὐδὲ τρίαιναν, ὡς ἔνιοι πλάττουσιν
ἑαυτοὺς καὶ γράφουσι τῷ ἀνεφίκτῳ ποιοῦντες
ἐπίφθονον τὸ ἀνόητον· νεμεσᾷ γὰρ ὁ θεὸς τοῖς
ἀπομιμουμένοις βροντὰς καὶ κεραυνοὺς καὶ
ἀκτινοβολίας, τοὺς δὲ τὴν ἀρετὴν ζηλοῦντας
αὐτοῦ καὶ πρὸς τὸ καλὸν καὶ φιλάνθρωπον

moon; and the sun arranges everything and mixes its own charm into all that grows. But of the good gifts which the gods give— gifts that are so great and so many—there is no enjoyment or proper use of them that is separate from law and justice and a leader. Justice, in fact, is the aim of the law, and law is the work of the leader, and the leader is the image of god, who gives order to everything. True leaders require no Phidias to fashion them, no Polyclitus and no Myron, because they on their own transform themselves into the likeness of god through virtue, creating a real-life statue that is the most pleasant to look upon and the most fitting image of a god.[5]

And so, just as god has established the sun in the sky as a beautiful image of himself, and the moon as well, so in cities there is a facsimile of god and a source of light:

ἀφομοιοῦντας ἑαυτοὺς ἡδόμενος αὔξει καὶ
μεταδίδωσι τῆς περὶ αὐτὸν εὐνομίας καὶ δίκης
καὶ ἀληθείας καὶ πραότητος· ὧν θειότερον
οὐ πῦρ ἐστιν οὐ φῶς οὐχ ἡλίου δρόμος οὐκ
ἀνατολαὶ καὶ δύσεις ἄστρων οὐ τὸ ἀίδιον καὶ
ἀθάνατον. οὐ γὰρ χρόνῳ ζωῆς ὁ θεὸς εὐδαίμων
ἀλλὰ τῆς ἀρετῆς τῷ ἄρχοντι· τοῦτο γὰρ θεῖόν
ἐστι, καλὸν δ᾽ αὐτῆς καὶ τὸ ἀρχόμενον.

the leader "who is god-fearing and upholds righteousness."[6] That is to say, the leader who possesses the Reason and the intellect of god, but not one who holds a scepter or lightning bolt or trident, as some fashion themselves in images and describe themselves in writing, thus making their foolishness odious by adding to it what in fact is unattainable. For god resents those who imitate thunder and lightning and shooting rays of light, but he is pleased with those who eagerly pursue his virtue and assimilate themselves to true beauty and benevolence. These he strengthens, and to these he gives a share of his order, justice, truth, and mildness. Fire is not more divine than they are, nor is light, nor the course of the sun, nor the risings and settings of stars, nor eternity and immortality. For god is fortunate not in his longevity, but in the governing ability

4. Ἀνάξαρχος μὲν οὖν ἐπὶ τῷ Κλείτου φόνῳ
δεινοπαθοῦντα παραμυθούμενος Ἀλέξανδρον
ἔφη καὶ τῷ Διὶ τὴν Δίκην εἶναι καὶ τὴν Θέμιν
παρέδρους, ἵνα πᾶν πραττόμενον ὑπὸ βασιλέως
θεμιτὸν δοκῇ καὶ δίκαιον, οὐκ ὀρθῶς οὐδ᾽
ὠφελίμως τὴν ἐφ᾽ οἷς ἥμαρτε μετάνοιαν αὐτοῦ
τῷ πρὸς τὰ ὅμοια θαρρύνειν ἰώμενος. εἰ δὲ δεῖ
ταῦτ᾽ εἰκάζειν, ὁ μὲν Ζεὺς οὐκ ἔχει τὴν Δίκην
πάρεδρον, ἀλλ᾽ αὐτὸς Δίκη καὶ Θέμις ἐστὶ
καὶ νόμων ὁ πρεσβύτατος καὶ τελειότατος. οἱ
δὲ παλαιοὶ οὕτω λέγουσι καὶ γράφουσι καὶ
διδάσκουσιν, ὡς ἄνευ Δίκης ἄρχειν μηδὲ τοῦ
Διὸς καλῶς δυναμένου· "ἡ δέ γε παρθένος
ἐστὶ" καθ᾽ Ἡσίοδον ἀδιάφθορος, αἰδοῦς καὶ
σωφροσύνης καὶ ὠφελείας σύνοικος· ὅθεν
"αἰδοίους" προσαγορεύουσι τοὺς βασιλεῖς·

of his virtue. For this is a divine thing, and noble, too, is the ability of his virtue to be governed.

4. When Anaxarchus was consoling Alexander, who was despondent over his murder of Cleitus,[7] he said that Justice and Right were attendants to Zeus, so that everything done by a king was by definition righteous and just.[8] But in his attempt to assuage Alexander's remorse for his crime, he encouraged similar actions in the future. This was wrong and harmful. For if we must find a model for this situation, it would not be to say that Zeus has Justice as an attendant, but that Zeus himself is Justice and Right, and that he is the eldest and most perfect of laws. The ancient authors and teachers tell us, however, that not even Zeus is able to govern nobly apart from Justice. "She is a

μάλιστα γὰρ αἰδεῖσθαι προσήκει τοῖς ἥκιστα
φοβουμένοις. φοβεῖσθαι δὲ δεῖ τὸν ἄρχοντα τοῦ
παθεῖν κακῶς μᾶλλον τὸ ποιῆσαι· τοῦτο γὰρ
αἴτιόν ἐστιν ἐκείνου καὶ οὗτός ἐστιν ὁ φόβος
τοῦ ἄρχοντος φιλάνθρωπος καὶ οὐκ ἀγεννής,
ὑπὲρ τῶν ἀρχομένων δεδιέναι μὴ λάθωσι
βλαβέντες,

ὡς δὲ κύνες περὶ μῆλα δυσωρήσονται ἐν
αὐλῇ,
θηρὸς ἀκούσαντες κρατερόφρονος,

οὐχ ὑπὲρ αὑτῶν ἀλλ᾽ ὑπὲρ τῶν φυλαττομένων.
Ὁ δ᾽ Ἐπαμεινώνδας, εἰς ἑορτήν τινα καὶ
πότον ἀνειμένως τῶν Θηβαίων ῥυέντων,
μόνος ἐφώδευε τὰ ὅπλα καὶ τὰ τείχη, νήφειν
λέγων καὶ ἀγρυπνεῖν ὡς ἂν ἐξῇ τοῖς ἄλλοις
μεθύειν καὶ καθεύδειν. καὶ Κάτων ἐν Ἰτύκῃ
τοὺς ἄλλους ἅπαντας ἀπὸ τῆς ἥττης ἐκήρυττε
πέμπειν ἐπὶ θάλατταν· καὶ ἐμβιβάσας,

maiden," writes Hesiod,[9] uncorrupted, and the companion of reverence, self-control, and profit. For this reason, they call kings "reverend," for it is appropriate that those who are least fearful should be most revered. Leaders, in fact, must be more afraid of inflicting harm than of suffering harm themselves. This is what causes them to be revered. This is the benevolent and noble sort of fear that leaders possess: to be afraid on behalf of those they govern, and so to remain vigilant and keep their constituents from harm, "just as dogs keep careful watch over flocks in the pen. When they've heard a stouthearted wild beast,"[10] they act not in their own interests but on behalf of those they are protecting.

Take Epaminondas, for example. When his fellow Thebans had abandoned themselves to a drunken festival, he alone kept watch

εὔπλοιαν εὐξάμενος ὑπὲρ αὐτῶν, εἰς οἶκον
ἐπανελθὼν ἑαυτὸν ἀπέσφαξε· διδάξας ὑπὲρ
τίνων δεῖ τὸν ἄρχοντα τῷ φόβῳ χρῆσθαι καὶ
τίνων δεῖ τὸν ἄρχοντα καταφρονεῖν. Κλέαρχος
δ᾽ ὁ Ποντικὸς τύραννος εἰς κιβωτὸν ἐνδυόμενος
ὥσπερ ὄφις ἐκάθευδε. καὶ Ἀριστόδημος ὁ
Ἀργεῖος εἰς ὑπερῷον οἴκημα θύραν ἔχον
ἐπιρρακτήν, ἧς ἐπάνω τιθεὶς τὸ κλινίδιον
ἐκάθευδε μετὰ τῆς ἑταίρας· ἡ δὲ μήτηρ ἐκείνης
ὑφεῖλκε κάτωθεν τὸ κλιμάκιον, εἶθ᾽ ἡμέρας
πάλιν προσετίθει φέρουσα. πῶς οὗτος, οἴεσθε,
τὸ θέατρον ἐπεφρίκει καὶ τὸ ἀρχεῖον, τὸ
βουλευτήριον, τὸ συμπόσιον, ὁ τὸν θάλαμον
ἑαυτῷ δεσμωτήριον πεποιηκώς; τῷ γὰρ ὄντι
δεδίασιν οἱ βασιλεῖς ὑπὲρ τῶν ἀρχομένων, οἱ
δὲ τύραννοι τοὺς ἀρχομένους· διὸ τῇ δυνάμει
τὸ δέος συναύξουσι· πλειόνων γὰρ ἄρχοντες
πλείονας φοβοῦνται.

over the city's weapons and walls, saying that by remaining sober and awake he was freeing the others to get drunk and sleep. Or consider Cato the Younger at Utica. Following their defeat in battle, he ordered that everyone be sent to the coast, and after embarking them on ships and praying for good sailing, he returned to his quarters and committed suicide. Thus, he has taught us on whose behalf a leader ought to be afraid and what things a leader ought to scorn.[11] But Clearchus, the tyrant of Heraclea Pontica, used to curl himself into a box like a snake when he went to sleep. And Aristodemus of Argos used to go up into a room on the second floor through a trap door, and after moving his bed on top of the door, he would sleep there with his mistress, while the woman's mother would take away the ladder from below and then put it back again in

5. Οὐ γὰρ εἰκὸς οὐδὲ πρέπον, ὥσπερ ἔνιοι
φιλόσοφοι λέγουσι, τὸν θεὸν ἐν ὕλῃ πάντα
πασχούσῃ καὶ πράγμασι μυρίας δεχομένοις
ἀνάγκας καὶ τύχας καὶ μεταβολὰς ὑπάρχειν
ἀναμεμιγμένον· ἀλλ᾽ ὁ μὲν ἄνω που περὶ τὴν ἀεὶ
κατὰ ταὐτὰ ὡσαύτως φύσιν ἔχουσαν ἱδρυμένος
ἐν βάθροις ἁγίοις ᾗ φησι Πλάτων, εὐθείᾳ
περαίνει κατὰ φύσιν περιπορευόμενος· οἷον δ᾽
ἥλιος ἐν οὐρανῷ μίμημα τὸ περικαλλὲς αὑτοῦ

the morning.[12] How much, do you suppose, the theater and the town hall and the council chamber and the drinking party frightened this man, who had converted his own bedroom into a personal prison? In truth, kings are afraid *for* their subjects, while tyrants are afraid *of* their subjects.[13] And so, tyrants increase their fear in proportion to their power: the more people they rule, the more people they fear.

5. It is, indeed, neither likely nor fitting, as some philosophers claim, that god should exist intermingled with matter that is entirely passive or with substances that are liable to countless acts of compulsion and changes of fortune and fluctuations. Rather, up on high, somewhere near that nature which ever and always remains the same, god is established upon a holy pedestal, as

δι' ἐσόπτρου εἴδωλον ἀναφαίνεται τοῖς ἐκεῖνον
ἐνορᾶν δι' αὐτοῦ δυνατοῖς, οὕτω τὸ ἐν πόλεσι
φέγγος εὐδικίας καὶ λόγου τοῦ περὶ αὐτὸν
ὥσπερ εἰκόνα κατέστησεν, ἣν οἱ μακάριοι καὶ
σώφρονες ἐκ φιλοσοφίας ἀπογράφονται πρὸς
τὸ κάλλιστον τῶν πραγμάτων πλάττοντες
ἑαυτούς. ταύτην δ' οὐδὲν ἐμποιεῖ τὴν διάθεσιν
ἢ λόγος ἐκ φιλοσοφίας παραγενόμενος·
ἵνα μὴ πάσχωμεν τὸ τοῦ Ἀλεξάνδρου, ὃς ἐν
Κορίνθῳ Διογένην θεασάμενος καὶ δι' εὐφυΐαν
ἀγαπήσας καὶ θαυμάσας τὸ φρόνημα καὶ τὸ
μέγεθος τοῦ ἀνδρὸς εἶπεν, "εἰ μὴ Ἀλέξανδρος
ἤμην, Διογένης ἂν ἤμην"· ὀλίγου δέον εἰπεῖν,
τὴν περὶ αὐτὸν εὐτυχίαν καὶ λαμπρότητα
καὶ δύναμιν ὡς κώλυσιν ἀρετῆς καὶ ἀσχολίαν
βαρυνόμενος καὶ ζηλοτυπῶν τὸν τρίβωνα
καὶ τὴν πήραν, ὅτι τούτοις ἦν ἀνίκητος καὶ
ἀνάλωτος Διογένης, οὐχ ὡς ἐκεῖνος ὅπλοις καὶ
ἵπποις καὶ σαρίσσαις. ἐξῆν οὖν φιλοσοφοῦντα
καὶ τῇ διαθέσει γίγνεσθαι Διογένην καὶ τῇ τύχῃ

Plato says,[14] and "making his way along a straight path in accordance with nature, he completes his course."[15] Just as the sun in the sky appears plainly as a beautiful facsimile and mirror-image of god to those who are able to perceive him in it, so god has established in cities the light of righteousness and of his own Reason. This light acts as an image, which those who are blessed and self-controlled seek to replicate in themselves through philosophy, reshaping themselves closer to the absolute standard of goodness.[16] Nothing other than Reason developed through philosophy creates this character within a person. If we understand this, we may avoid making the same mistake as Alexander. For when he saw Diogenes at Corinth, he admired him for his natural abilities and marveled at his intellect and stature. Then he declared, "If I

μένειν Ἀλέξανδρον, καὶ διὰ τοῦτο γενέσθαι
Διογένην μᾶλλον, ὅτι ἦν Ἀλέξανδρος, ὡς
πρὸς τύχην μεγάλην πολὺ πνεῦμα καὶ σάλον
ἔχουσαν ἕρματος πολλοῦ καὶ κυβερνήτου
μεγάλου δεόμενον.

were not Alexander, I would be Diogenes." In saying this, he essentially affirmed that he was weighed down by his own good fortune, fame, and power, which acted as impediments to virtue and left him no time for anything else. He was further declaring that he envied the philosopher's ragged cloak and leather bag, because Diogenes was neither conquered nor held captive by them, while he himself was restrained by armor and horses and spears.[17] But it was, in fact, possible for him to practice philosophy, and so to become Diogenes in his character while remaining Alexander in his success. Indeed, because he was Alexander, he had all the more reason to become Diogenes, because with respect to his great success, which like a ship is subject to strong winds and rough seas, he was in need of heavy ballast and a stout pilot.

6. Ἐν μὲν γὰρ τοῖς ἀσθενέσι καὶ ταπεινοῖς καὶ
ἰδιώταις τῷ ἀδυνάτῳ μιγνύμενον τὸ ἀνόητον εἰς
τὸ ἀναμάρτητον τελευτᾷ, ὥσπερ ἐν ὀνείρασι
φαύλοις τις ἀνία τὴν ψυχὴν διαταράττει
συνεξαναστῆναι ταῖς ἐπιθυμίαις μὴ δυναμένην·
ἡ δ' ἐξουσία παραλαβοῦσα τὴν κακίαν νεῦρα
τοῖς πάθεσι προστίθησι· καὶ τὸ τοῦ Διονυσίου
ἀληθές ἐστιν· ἔφη γὰρ ἀπολαύειν μάλιστα τῆς
ἀρχῆς, ὅταν ταχέως ἃ βούλεται ποιῇ. μέγας οὖν
ὁ κίνδυνος βούλεσθαι ἃ μὴ δεῖ τὸν ἃ βούλεται
ποιεῖν δυνάμενον· "αὐτίκ' ἔπειτά γε μῦθος
ἔην, τετέλεστο δὲ ἔργον." ὀξὺν ἡ κακία διὰ τῆς
ἐξουσίας δρόμον ἔχουσα πᾶν πάθος ἐξωθεῖ,
ποιοῦσα τὴν ὀργὴν φόνον τὸν ἔρωτα μοιχείαν
τὴν πλεονεξίαν δήμευσιν. "αὐτίκ' ἔπειθ' ἅμα
μῦθος ἔην," καὶ ἀπόλωλεν ὁ προσκρούσας·
ὑπόνοια, καὶ τέθνηκεν ὁ διαβληθείς. ἀλλ'
ὥσπερ οἱ φυσικοὶ λέγουσι τὴν ἀστραπὴν
τῆς βροντῆς ὑστέραν μὲν ἐκπίπτειν ὡς αἷμα
τραύματος, προτέραν δὲ φαίνεσθαι, τὸν μὲν

6. For private citizens who are weak and obscure, however, lack of intelligence combines with a lack of power to result in no harm being done, just as in bad dreams when a sense of grief disturbs the soul, but the soul, though it has the will, is unable to respond. But political power, once it has latched onto depravity, gives physical strength to one's emotions. Thus, the saying of Dionysius proves to be true, for he declared that whenever he achieved his desires quickly, that was when he most enjoyed being tyrant. There is a great danger, then, when people who are able to accomplish what they wish in fact wish for things that are improper. "Then as soon as the word was spoken, the deed was accomplished."[18] Depravity, once combined with political power, races to give expression to every emotion: it converts anger into

ψόφον ἐκδεχομένης τῆς ἀκοῆς τῷ δὲ φωτὶ
τῆς ὄψεως ἀπαντώσης· οὕτως ἐν ταῖς ἀρχαῖς
φθάνουσιν αἱ κολάσεις τὰς κατηγορίας καὶ
προεκπίπτουσιν αἱ καταδίκαι τῶν ἀποδείξεων.

εἴκει γὰρ ἤδη θυμὸς οὐδ᾽ ἔτ᾽ ἀντέχει,
θινῶδες ὡς ἄγκιστρον ἀγκύρας σάλῳ,

ἂν μὴ βάρος ἔχων ὁ λογισμὸς ἐπιθλίβῃ καὶ
πιέζῃ τὴν ἐξουσίαν, μιμουμένου τὸν ἥλιον
τοῦ ἄρχοντος, ὃς ὅταν ὕψωμα λάβῃ μέγιστον,
ἐξαρθεὶς ἐν τοῖς βορείοις, ἐλάχιστα κινεῖται,
τῷ σχολαιοτέρῳ τὸν δρόμον εἰς ἀσφαλὲς
καθιστάμενος.

murder, love into adultery, and greed into the confiscation of property.[19] "Then as soon as the word was spoken," the offender was put to death. As soon as the suspicion was raised, the one who was slandered was killed. Scientists declare that lightning follows thunder, as blood flows after a wound is inflicted, even though we see the lightning first, because our sense of hearing passively awaits sound while our sense of sight actively encounters light.[20] Likewise, in the sphere of government, punishments may come before formal accusations, and indictments may precede the presentation of proof. "For the spirit is already yielding and no longer holds out, as the hook of an anchor lodged in sand yields when seas are rough," unless a weighty Reason presses down on and applies pressure to political power. For then a leader imitates the sun,

7. Οὐδὲ γὰρ λαθεῖν οἷόν τε τὰς κακίας ἐν
ταῖς ἐξουσίαις· ἀλλὰ τοὺς μὲν ἐπιληπτικούς,
ἂν ἐν ὕψει τινὶ γένωνται καὶ περιενεχθῶσιν,
ἴλιγγος ἴσχει καὶ σάλος, ἐξελέγχων τὸ πάθος
αὐτῶν, τοὺς δ᾽ ἀπαιδεύτους καὶ ἀμαθεῖς ἡ
τύχη μικρὸν ἐκκουφίσασα πλούτοις τισὶν
ἢ δόξαις ἢ ἀρχαῖς μετεώρους γενομένους
εὐθὺς ἐπιδείκνυσι πίπτοντας· μᾶλλον δ᾽,
ὥσπερ τῶν κενῶν ἀγγείων οὐκ ἂν διαγνοίης
τὸ ἀκέραιον καὶ πεπονηκός, ἀλλ᾽ ὅταν
ἐγχέῃς, φαίνεται τὸ ῥέον· οὕτως αἱ σαθραὶ
ψυχαὶ τὰς ἐξουσίας μὴ στέγουσαι ῥέουσιν
ἔξω ταῖς ἐπιθυμίαις, ταῖς ὀργαῖς, ταῖς
ἀλαζονείαις, ταῖς ἀπειροκαλίαις. καίτοι τί δεῖ
ταῦτα λέγειν, ὅπου καὶ τὰ σμικρότατα τῶν

which moves least when it achieves its greatest height, once it has ascended high into the northerly sky, and by taking its time, it makes its path more certain.

7. It is, of course, impossible for vices to go unnoticed when people hold positions of power. Epileptics begin to spin and rock back and forth when they go to high places and move around, and so height and motion expose their disease. Fortune, likewise, after elevating uneducated and unlearned people to even slight prominence through some wealth or glory or political office, immediately makes a show of their downfall. Or to put it another way, when jars are empty you cannot distinguish between those that are intact and those that are damaged, but once you fill them, then the leaks appear. Just so, cracked souls cannot

ἐλλειμμάτων περὶ τοὺς ἐπιφανεῖς καὶ ἐνδόξους
συκοφαντεῖται; Κίμωνος ἦν ὁ οἶνος διαβολή,
Σκιπίωνος ὁ ὕπνος, Λεύκολλος ἐπὶ τῷ δειπνεῖν
πολυτελέστερον ἤκουε κακῶς.

contain political power, but they leak with desire, anger, boasting, and vulgarity. But why must I go on about this, when we know that people criticize even the smallest of defects in prominent and famous leaders? Wine, for example, became a slander against Cimon, and sleep against Scipio,[21] while Lucullus was criticized for his overly luxurious dinners.

HOW TO BE A GOOD LEADER

The principles explained here are addressed
to Menemachus, a young man from Sardis in Asia Minor (modern Turkey), who
was just beginning his political career. As
we read both in this essay and in *Should
an Old Man Engage in Politics?*, Plutarch
firmly believed that the best way to learn
about the political life was to serve as an
apprentice to an experienced leader who
was willing to guide newcomers and build
up their confidence, while also shielding
them from hard realities until they could
stand on their own. Menemachus lacked
the time for this sort of on-the-job training, however, and so Plutarch agreed to

write this essay as a textbook of political leadership. As a substitute for observing actual leaders in action, Plutarch here offers numerous examples, both positive and negative, from the Greek and Roman past. All of his examples come from a time when Greek cities were independent states and the Roman Republic had not yet become an empire. Nonetheless, by emphasizing general principles, Plutarch attempts to make the experiences of leaders from the past relevant to the politicians of his own day. Topics that he discusses include personal integrity, the importance of friendships, how best to persuade one's fellow citizens, how not to provoke one's superiors, and the dangers inherent in rivalry and envy. The essay's overarching lesson is that the successful management of public affairs demands respect for the state's institutions, cooperation among politicians, and the subordination of one's own ambition to the welfare of the state.

Plutarch had much to say and many examples from which to choose. I have selected passages from the full essay that connect to themes in the other essays of this collection and that are most relevant to political life in a modern democracy or large organization. I have organized the various topics under separate headings to make them easier to identify, though the headings do not appear in the original Greek.

■ ■ ■

ΠΟΛΙΤΙΚΑ ΠΑΡΑΓΓΕΛΜΑΤΑ

Εἰ πρὸς ἄλλο τι χρήσασθαι καλῶς ἐστιν ἔχον, ὦ
Μενέμαχε, τῷ

οὔτις τοι τὸν μῦθον ὀνόσσεται ὅσσοι
 Ἀχαιοί,
οὐδὲ πάλιν ἐρέει· ἀτὰρ οὐ τέλος ἵκεο
 μύθων,

καὶ πρὸς τοὺς προτρεπομένους τῶν φιλοσόφων
διδάσκοντας δὲ μηδὲν μηδ' ὑποτιθεμένους·
ὅμοιοι γάρ εἰσι τοῖς τοὺς λύχνους προμύττουσιν
ἔλαιον δὲ μὴ ἐγχέουσιν. ὁρῶν οὖν σε
παρωρμημένον ἀξίως τῆς εὐγενείας ἐν τῇ
πατρίδι "μύθων τε ῥητῆρ' ἔμεναι πρηκτῆρά
τε ἔργων," ἐπειδὴ χρόνον οὐκ ἔχεις ἀνδρὸς

If it is right in any situation, Menemachus, to invoke these verses, "No one of all the Achaeans will reproach your speech, nor speak against it, though you have not had the final word,"[1] then we should invoke them in the case of philosophers who seek to influence us but neither teach nor explain anything. For they are like people who trim their lamps but add no oil. I see, then, that in accord with your noble status, you are motivated "to be a speaker of words and doer of deeds"[2] in your native city. Since you have time neither to master the philosopher's life at first hand through political activity and public contests, nor to

φιλοσόφου βίον ὕπαιθρον ἐν πράξεσι
πολιτικαῖς καὶ δημοσίοις ἀγῶσι κατανοῆσαι
καὶ γενέσθαι παραδειγμάτων ἔργῳ μὴ λόγῳ
περαινομένων θεατής, ἀξιοῖς δὲ παραγγέλματα
λαβεῖν πολιτικά, τὴν μὲν ἄρνησιν οὐδαμῶς
ἐμαυτῷ προσήκουσαν εἶναι νομίζω, τὸ δ᾽ ἔργον
εὔχομαι καὶ τῆς σῆς ἄξιον σπουδῆς καὶ τῆς
ἐμῆς προθυμίας γενέσθαι· τοῖς δὲ παραδείγμασι
ποικιλωτέροις, ὥσπερ ἠξίωσας, ἐχρησάμην.

Πρῶτον μὲν οὖν ὑποκείσθω πολιτείᾳ καθάπερ
ἔδαφος βέβαιον καὶ ἰσχυρὸν ἡ προαίρεσις
ἀρχὴν ἔχουσα κρίσιν καὶ λόγον, ἀλλὰ μὴ πτοίαν
ὑπὸ δόξης κενῆς ἢ φιλονεικίας τινὸς ἢ πράξεων
ἑτέρων ἀπορίας. ὥσπερ γὰρ οἷς οὐδὲν ἔστιν
οἴκοι χρηστόν, ἐν ἀγορᾷ διατρίβουσι, κἂν μὴ
δέωνται, τὸν πλεῖστον χρόνον, οὕτως ἔνιοι τῷ

become an observer of examples executed in deed rather than in word, and since you are asking me for political advice, I think that I cannot properly refuse. I pray, then, that my effort does justice both to your seriousness for politics and to my eagerness to help. I have, moreover, employed a rather wide variety of examples, as you have requested.

THE PROPER MOTIVATION
FOR A POLITICAL CAREER

First of all, let conscious choice, like a firm and strong foundation, be the basis of your political activity. Moreover, let your choice have its origin in judgment and reason, rather than in the excitement aroused by the vain pursuit of glory, a sense of rivalry, or a lack of other meaningful activities. For

μηδὲν ἔχειν ἴδιον ἄλλο πράττειν ἄξιον σπουδῆς
ἐμβάλλουσιν ἑαυτοὺς εἰς δημόσια πράγματα,
τῇ πολιτείᾳ διαγωγῇ χρώμενοι. πολλοὶ δ᾽ ἀπὸ
τύχης ἁψάμενοι τῶν κοινῶν καὶ ἀναπλησθέντες
οὐκέτι ῥᾳδίως ἀπελθεῖν δύνανται, ταὐτὸ
τοῖς ἐμβᾶσιν εἰς πλοῖον αἰώρας χάριν εἶτ᾽
ἀποσπασθεῖσιν εἰς πέλαγος πεπονθότες· ἔξω
βλέπουσι ναυτιῶντες καὶ ταραττόμενοι, μένειν
δὲ καὶ χρῆσθαι τοῖς παροῦσιν ἀνάγκην ἔχοντες·

    λευκᾶς καθύπερθε γαλάνας
    εὐπρόσωποι σφᾶς παρῇσαν ἔρωτες ναΐας
    κλᾷδος χαραξιπόντου δαιμονίαν ἐς ὕβριν.

οὗτοι καὶ μάλιστα διαβάλλουσι τὸ πρᾶγμα
τῷ μετανοεῖν καὶ ἀσχάλλειν, ὅταν ἢ δόξαν
ἐλπίσαντες ἀδοξίᾳ περιπέσωσιν, ἢ φοβεροὶ
προσδοκήσαντες ἑτέροις ἔσεσθαι διὰ δύναμιν
εἰς πράγματα κινδύνους ἔχοντα καὶ ταραχὰς
ἄγωνται.

just as there are people who have nothing worthwhile to do at home and so pass most of their time in the marketplace, even when they have no need to buy anything, so other people, because they have no private business that is worthy of their attention, throw themselves into public affairs and occupy themselves with politics to pass the time. And many of these people, once they have taken up public affairs on a whim and have had their fill, are not able to retire easily. They suffer the same thing that happens to those who board a ship for a pleasure cruise but then are drawn out to deeper waters. Seasick and distressed, they gaze towards shore, but they are forced to remain onboard and to suffer the reality of their circumstances: "Upon the foaming sea their handsome lovers passed them by, as they went to the divine violence of the ship's

ΠΟΛΙΤΙΚΑ ΠΑΡΑΓΓΕΛΜΑΤΑ

Ὁ δ' ὡς μάλιστα προσῆκον ἑαυτῷ καὶ
κάλλιστον ἔργον ἀπὸ γνώμης καὶ λογισμῷ
τὰ κοινὰ πράσσειν ἀρξάμενος ὑπ' οὐδενὸς
ἐκπλήττεται τούτων οὐδ' ἀναστρέφεται τὴν
γνώμην. οὔτε γὰρ ἐπ' ἐργασίᾳ καὶ χρηματισμῷ
προσιτέον τοῖς κοινοῖς, ὡς οἱ περὶ Στρατοκλέα
καὶ Δρομοκλείδην ἐπὶ τὸ χρυσοῦν θέρος,
τὸ βῆμα μετὰ παιδιᾶς οὕτως ὀνομάζοντες,
ἀλλήλους παρεκάλουν· οὔθ' οἷον ἐπιλήπτους
ὑπὸ πάθους ἄφνω γενομένους, ὡς Γάιος
Γράκχος ἐπὶ θερμοῖς τοῖς περὶ τὸν ἀδελφὸν
ἀτυχήμασιν ἀπωτάτω τῶν κοινῶν τὸν βίον
θέμενος, εἶθ' ὕβρει τινῶν καὶ λοιδορίᾳ πρὸς

50

benches that plow the sea."³ These people greatly denigrate politics because of their displeasure and change of heart, when they fall into disrepute after hoping for glory, or when they are drawn into dangerous and tumultuous affairs after expecting others to fear them on account of their power.

But those who enter politics on the basis of a reasoned judgment, considering it to be the most suitable and honorable task, are surprised by neither of those outcomes and do not change their mind. For we must not enter into public affairs as a money-making occupation, in the way that Stratocles and Dromoclides used to invite each other to ascend the "golden harvest," as they jokingly used to call the speaker's platform.⁴ Nor should we act hastily under the influence of a sudden emotion, as Gaius Gracchus did. For he removed himself as far away

αὐτὸν ἀναφλεχθεὶς ὑπ᾽ ὀργῆς, ἐνέπεσε τοῖς
κοινοῖς· καὶ ταχὺ μὲν ἐπλήσθη πραγμάτων
καὶ δόξης, ζητῶν δὲ παύσασθαι καὶ δεόμενος
μεταβολῆς καὶ ἡσυχίας οὐχ εὗρε καταθέσθαι
τὴν δύναμιν αὐτοῦ διὰ μέγεθος ἀλλὰ
προαπώλετο· τούς τε πρὸς ἅμιλλαν ἢ δόξαν
ὥσπερ ὑποκριτὰς εἰς θέατρον ἀναπλάττοντας
ἑαυτοὺς ἀνάγκη μετανοεῖν, ἢ δουλεύοντας ὧν
ἄρχειν ἀξιοῦσιν ἢ προσκρούοντας οἷς ἀρέσκειν
ἐθέλουσιν. ἀλλ᾽ ὥσπερ εἰς φρέαρ οἶμαι τὴν
πολιτείαν τοὺς μὲν ἐμπίπτοντας αὐτομάτως
καὶ παραλόγως ταράττεσθαι καὶ μετανοεῖν,
τοὺς δὲ καταβαίνοντας ἐκ παρασκευῆς
καὶ λογισμοῦ καθ᾽ ἡσυχίαν χρῆσθαί τε
τοῖς πράγμασι μετρίως καὶ πρὸς μηδὲν
δυσκολαίνειν, ἅτε δὴ τὸ καλὸν αὐτὸ καὶ μηδὲν
ἄλλο τῶν πράξεων ἔχοντας τέλος.

as possible from politics while the trouble surrounding his brother was still a current affair, but then inflamed with anger at the arrogance of certain people and the insults made against him, he threw himself into public life. He quickly had his fill of governing and glory, however, and although he needed a change of lifestyle and some peace and was seeking to retire, he could not find a way to lay down his power because it had become so great. And so, he was killed before he found a way out.[5] And those who create personas for themselves to enter political contests and earn glory, as actors do for the theater, are guaranteed to suffer a change of heart, either because they have become enslaved to the people they thought they would rule, or because they have clashed with the people they wished to please. But I think that those who fall into

Οὕτω δὴ τὴν προαίρεσιν ἀπερείσαντας
ἐν ἑαυτοῖς καὶ ποιήσαντας ἄτρεπτον καὶ
δυσμετάθετον, τρέπεσθαι χρὴ πρὸς κατανόησιν
τοῦ ἤθους τῶν πολιτῶν, ὃ μάλιστα συγκραθὲν
ἐκ πάντων ἐπιφαίνεται καὶ ἰσχύει. τὸ μὲν
γὰρ εὐθὺς αὐτὸν ἐπιχειρεῖν ἠθοποιεῖν καὶ
μεθαρμόττειν τοῦ δήμου τὴν φύσιν οὐ ῥᾴδιον
οὐδ᾽ ἀσφαλές, ἀλλὰ καὶ χρόνου δεόμενον

politics accidentally and rashly, as though they have fallen into a well, are confounded and change their minds, while those who make a calm descent, with preparation and deliberation, manage affairs prudently and remain always untroubled, because they have absolute goodness[6] and nothing else as the purpose of their endeavor.

THE CHARACTER OF THE CITIZENS AND THE LEADERS

Once they have made a fixed and inflexible decision to enter politics, politicians must turn themselves to understanding the character of the citizens, which reveals itself in a blending of all their individual characters and is quite powerful. For undertaking to mold the character and adapt the nature of the people straightaway is neither easy

πολλοῦ καὶ μεγάλης δυνάμεως. δεῖ δ᾽,
ὥσπερ οἶνος ἐν ἀρχῇ μὲν ὑπὸ τῶν ἠθῶν
κρατεῖται τοῦ πίνοντος ἡσυχῇ δὲ διαθάλπων
καὶ κατακεραννύμενος αὐτὸς ἠθοποιεῖ τὸν
πίνοντα καὶ μεθίστησιν, οὕτω τὸν πολιτικόν,
ἕως ἂν ἰσχὺν ἀγωγὸν ἐκ δόξης καὶ πίστεως
κατασκευάσηται, τοῖς ὑποκειμένοις ἤθεσιν
εὐάρμοστον εἶναι καὶ στοχάζεσθαι τούτων,
ἐπιστάμενον οἷς χαίρειν ὁ δῆμος καὶ ὑφ᾽ ὧν
ἄγεσθαι πέφυκεν· οἷον ὁ Ἀθηναίων εὐκίνητός
ἐστι πρὸς ὀργήν, εὐμετάθετος πρὸς ἔλεον,
μᾶλλον ὀξέως ὑπονοεῖν ἢ διδάσκεσθαι καθ᾽
ἡσυχίαν βουλόμενος· ὥσπερ τῶν ἀνδρῶν τοῖς
ἀδόξοις καὶ ταπεινοῖς βοηθεῖν προθυμότερος,
οὕτω τῶν λόγων τοὺς παιγνιώδεις καὶ γελοίους
ἀσπάζεται καὶ προτιμᾷ· τοῖς μὲν ἐπαινοῦσιν
αὐτὸν μάλιστα χαίρει, τοῖς δὲ σκώπτουσιν
ἥκιστα δυσχεραίνει· φοβερός ἐστιν ἄχρι
τῶν ἀρχόντων, εἶτα φιλάνθρωπος ἄχρι τῶν
πολεμίων.

nor risk-free, but it requires much time and great authority. Just as wine at first is controlled by the nature of those who are drinking it, but then stealthily, by warming and mixing into the drinkers' bodies, comes to control the drinkers' character and to change their state, so politicians, until they have established themselves through reputation and trust as steady guides, must adapt themselves to, and work with, the existing character of the people, understanding what pleases them and how they are naturally suited to be led. The Athenian people, for example, are easily excited to anger, easily moved to show mercy, and prefer to make a quick conjecture about something rather than to be calmly taught the facts; they are very eager to assist humble people who lack reputation, and in the same way they welcome and think highly of speeches that

ΠΟΛΙΤΙΚΑ ΠΑΡΑΓΓΕΛΜΑΤΑ

Ἕτερον ἦθος τοῦ Καρχηδονίων δήμου,
πικρόν, σκυθρωπόν, ὑπήκοον τοῖς ἄρχουσι,
βαρὺ τοῖς ὑπηκόοις, ἀγεννέστατον ἐν φόβοις,
ἀγριώτατον ἐν ὀργαῖς, ἐπίμονον τοῖς γνωσθεῖσι,
πρὸς παιδιὰν καὶ χάριν ἀνήδυντον καὶ σκληρόν·
οὐκ ἂν οὗτοι, Κλέωνος ἀξιοῦντος αὐτούς, ἐπεὶ
τέθυκε καὶ ξένους ἑστιᾶν μέλλει, τὴν ἐκκλησίαν
ὑπερθέσθαι, γελάσαντες ἂν καὶ κροτήσαντες
ἀνέστησαν· οὐδ' Ἀλκιβιάδην ὄρτυγος ἐν τῷ
λέγειν διαφυγόντος ἐκ τοῦ ἱματίου, φιλοτίμως
συνθηρεύσαντες ἀπέδωκαν ἄν· ἀλλὰ καὶ
ἀπέκτειναν ἄν, ὡς ὑβρίζοντας καὶ τρυφῶντας·
ὅπου καὶ Ἄννωνα λέοντι χρώμενον σκευοφόρῳ
παρὰ τὰς στρατείας αἰτιασάμενοι τυραννικὰ
φρονεῖν ἐξήλασαν. οἶμαι δ' ἂν ἔγωγε μηδὲ

are playful and humorous; they take the greatest delight in people who offer praise, and take hardly any offense at those who mock them; they are dreadful even to their leaders, then kindly even to their enemies.

The character of the Carthaginians, however, is quite different: they are bitter, sullen, obedient to their leaders, harsh to their subjects, most ignoble when facing their fears, most wild when angry, insistent in their judgments, and unpleasant and austere with respect to amusement and joy. The Carthaginians would not have left their seats with laughter and applause if Cleon had asked them to postpone the assembly because he had just sacrificed and was about to entertain guests at dinner. Nor, if Alcibiades had let a quail escape from his cloak while speaking, would they have joined eagerly in the hunt and given it back

Θηβαίους ἀποσχέσθαι γραμμάτων πολεμίων
κυρίους γενομένους, ὡς Ἀθηναῖοι Φιλίππου
γραμματοφόρους λαβόντες ἐπιστολὴν
ἐπιγεγραμμένην Ὀλυμπιάδι κομίζοντας οὐκ
ἔλυσαν οὐδ' ἀπεκάλυψαν ἀπόρρητον ἀνδρὸς
ἀποδήμου πρὸς γυναῖκα φιλοφροσύνην· οὐδέ
γ' αὖ πάλιν Ἀθηναίους, Ἐπαμεινώνδου πρὸς
τὴν κατηγορίαν ἀπολογεῖσθαι μὴ θέλοντος
ἀλλ' ἀναστάντος ἐκ τοῦ θεάτρου καὶ διὰ τῆς
ἐκκλησίας εἰς τὸ γυμνάσιον ἀπιόντος, εὐκόλως
ἐνεγκεῖν τὴν ὑπεροψίαν καὶ τὸ φρόνημα τοῦ
ἀνδρός· πολλοῦ δ' ἂν ἔτι καὶ Σπαρτιάτας
δεῆσαι τὴν Στρατοκλέους ὕβριν ὑπομεῖναι
καὶ βωμολοχίαν, πείσαντος μὲν αὐτοὺς
εὐαγγέλια θύειν ὡς νενικηκότας, ἐπεὶ δέ, τῆς
ἥττης ἀληθῶς ἀπαγγελθείσης, ἠγανάκτουν,
ἐρωτῶντος τὸν δῆμον τί ἠδίκηται, τρεῖς ἡμέρας
δι' αὐτὸν ἡδέως γεγονώς. οἱ μὲν οὖν αὐλικοὶ
κόλακες ὥσπερ ὀρνιθοθῆραι μιμούμενοι τῇ
φωνῇ καὶ συνεξομοιοῦντες ἑαυτοὺς ὑποδύονται

to him.[7] On the contrary, they would have killed both men for behaving arrogantly and extravagantly. We know this from the example of their own Hanno, whom they accused of tyrannical intentions and banished because he was using a lion as his pack animal on military campaigns. And I personally do not think that the Thebans, having come into possession of their enemies' letters, would have left them unread, unlike the Athenians who, having captured Philip's messengers as they were carrying a letter written to Olympias, neither opened the letter nor revealed the intimate message sent by a man abroad to his wife. On the other hand, when Epaminondas was unwilling to defend himself against his accusers but left the theater and went out through the assembly to the gymnasium, I do not think that the Athenians would easily have

μάλιστα καὶ προσάγουσι δι᾽ ἀπάτης τοῖς
βασιλεῦσι· τῷ δὲ πολιτικῷ μιμεῖσθαι μὲν οὐ
προσήκει τοῦ δήμου τὸν τρόπον, ἐπίστασθαι δὲ
καὶ χρῆσθαι πρὸς ἕκαστον, οἷς ἁλώσιμός ἐστιν·
ἡ γὰρ ἄγνοια τῶν ἠθῶν ἀστοχίας φέρει καὶ
διαπτώσεις οὐχ ἥττονας ἐν ταῖς πολιτείαις ἢ
ταῖς φιλίαις τῶν βασιλέων.

endured his contempt and pride.[8] And I think the Spartans were still farther from tolerating the arrogance and buffoonery of Stratocles, who convinced the Athenians to make a thanks-offering for receiving the good news that they had won a victory. Later, when it was announced that Athens had actually been defeated and the people were upset, he asked them what injustice had been done if on his account they had enjoyed themselves for a few days. Now court flatterers, like people who hunt birds, imitate the speech of kings and act the way they do, and so they closely insinuate themselves and lead kings on through deception. But it is inappropriate for the politician to imitate the manners of the people. It is fitting instead to understand them and to take the approach that is most effective for winning over each individual. For ignorance

ΠΟΛΙΤΙΚΑ ΠΑΡΑΓΓΕΛΜΑΤΑ

Τὸ μὲν οὖν τῶν πολιτῶν ἦθος ἰσχύοντα δεῖ
καὶ πιστευόμενον ἤδη πειρᾶσθαι ῥυθμίζειν
ἀτρέμα πρὸς τὸ βέλτιον ὑπάγοντα καὶ πράως
μεταχειριζόμενον· ἐργώδης γὰρ ἡ μετάθεσις
τῶν πολλῶν. αὐτὸς δ᾽ ὥσπερ ἐν θεάτρῳ τὸ
λοιπὸν ἀναπεπταμένῳ βιωσόμενος, ἐξάσκει
καὶ κατακόσμει τὸν τρόπον· εἰ δὲ μὴ ῥάδιον
ἀπαλλάξαι παντάπασι τῆς ψυχῆς τὴν κακίαν,
ὅσα γοῦν ἐπανθεῖ μάλιστα καὶ προπίπτει
τῶν ἁμαρτημάτων ἀφαιρῶν καὶ κολούων.
ἀκούεις γάρ, ὅτι καὶ Θεμιστοκλῆς ἅπτεσθαι
τῆς πολιτείας διανοούμενος ἀπέστησε τῶν
πότων καὶ τῶν κώμων ἑαυτόν, ἀγρυπνῶν
δὲ καὶ νήφων καὶ πεφροντικὼς ἔλεγε πρὸς
τοὺς συνήθεις, ὡς οὐκ ἐᾷ καθεύδειν αὐτὸν τὸ
Μιλτιάδου τρόπαιον· Περικλῆς δὲ καὶ περὶ
τὸ σῶμα καὶ τὴν δίαιταν ἐξήλλαξεν αὑτὸν

of people's character leads to missteps and mistakes no less in our political systems than in the entourages of kings.

And so the politician, after gaining power and trust, must then attempt to train the character of the citizens, guiding it calmly towards improvement and handling it gently, for changing the disposition of the people is difficult. And you, since you will be living the rest of your life in public as upon a stage, must adorn and arrange your own way of life. If you cannot easily clear your soul entirely of its defects, then remove and curtail the faults that are especially obvious and prominent. For you hear that even Themistocles, when he was intending to get involved in politics, kept himself away from drinking and revelry, but remaining watchful, sober, and reflective, he used to tell his friends that Miltiades's

ἠρέμα βαδίζειν καὶ πράως διαλέγεσθαι καὶ τὸ
πρόσωπον ἀεὶ συνεστηκὸς ἐπιδείκνυσθαι καὶ
τὴν χεῖρα συνέχειν ἐντὸς τῆς περιβολῆς καὶ
μίαν ὁδὸν πορεύεσθαι τὴν ἐπὶ τὸ βῆμα καὶ τὸ
βουλευτήριον. οὐ γὰρ εὐμεταχείριστον οὐδὲ
ῥάδιον ἁλῶναι τὴν σωτήριον ἅλωσιν ὑπὸ τοῦ
τυχόντος ὄχλος, ἀλλ᾽ ἀγαπητόν, εἰ μήτ᾽ ὄψει
μήτε φωνῇ πτυρόμενος ὥσπερ θηρίον ὕποπτον
καὶ ποικίλον ἐνδέχοιτο τὴν ἐπιστασίαν.

Ὧι τοίνυν οὐδὲ τούτων ἐπιμελητέον ἐστὶ
παρέργως, ἦπου τῶν περὶ τὸν βίον καὶ τὸ
ἦθος ἀμελητέον ὅπως ᾖ ψόγου καθαρὰ καὶ
διαβολῆς ἁπάσης; οὐ γὰρ ὧν λέγουσιν ἐν
κοινῷ καὶ πράττουσιν οἱ πολιτευόμενοι μόνον

trophy would not allow him to sleep.[9] And Pericles transformed himself with respect to both his body and his daily routine, so that he walked slowly, engaged in dialogue mildly, always presented a composed appearance, kept his hand inside his clothing, and made his way along only a single road, the one that led to the speaker's platform and the council chamber. For a multitude is not easily manipulated by just anybody or easily placed in a captivity that keeps it safe. You must instead be content if the people are not startled by your sight or your voice, as a fearful and wily animal is, and if they accept your authority.

Should politicians, who must pay careful attention to these matters, then neglect the condition of their own life and character, and not worry about how they may be cleansed of all blame and slander? For

εὐθύνας διδόασιν, ἀλλὰ καὶ δεῖπνον αὐτῶν
πολυπραγμονεῖται καὶ κοίτη καὶ γάμος
καὶ παιδιὰ καὶ σπουδὴ πᾶσα. τί γὰρ δεῖ
λέγειν Ἀλκιβιάδην, ὃν περὶ τὰ κοινὰ πάντων
ἐνεργότατον ὄντα καὶ στρατηγὸν ἀήττητον
ἀπώλεσεν ἡ περὶ τὴν δίαιταν ἀναγωγία καὶ
θρασύτης, καὶ τῶν ἄλλων ἀγαθῶν αὐτοῦ τὴν
πόλιν ἀνόνητον ἐποίησε διὰ τὴν πολυτέλειαν
καὶ τὴν ἀκολασίαν; ὅπου καὶ Κίμωνος οὗτοι
τὸν οἶνον, καὶ Ῥωμαῖοι Σκιπίωνος οὐδὲν
ἄλλο ἔχοντες λέγειν τὸν ὕπνον ᾐτιῶντο·
Πομπήιον δὲ Μάγνον ἐλοιδόρουν οἱ ἐχθροί,
παραφυλάξαντες ἑνὶ δακτύλῳ τὴν κεφαλὴν
κνώμενον. ὡς γὰρ ἐν προσώπῳ φακὸς καὶ
ἀκροχορδὼν δυσχεραίνεται μᾶλλον ἢ στίγματα
καὶ κολοβότητες καὶ οὐλαὶ τοῦ λοιποῦ
σώματος, οὕτω τὰ μικρὰ φαίνεται μεγάλα τῶν
ἁμαρτημάτων ἐν ἡγεμονικοῖς καὶ πολιτικοῖς
ὁρώμενα βίοις διὰ δόξαν, ἣν οἱ πολλοὶ περὶ
ἀρχῆς καὶ πολιτείας ἔχουσιν, ὡς πράγματος

politicians do not give an accounting only for the things they say and do in the public sphere, but we even inquire into their dinners, sexual activity, marriages, amusements, and all their interests. Do I have to mention Alcibiades? Though he was more effective than anyone else on the public's behalf and undefeated as a general, his lack of discipline and the audacity of his way of life destroyed him, and he deprived the city of all his benefits on account of his extravagance and licentiousness. And there's the case of Cimon, whom the Athenians reproached for his wine, and of Scipio, whom the Romans (having nothing else to say) reproached for sleeping. And Pompey the Great's political enemies used to rebuke him after they observed him scratching his head with one finger.[10] For just as a mole or wart on the face causes more disgust than

μεγάλου καὶ καθαρεύειν ἀξίου πάσης ἀτοπίας
καὶ πλημμελείας. εἰκότως οὖν Λιούιος Δροῦσος
ὁ δημαγωγὸς εὐδοκίμησεν ὅτι, τῆς οἰκίας
αὐτοῦ πολλὰ μέρη κάτοπτα τοῖς γειτνιῶσιν
ἐχούσης καὶ τῶν τεχνιτῶν τινος ὑπισχνουμένου
ταῦτ' ἀποστρέψειν καὶ μεταθήσειν ἀπὸ πέντε
μόνων ταλάντων, "δέκα," ἔφη, "λαβὼν ὅλην
μου ποίησον καταφανῆ τὴν οἰκίαν, ἵνα πάντες
ὁρῶσιν οἱ πολῖται πῶς διαιτῶμαι"· καὶ γὰρ
ἦν ἀνὴρ σώφρων καὶ κόσμιος. ἴσως δὲ ταύτης
οὐδὲν ἔδει τῆς καταφανείας αὐτῷ· διορῶσι γὰρ
οἱ πολλοὶ καὶ τὰ πάνυ βαθέως περιαμπέχεσθαι
δοκοῦντα τῶν πολιτευομένων ἤθη καὶ
βουλεύματα καὶ πράξεις καὶ βίους, οὐχ ἧττον
ἀπὸ τῶν ἰδίων ἢ τῶν δημοσίων ἐπιτηδευμάτων
τὸν μὲν φιλοῦντες καὶ θαυμάζοντες τὸν δὲ
δυσχεραίνοντες καὶ καταφρονοῦντες.

marks, growths, and scars on other parts of the body, so small faults appear great when observed in the lives of leaders and politicians. This is because the majority believe that important business, such as leadership and politics, also deserves to be free of every oddity and fault. Consider the tribune Livius Drusus, whose house had many rooms that were visible to his neighbors. He was rightly held in high esteem, because when a certain craftsman was promising to rearrange and relocate those rooms for a cost of only five talents,[11] Drusus said, "Take ten, and make my whole house visible, so that every citizen may see how I live my life." For he was a self-controlled and disciplined man. But perhaps he had no need of such visibility, since the people very clearly see in politicians even those character traits, counsels, deeds, and ways of life that appear

Τί οὖν δή; οὐχὶ καὶ τοῖς ἀσελγῶς καὶ
τεθρυμμένως ζῶσιν αἱ πόλεις χρῶνται; καὶ
γὰρ αἱ κιττῶσαι λίθους καὶ οἱ ναυτιῶντες
ἁλμυρίδας καὶ τὰ τοιαῦτα βρώματα διώκουσι
πολλάκις, εἶτ᾽ ὀλίγον ὕστερον ἐξέπτυσαν καὶ
ἀπεστράφησαν· οὕτω καὶ οἱ δῆμοι διὰ τρυφὴν
καὶ ὕβριν ἢ βελτιόνων ἀπορίᾳ δημαγωγῶν
χρῶνται τοῖς ἐπιτυχοῦσι βδελυττόμενοι καὶ
καταφρονοῦντες, εἶτα χαίρουσι τοιούτων εἰς
αὑτοὺς λεγομένων, οἷα Πλάτων ὁ κωμικὸς τὸν
Δῆμον αὐτὸν λέγοντα ποιεῖ·

λαβοῦ, λαβοῦ τῆς χειρὸς ὡς τάχιστά μου,
μέλλω στρατηγὸν χειροτονεῖν Ἀγύρριον·

to be deeply concealed. Judging politicians no less by their private than by their public habits, the people love and admire some, while towards others they feel disgust and scorn.

"What's this? Don't cities also employ people who live licentious and dissolute lives?" Of course they do—and pregnant women often crave stones, and people who are nauseated seek out salty or similarly spiced foods, but shortly thereafter they spit them out and reject them. Thus, the people also, because of licentiousness and arrogance or the lack of better leaders, make use of the politicians who are available, even though they find them loathsome and contemptible, but then they are glad when they hear words such as Plato the comic poet makes his character "The People" say:

καὶ πάλιν αἰτοῦντα λεκάνην καὶ πτερόν, ὅπως
ἐμέσῃ, λέγοντα, "προσίσταταί μου πρὸς τὸ
βῆμα Μαντίας" καὶ "βόσκει δυσώδη Κέφαλον,
ἐχθίστην νόσον." ὁ δὲ Ῥωμαίων δῆμος,
ὑπισχνουμένου τι Κάρβωνος καὶ προστιθέντος
ὅρκον δή τινα καὶ ἀράν, ἀντώμοσεν ὁμοῦ μὴ
πιστεύειν. ἐν δὲ Λακεδαίμονι τινὸς ἀνδρὸς
ἀκολάστου γνώμην εἰπόντος ἁρμόζουσαν,
ἀπέρριψεν ὁ δῆμος, οἱ δ᾽ Ἔφοροι κληρώσαντες
ἕνα τῶν γερόντων ἐκέλευσαν εἰπεῖν τὸν αὐτὸν
λόγον ἐκεῖνον, ὥσπερ εἰς καθαρὸν ἀγγεῖον ἐκ
ῥυπαροῦ μετεράσαντες, ὅπως εὐπρόσδεκτος
γένηται τοῖς πολλοῖς. οὕτω μεγάλην ἔχει ῥοπὴν
ἐν πολιτείᾳ πίστις ἤθους καὶ τοὐναντίον.

"Grab, grab my hand as quickly as you can! I'm about to elect Agyrrius general!" And again, when "The People" are asking for a basin and a feather in order to vomit, they say, "Mantias has approached my speaker's platform" and "He feeds foul Cephalus, a most hateful malady." And when Carbo was promising something to the Roman people and backing his promise with an oath and a curse, the people all took a counter oath not to trust him. In Lacedaemon, when a certain licentious person made an acceptable proposal, the people rejected it, and so the ephors selected one of the elders by lot and ordered him to make the same proposal, thus pouring the proposal, so to speak, from a dirty vessel into a clean one, so that it would be well received by the multitude. Thus, trust in a person's character and a lack of trust both have great influence in politics.

Οὐ μὴν ἀμελητέον γε διὰ τοῦτο τῆς περὶ τὸν
λόγον χάριτος καὶ δυνάμεως ἐν ἀρετῇ θεμένους
τὸ σύμπαν, ἀλλὰ τὴν ῥητορικὴν νομίσαντας μὴ
δημιουργὸν ἀλλά τοι συνεργὸν εἶναι πειθοῦς,
ἐπανορθωτέον τὸ τοῦ Μενάνδρου "τρόπος
ἔσθ᾽ ὁ πείθων τοῦ λέγοντος, οὐ λόγος"· καὶ
γὰρ ὁ τρόπος καὶ ὁ λόγος· εἰ μὴ νὴ Δία φήσει
τις, ὡς τὸν κυβερνήτην ἄγειν τὸ πλοῖον οὐ τὸ
πηδάλιον, καὶ τὸν ἱππέα στρέφειν τὸν ἵππον οὐ
τὸν χαλινόν, οὕτω πόλιν πείθειν οὐ λόγῳ, ἀλλὰ
τρόπῳ χρωμένην ὥσπερ οἴακι καὶ χαλινῷ τὴν
πολιτικὴν ἀρετήν, ᾗπερ εὐστροφώτατον ζῷον,
ὥς φησι Πλάτων, οἷον ἐκ πρύμνης ἁπτομένην
καὶ κατευθύνουσαν. ὅπου γὰρ οἱ μεγάλοι
βασιλεῖς ἐκεῖνοι καὶ διογενεῖς, ὡς Ὅμηρός
φησιν, ἀλουργίσι καὶ σκήπτροις καὶ δορυφόροις
καὶ θεῶν χρησμοῖς ἐξογκοῦσιν ἑαυτούς, καὶ
δουλούμενοι τῇ σεμνότητι τοὺς πολλοὺς ὡς

THE POWER OF SPEECH

Even with this being the case, we must not neglect the grace and power of speech by placing all of our emphasis on virtue. Rather, believing rhetoric to be not the creator of persuasion but a collaborator, we should correct Menander, who said that "the character of the speaker is what persuades, not the speech itself." In fact, both the character *and* the speech are important. Unless, by Zeus, someone will argue that just as the pilot not the rudder steers the ship and the rider not the bit turns the horse, so in the art of politics, you persuade a city not with speech but by employing only your character as the tiller and bit. And so, the argument goes, you must take hold of and direct the city from behind, which, as Plato says, is the best way to drive an animal. But

κρείττονες, ὅμως ἐβούλοντο "μύθων ῥητῆρες"
εἶναι καὶ οὐκ ἠμέλουν τῆς τοῦ λέγειν χάριτος,
"οὐδ᾽ ἀγορέων, ἵνα τ᾽ ἄνδρες ἀριπρεπέες
τελέθουσιν," οὐδὲ Διὸς Βουλαίου μόνον ἔχρῃζον
οὐδ᾽ Ἄρεος Ἐνυαλίου καὶ Στρατίας Ἀθηνᾶς,
ἀλλὰ καὶ τὴν Καλλιόπην παρεκάλουν "ἣ δὴ
βασιλεῦσιν ἅμ᾽ αἰδοίοισιν ὀπηδεῖ," πραΰνουσα
πειθοῖ καὶ κατάδουσα τῶν δήμων τὸ αὔθαδες
καὶ βίαιον· ἢ που δυνατὸν ἄνθρωπον ἰδιώτην
ἐξ ἱματίου καὶ σχήματος δημοτικοῦ πόλιν
ἄγειν βουλόμενον ἐξισχῦσαι καὶ κρατῆσαι
τῶν πολλῶν, εἰ μὴ λόγον ἔχοι συμπείθοντα
καὶ προσαγόμενον; οἱ μὲν οὖν τὰ πλοῖα
κυβερνῶντες ἑτέροις χρῶνται κελευσταῖς,
ὁ δὲ πολιτικὸς ἐν ἑαυτῷ μὲν ὀφείλει τὸν
κυβερνῶντα νοῦν ἔχειν ἐν ἑαυτῷ δὲ τὸν
ἐγκελευόμενον λόγον, ὅπως μὴ δέηται φωνῆς
ἀλλοτρίας μηδ᾽ ὥσπερ Ἰφικράτης ὑπὸ τῶν
περὶ Ἀριστοφῶντα καταρρητορευόμενος λέγῃ,
"βελτίων μὲν ὁ τῶν ἀντιδίκων ὑποκριτὴς δρᾶμα

I disagree, for those kings who were great and, as Homer says, born-from-Zeus built themselves up with purple robes, scepters, bodyguards, and oracles from the gods, and believing themselves superior they made the multitude their subjects by means of their majesty. Nonetheless, they still wished to be "speakers of words" and did not neglect the grace of speaking "nor the assemblies, so they might become highly distinguished men."[12] Not only did they long for Zeus of the Council, Warlike Ares, and Athena Patron of the Army, but they also called upon Calliope, "who attends reverend kings"[13] and who by persuasion tames and charms the arrogance and violence of the people. How, then, can private individuals who wish to lead the city, wearing ordinary clothing and having an ordinary appearance, prevail over and control the people,

δὲ τοὐμὸν ἄμεινον," μηδὲ πολλάκις δέηται τῶν
Εὐριπιδείων ἐκείνων "εἴθ᾽ ἦν ἄφωνον σπέρμα
δυστήνων βροτῶν"· καὶ

    φεῦ φεῦ, τὸ μὴ τὰ πράγματ᾽ ἀνθρώποις
      ἔχειν
    φωνήν, ἵν᾽ ἦσαν μηδὲν οἱ δεινοὶ λέγειν.

Διὰ τοῦτ᾽ ἦν ἡ κατὰ Περικλέα πολιτεία
"λόγῳ μέν," ὥς φησι Θουκυδίδης, "δημοκρατία,
ἔργῳ δ᾽ ὑπὸ τοῦ πρώτου ἀνδρὸς ἀρχὴ" διὰ

unless they possess a persuasive and winning ability to speak? Now those who pilot ships have other people give their orders, but politicians ought to possess within themselves both a piloting mind and a commanding speech. Otherwise, they might require the aid of someone else's voice or end up saying, as Iphicrates did when he was out-spoken by Aristophon, "My opponents have the better actor, but I have the better play." And thus, they would not often require those verses of Euripides: "I wish the children of wretched mortals were mute," and "It's a pity that human deeds cannot speak for themselves. Then, those who are clever at speaking would amount to nothing."

And so, the Athenian political system under Pericles was "in name a democracy," as Thucydides says, "but in fact

τὴν τοῦ λόγου δύναμιν. ἐπεὶ καὶ Κίμων
ἀγαθὸς ἦν καὶ Ἐφιάλτης καὶ Θουκυδίδης,
ἀλλ᾿ ἐρωτηθεὶς οὗτος ὑπ᾿ Ἀρχιδάμου τοῦ
βασιλέως τῶν Σπαρτιατῶν πότερον αὐτὸς ἢ
Περικλῆς παλαίει βέλτιον "οὐκ ἂν εἰδείη τις,"
εἶπεν· "ὅταν γὰρ ἐγὼ καταβάλω παλαίων,
ἐκεῖνος λέγων μὴ πεπτωκέναι νικᾷ καὶ πείθει
τοὺς θεωμένους." τοῦτο δ᾿ οὐκ αὐτῷ μόνον
ἐκείνῳ δόξαν ἀλλὰ καὶ τῇ πόλει σωτηρίαν
ἔφερε· πειθομένη γὰρ αὐτῷ τὴν ὑπάρχουσαν
εὐδαιμονίαν ἔσῳζε, τῶν δ᾿ ἐκτὸς ἀπείχετο.
Νικίας δὲ τὴν αὐτὴν προαίρεσιν ἔχων, πειθοῦς
δὲ τοιαύτης ἐνδεὴς ὢν καὶ καθάπερ ἀμβλεῖ
χαλινῷ τῷ λόγῳ πειρώμενος ἀποστρέφειν
τὸν δῆμον, οὐ κατέσχεν οὐδ᾿ ἐκράτησεν,
ἀλλ᾿ ᾤχετο βίᾳ φερόμενος εἰς Σικελίαν καὶ
συνεκτραχηλιζόμενος. τὸν μὲν οὖν λύκον οὔ
φασι τῶν ὤτων κρατεῖν, δῆμον δὲ καὶ πόλιν
ἐκ τῶν ὤτων ἄγειν δεῖ μάλιστα, μή, καθάπερ
ἔνιοι τῶν ἀγυμνάστων περὶ λόγον λαβὰς

it was government by the leading man"[14] thanks to the power of his speech. Now Cimon was a good man, and Ephialtes and Thucydides,[15] too, but when Archidamus the Spartan king asked Thucydides whether he or Pericles was the better wrestler, he replied, "No one knows, because whenever we're wrestling and I throw him down, he argues that he wasn't thrown, persuades the spectators, and wins the match!" This skill brought not only glory to Pericles but also salvation to the city: convinced by his arguments, Athens preserved the wealth that it possessed and kept itself out of trouble abroad. By contrast, Nicias had the same plan, but lacking a similar ability to persuade and attempting to guide the people with his speech as though with a feeble bit, he could not gain mastery or control, but carried away by the people's violence, he

ἀμούσους καὶ ἀτέχνους ζητοῦντες ἐν τοῖς
πολλοῖς τῆς γαστρὸς ἕλκουσιν εὐωχοῦντες
ἢ τοῦ βαλλαντίου διδόντες, ἢ πυρρίχας τινὰς
ἢ μονομάχων θεάματα παρασκευάζοντες
ἀεὶ δημαγωγοῦσι, μᾶλλον δὲ δημοκοποῦσι.
δημαγωγία γὰρ ἡ διὰ λόγου πειθομένων
ἐστίν, αἱ δὲ τοιαῦται τιθασεύσεις τῶν ὄχλων
οὐδὲν ἀλόγων ζῴων ἄγρας καὶ βουκολήσεως
διαφέρουσιν.

    Δεῖ δὲ καὶ φωνῆς εὐεξίᾳ καὶ πνεύματος ῥώμῃ
πρὸς οὐ φαῦλον ἀλλὰ πάμμαχον ἀγῶνα τὸν
τῆς πολιτείας ἠθληκότα κομίζειν τὸν λόγον, ὡς

went off to Sicily and was thrown from the horse.[16] They say not to hold a wolf by the ears, but by the ears is just how one must control the people and a city. Some, who are unpracticed in speaking, seek inelegant and unsophisticated means of getting a hold on the people. By giving feasts, they pull the people by the stomach, or by making donations they pull them by the wallet, or they are constantly putting on war dances or gladiatorial shows, and in this way they lead the people, or rather they court the mob. For true leadership of the people is leadership of those persuaded through speech, while taming the mob as described above is no different from hunting and herding irrational animals.

And so, you must bring to the political contest, which is not a skirmish but an all-out battle, a speaking ability that is well trained

μὴ πολλάκις ἀπαγορεύοντα καὶ σβεννύμενον
ὑπερβάλλῃ τις αὐτὸν "ἅρπαξ κεκράκτης,
Κυκλοβόρου φωνὴν ἔχων." Κάτων δέ, περὶ ὧν
οὐκ ἤλπιζε πείσειν τῷ προκατέχεσθαι χάρισι
καὶ σπουδαῖς τὸν δῆμον ἢ τὴν βουλήν, ἔλεγε
τὴν ἡμέραν ὅλην ἀναστὰς καὶ τὸν καιρὸν
οὕτως ἐξέκρουε. περὶ μὲν οὖν τῆς τοῦ λόγου
παρασκευῆς καὶ χρείας ἱκανὰ ταῦτα τῷ
δυναμένῳ τὸ ἀκόλουθον προσεξευρίσκειν.

Εἰσβολαὶ δὲ καὶ ὁδοὶ δύο τῆς πολιτείας εἰσίν,
ἡ μὲν ταχεῖα καὶ λαμπρὰ πρὸς δόξαν οὐ μὴν
ἀκίνδυνος, ἡ δὲ πεζοτέρα καὶ βραδυτέρα τὸ

in vigor of voice and strength of breath, so that, weary and quenched, you are not overpowered by some "grasping brawler with the voice of the Cycloborus."[17] Cato the Younger, for instance, when he did not expect to persuade the people or the senate because they had already been influenced by favors and lobbying, used to rise and speak the whole day, and thus he kept them from making a decision. Concerning the preparation and use of your speaking ability, then, what I have written is sufficient, since you are capable of discovering for yourself what follows from it.

ENTERING THE ARENA

There are two routes by which you may enter politics: one, swift and dazzling, leads to glory though not without risk, while

δ' ἀσφαλὲς ἔχουσα μᾶλλον. οἱ μὲν γὰρ εὐθὺς
ὥσπερ ἐξ ἄκρας πελαγίου πράξεως ἐπιφανοῦς
καὶ μεγάλης ἐχούσης δὲ τόλμαν ἄραντες
ἀφῆκαν ἐπὶ τὴν πολιτείαν, ἡγούμενοι λέγειν
ὀρθῶς τὸν Πίνδαρον ὡς

ἀρχομένου δ' ἔργου πρόσωπον
χρὴ θέμεν τηλαυγές·

καὶ γὰρ δέχονται προθυμότερον οἱ πολλοὶ
κόρῳ τινὶ καὶ πλησμονῇ τῶν συνήθων τὸν
ἀρχόμενον, ὥσπερ ἀγωνιστὴν θεαταί, καὶ τὸν
φθόνον ἐκπλήττουσιν αἱ λαμπρὰν ἔχουσαι
καὶ ταχεῖαν αὔξησιν ἀρχαὶ καὶ δυνάμεις. οὔτε
γὰρ πῦρ φησιν ὁ Ἀρίστων καπνὸν ποιεῖν οὔτε
δόξαν φθόνον, ἢν εὐθὺς ἐκλάμψῃ καὶ ταχέως,
ἀλλὰ τῶν κατὰ μικρὸν αὐξανομένων καὶ
σχολαίως ἄλλον ἀλλαχόθεν ἐπιλαμβάνεσθαι·
διὸ πολλοὶ πρὶν ἀνθῆσαι περὶ τὸ βῆμα
κατεμαράνθησαν. ὅπου δ', ὥσπερ ἐπὶ τοῦ

the other is slower and more prosaic but provides surer footing. Those who take the first route set forth straightaway from some illustrious, great, and daring deed, as though sailing out from a cape along the sea, and they make their arrival into politics believing that Pindar had it right when he said, "At the start of an undertaking, one must present a brilliant facade."[18] For the people welcome the newcomer all the more eagerly because they have had enough of the usual politicians, just as the audience at a play welcomes a new actor. Moreover, the offices and powers that accumulate brilliantly and swiftly drive away envy. For Ariston says that fire does not produce smoke nor does glory provoke envy if it flares up promptly and swiftly, but when people build their reputations little by little and at a leisurely pace, other people attack

Λάδα λέγουσιν, "ὁ ψόφος ἦν ὕσπληγος ἐν
οὔασιν," ἔνθα κἀστεφανοῦτο πρεσβεύων ἢ
θριαμβεύων ἢ στρατηγῶν ἐπιφανῶς, οὔθ᾽ οἱ
φθονοῦντες οὔθ᾽ οἱ καταφρονοῦντες ὁμοίως
ἐπὶ τοιούτων ἰσχύουσιν. οὕτω παρῆλθεν
εἰς δόξαν Ἄρατος, ἀρχὴν ποιησάμενος
πολιτείας τὴν Νικοκλέους τοῦ τυράννου
κατάλυσιν· οὕτως Ἀλκιβιάδης, τὰ Μαντινικὰ
συστήσας ἐπὶ Λακεδαιμονίους. Πομπήιος
δὲ καὶ θριαμβεύειν ἠξίου μήπω παριὼν εἰς
σύγκλητον· οὐκ ἐῶντος δὲ Σύλλα, "πλείονες,"
ἔφη, "τὸν ἥλιον ἀνατέλλοντα προσκυνοῦσιν ἢ
δυόμενον"· καὶ Σύλλας ὑπεῖξε τοῦτ᾽ ἀκούσας.
καὶ Σκιπίωνα δὲ Κορνήλιον οὐκ ἀφ᾽ ἧς
ἔτυχεν ἀρχῆς ὁ Ῥωμαίων δῆμος ἀγορανομίαν
μετερχόμενον ἐξαίφνης ὕπατον ἀπέδειξε παρὰ
τὸν νόμον, ἀλλὰ θαυμάσας αὐτοῦ μειρακίου
μὲν ὄντος τὴν ἐν Ἰβηρίᾳ μονομαχίαν καὶ
νίκην, μικρὸν δ᾽ ὕστερον τὰ πρὸς Καρχηδόνι
χιλιαρχοῦντος ἔργα, περὶ ὧν καὶ Κάτων ὁ

them from all sides. On this account, many aspiring leaders wither and die around the speaker's platform before they have the chance to bloom. And just as they say about the sprinter Ladas, that "the sound of the race's start filled his ears," so when people are crowned for serving on an embassy, celebrating a triumph, or performing brilliantly as general, neither those who are envious nor those heaping scorn can exert any influence. Thus, Aratus earned his reputation by making the downfall of the tyrant Nicocles his first political act; and thus, Alcibiades's first act was to make an alliance with the Mantineans against the Lacedaemonians. Pompey thought he deserved a triumph when he had not yet been elected to the senate, and when Sulla would not allow it, Pompey declared, "More people worship the sun as it rises

πρεσβύτερος ἀνεφώνησεν, "οἷος πέπνυται, τοὶ δὲ σκιαὶ ἀίσσουσιν."

Νῦν οὖν ὅτε τὰ πράγματα τῶν πόλεων οὐκ ἔχει πολέμων ἡγεμονίας οὐδὲ τυραννίδων καταλύσεις οὐδὲ συμμαχικὰς πράξεις, τίν᾽ ἄν τις ἀρχὴν ἐπιφανοῦς λάβοι καὶ λαμπρᾶς πολιτείας; αἱ δίκαι τε λείπονται αἱ δημόσιαι καὶ πρεσβεῖαι πρὸς αὐτοκράτορα ἀνδρὸς διαπύρου καὶ θάρσος ἅμα καὶ νοῦν ἔχοντος δεόμεναι. πολλὰ δ᾽ ἔστι καὶ τῶν παρειμένων ἐν

than as it sets." And the Roman people illegally elected Scipio Aemilianus consul when he was only running for aedile, not as the result of any ordinary political start, but because they marveled at his winning a single combat in Iberia while he was yet a young man, and at the deeds he performed soon after as military tribune fighting against Carthage. These accomplishments made Cato the Elder exclaim that Scipio "alone possesses intelligence, while the rest flit around like shadows."[19]

But in our time, when the affairs of cities do not include leadership in war or bringing down tyrants or campaigning with allies, what conspicuous and brilliant entry into politics can we make? There remain public trials and embassies to the emperor, which require people who are eager yet possess both courage and sense. And there

ταῖς πόλεσι καλῶν ἀναλαμβάνοντα καὶ τῶν ἐξ
ἔθους φαύλου παραδυομένων ἐπ᾽ αἰσχύνῃ τινὶ
τῆς πόλεως ἢ βλάβῃ μεθιστάντα πρὸς αὑτὸν
ἐπιστρέφειν. ἤδη δὲ καὶ δίκη μεγάλη καλῶς
δικασθεῖσα καὶ πίστις ἐν συνηγορίᾳ πρὸς
ἀντίδικον ἰσχυρὸν ὑπὲρ ἀσθενοῦς καὶ παρρησία
πρὸς ἡγεμόνα μοχθηρὸν ὑπὲρ τοῦ δικαίου
κατέστησεν ἐνίους εἰς ἀρχὴν πολιτείας ἔνδοξον.

Τὴν δ᾽ ἀσφαλῆ καὶ σχολαίαν εἵλοντο πολλοὶ
τῶν ἐνδόξων, Ἀριστείδης, Φωκίων, Παμμένης
ὁ Θηβαῖος, Λεύκολλος ἐν Ῥώμῃ, Κάτων,
Ἀγησίλαος ὁ Λακεδαιμόνιος· τούτων γὰρ
ἕκαστος, ὥσπερ οἱ κιττοὶ τοῖς ἰσχύουσι τῶν
δένδρων περιπλεκόμενοι συνεξανίστανται,
προσδραμὼν ἀνδρὶ πρεσβυτέρῳ νέος ἔτι

are many other opportunities that you may turn to your benefit, either by reviving good practices that have been neglected in our cities, or by discontinuing practices acquired through bad habit that cause the city shame or harm. Consider also an important court case that is well pleaded, a show of good faith as a legal advocate for a weaker person against a stronger opponent, or a frank speech delivered against a corrupt leader in support of justice. All of these things have given some people glorious starts in politics.

But many people who achieved great glory chose the slow and steady route; for example, Aristides, Phocion, Pammenes the Theban, Lucullus the Roman, Cato the Elder, and Agesilaus the Lacedaemonian. Just as ivy intertwines itself with strong trees and climbs upwards with them, so each of

καὶ ἄδοξος ἐνδόξῳ, κατὰ μικρὸν αἰρόμενος
ὑπὸ τῆς περὶ ἐκεῖνον δυνάμεως καὶ
συναυξανόμενος ἤρεισε καὶ κατερρίζωσεν
ἑαυτὸν εἰς τὴν πολιτείαν. Ἀριστείδην μὲν γὰρ
ηὔξησε Κλεισθένης καὶ Φωκίωνα Χαβρίας,
Λεύκολλον δὲ Σύλλας, Κάτωνα δὲ Μάξιμος,
Ἐπαμεινώνδας δὲ Παμμένη, καὶ Λύσανδρος
Ἀγησίλαον· ἀλλ᾽ οὗτος μὲν ὑπὸ φιλοτιμίας
ἀκαίρου καὶ ζηλοτυπίας διὰ δόξαν ὑβρίσας
ἀπέρριψε ταχὺ τὸν καθηγεμόνα τῶν πράξεων·
οἱ δ᾽ ἄλλοι καλῶς καὶ πολιτικῶς καὶ ἄχρι
τέλους ἐθεράπευσαν καὶ συνεπεκόσμησαν,
ὥσπερ τὰ πρὸς ἥλιον ὑφιστάμενα σώματα,
τὸ λαμπρῦνον αὐτοὺς πάλιν ἀφ᾽ ἑαυτῶν
αὔξοντες καὶ συνεκφωτίζοντες. οἱ γοῦν
Σκιπίωνι βασκαίνοντες ὑποκριτὴν αὐτὸν
ἀπεφαίνοντο τῶν πράξεων ποιητὴν δὲ Λαίλιον
τὸν ἑταῖρον, ὁ δὲ Λαίλιος ὑπ᾽ οὐδενὸς ἐπήρθη
τούτων ἀλλ᾽ ἀεὶ διετέλεσε τῇ Σκιπίωνος
ἀρετῇ καὶ δόξῃ συμφιλοτιμούμενος. Ἀφράνιος

these men, while still young and unknown, approached an older man of good reputation, and being gradually elevated by the older man's authority and increasing in stature by cooperating with him, fixed and rooted himself firmly into political life. In this way, Cleisthenes helped Aristides to grow and Chabrias helped Phocion; Sulla helped Lucullus; Fabius Maximus helped Cato the Elder; Epaminondas helped Pammenes; and Lysander helped Agesilaus. Now Agesilaus, because of ill-timed ambition and jealousy over Lysander's reputation, insulted and cast aside the man who had been his mentor, but the rest of these men nobly, politically, and until the very end cultivated and helped to adorn the men who had made them brilliant. They were like heavenly bodies that reflect the sun, and in honoring their mentors, they further

δὲ Πομπηίου φίλος, εἰ καὶ πάνυ ταπεινὸς
ἦν, ὅμως ἐπίδοξος ὢν ὕπατος αἱρεθήσεσθαι,
Πομπηίου σπουδάζοντος ἑτέροις, ἀπέστη τῆς
φιλοτιμίας εἰπὼν οὐκ ἂν οὕτω λαμπρὸν αὑτῷ
γενέσθαι τὸ τυχεῖν ὑπατείας, ὡς ἀνιαρὸν ἅμα
καὶ δυσχερές, εἰ Πομπηίου μὴ θέλοντος μηδὲ
συμπράττοντος· ἐνιαυτὸν οὖν ἀνασχόμενος
μόνον οὔτε τῆς ἀρχῆς ἀπέτυχε καὶ τὴν φιλίαν
διετήρησε. τοῖς δ᾽ οὕτω χειραγωγουμένοις ὑφ᾽
ἑτέρων ἐπὶ δόξαν ἅμα συμβαίνει χαρίζεσθαί
τε πολλοῖς, κἄν τι συμβαίνῃ δύσκολον, ἧττον
ἀπεχθάνεσθαι· διὸ καὶ Φίλιππος Ἀλεξάνδρῳ
παρῄνει κτᾶσθαι φίλους, ἕως ἔξεστι,
βασιλεύοντος ἑτέρου πρὸς χάριν ὁμιλοῦντα καὶ
φιλοφρονούμενον.

increased their own stature and made themselves radiant too. Those who disparaged Scipio Aemilianus declared that he was only an actor and that his friend Laelius was the author of his deeds, but Laelius was never flattered by any of these people and never ceased to associate himself with Scipio's virtue and glory. And Afranius, the friend of Pompey, although he was very humble nonetheless was expecting to be elected consul. But when Pompey was supporting other candidates, Afranius renounced his ambition, declaring that gaining the consulship would not be glorious but would instead cause him grief and distress, if Pompey did not want him to hold the office and was not supporting him. Then, after holding out for just one year, he both won the consulship and preserved Pompey's friendship.[20] And so it happens that

ΠΟΛΙΤΙΚΑ ΠΑΡΑΓΓΕΛΜΑΤΑ

Αἱρεῖσθαι δὲ δεῖ τὸν ἀρχόμενον πολιτείας
ἡγεμόνα μὴ ἁπλῶς τὸν ἔνδοξον καὶ δυνατόν,
ἀλλὰ καὶ τὸν δι' ἀρετὴν τοιοῦτον. ὡς γὰρ οὐ
πᾶν δένδρον ἐθέλει προσίεσθαι καὶ φέρειν
περιπλεκομένην τὴν ἄμπελον ἀλλ' ἔνια
καταπνίγει καὶ διαφθείρει τὴν αὔξησιν αὐτῆς,
οὕτως ἐν ταῖς πόλεσιν οἱ μὴ φιλόκαλοι,
φιλότιμοι δὲ καὶ φίλαρχοι μόνον, οὐ προΐενται
τοῖς νέοις πράξεων ἀφορμάς, ἀλλ' ὥσπερ
τροφὴν ἑαυτῶν τὴν δόξαν ἀφαιρουμένους
πιέζουσιν ὑπὸ φθόνου καὶ καταμαραίνουσιν· ὡς

those who are mentored by others as they build their reputations are well received by the people and, if they run into trouble, encounter less hostility. For this reason, Philip advised Alexander to take advantage of the fact that someone else was king and, while he was able, to make friends by engaging in pleasant conversation and treating others kindly.

But those starting out in politics must not select as a guide someone who is merely highly esteemed and powerful. Rather, they must select someone who has become esteemed and powerful on account of their virtue. Not every tree is willing to accept and support the vine that wraps itself around its branches, but some actually choke and destroy the vine's growth. Similarly, there are people in our cities who do not love goodness,[21] but who only love

Μάριος ἐν Λιβύῃ καὶ πάλιν ἐν Γαλατίᾳ πολλὰ
διὰ Σύλλα κατορθώσας ἐπαύσατο χρώμενος,
ἀχθεσθεὶς μὲν αὐτοῦ τῇ αὐξήσει, πρόφασιν δὲ
τὴν σφραγῖδα ποιησάμενος ἀπέρριψεν· ὁ γὰρ
Σύλλας, ὅτε τῷ Μαρίῳ στρατηγοῦντι συνῆν
ταμιεύων ἐν Λιβύῃ, πεμφθεὶς ὑπ᾽ αὐτοῦ πρὸς
Βῶκχον ἤγαγεν Ἰογόρθαν αἰχμάλωτον· οἷα δὲ
νέος φιλότιμος, ἄρτι δόξης γεγευμένος, οὐκ
ἤνεγκε μετρίως τὸ εὐτύχημα, γλυψάμενος δ᾽
εἰκόνα τῆς πράξεως ἐν σφραγῖδι τὸν Ἰογόρθαν
αὐτῷ παραδιδόμενον ἐφόρει· καὶ τοῦτ᾽
ἐγκαλῶν ὁ Μάριος ἀπέρριψεν αὐτόν· ὁ δὲ πρὸς
Κάτουλον καὶ Μέτελλον ἄνδρας ἀγαθοὺς καὶ
Μαρίῳ διαφόρους μεταστὰς ταχὺ τὸν Μάριον
ἐξήλασε καὶ κατέλυσε τῷ ἐμφυλίῳ πολέμῳ
μικροῦ δεήσαντα τὴν Ῥώμην ἀνατρέψαι.
Σύλλας μέντοι καὶ Πομπήιον ἐκ νέου μὲν
ἦρεν ὑπεξανιστάμενος αὐτῷ καὶ τὴν κεφαλὴν
ἀποκαλυπτόμενος ἐπιόντι, καὶ τοῖς ἄλλοις νέοις
πράξεων ἡγεμονικῶν μεταδιδοὺς ἀφορμάς,

being honored and holding office, and so they do not concede to young people opportunities to perform civic duties. Rather, out of envy they suppress them and make them wither away, as though the young people were depriving them of their own glory, which is like their food. Thus, Marius in Libya and again in Gaul accomplished much through the agency of Sulla, but he stopped giving Sulla duties and dismissed him. He was agitated by his increased stature, but he used Sulla's seal-ring as a pretext. For when Sulla was serving as quaestor on campaign with Marius in Libya, Marius sent him on a mission that led to the capture of Jugurtha. Because he was young, ambitious, and had experienced his first taste of glory, Sulla did not handle his success with moderation. Instead, he had a seal-ring engraved with an image of the event, that is, with an

ἐνίους δὲ καὶ παροξύνων ἄκοντας, ἐνέπλησε
φιλοτιμίας καὶ ζήλου τὰ στρατεύματα· καὶ
πάντων ἐκράτησε βουλόμενος εἶναι μὴ μόνος
ἀλλὰ πρῶτος καὶ μέγιστος ἐν πολλοῖς καὶ
μεγάλοις. τούτων οὖν ἔχεσθαι δεῖ τῶν ἀνδρῶν
καὶ τούτοις ἐμφύεσθαι, μή, καθάπερ ὁ Αἰσώπου
βασιλίσκος ἐπὶ τῶν ὤμων τοῦ ἀετοῦ κομισθεὶς
αἰφνίδιον ἐξέπτη καὶ προέφθασεν, οὕτω τὴν
ἐκείνων δόξαν ὑφαρπάζοντας αὐτοὺς ἀλλὰ
παρ᾽ ἐκείνων ἅμα μετ᾽ εὐνοίας καὶ φιλίας
λαμβάνοντας, ὡς οὐδ᾽ ἄρξαι καλῶς τοὺς μὴ
πρότερον ὀρθῶς δουλεύσαντας, ᾗ φησιν ὁ
Πλάτων, δυναμένους.

image of Jugurtha being handed over into his custody, and he used to wear it. Citing this offense, Marius dismissed him. Then Sulla transferred his allegiance to Catulus and Metellus, good men who were opponents of Marius, and swiftly drove Marius into exile and deposed him by means of civil war, after he had very nearly overthrown Rome. Sulla, however, was building up Pompey from the time he was a young man, rising when Pompey came into his presence and uncovering his head,[22] and he was also granting to other young men opportunities to play leadership roles. He even encouraged some young men who were reluctant, and so he filled his armies with ambition and zeal. In the end he dominated everyone because he wished not to be alone in power but to be first and greatest among many great men. This is the sort of mentor that we

Ἕπεται δὲ τούτοις ἡ περὶ φίλων κρίσις,
μήτε τὴν Θεμιστοκλέους ἐπαινοῦσα μήτε
τὴν Κλέωνος διάνοιαν. ὁ μὲν γὰρ Κλέων, ὅτε
πρῶτον ἔγνω τῆς πολιτείας ἅπτεσθαι, τοὺς
φίλους συναγαγὼν εἰς ταὐτὸ διελύσατο τὴν
φιλίαν πρὸς αὐτούς, ὡς πολλὰ τῆς ὀρθῆς
καὶ δικαίας προαιρέσεως μαλάσσουσαν ἐν

must hold fast and cling to. Now Aesop's wren was being conveyed on the back of an eagle but then it suddenly flew off and got out in front.[23] We must not, in that manner, snatch glory away from our mentors. We must instead receive glory from them, together with their goodwill and friendship, since, as Plato says, people cannot be good leaders unless they have first been good servants.[24]

POLITICAL FRIENDSHIPS

Your next step is to make a judgment concerning your friends, for which the attitude neither of Themistocles nor of Cleon is recommended. For Cleon, when he first decided to enter politics, gathered his friends together and then dissolved his friendship with them, on the ground

τῇ πολιτείᾳ καὶ παράγουσαν· ἄμεινον δ᾽
ἂν ἐποίησε τὴν φιλοπλουτίαν ἐκβαλὼν τῆς
ψυχῆς καὶ τὴν φιλονεικίαν καὶ φθόνου καὶ
κακοηθείας καθήρας αὑτόν· οὐ γὰρ ἀφίλων
αἱ πόλεις ἀνδρῶν καὶ ἀνεταίρων ἀλλὰ
χρηστῶν καὶ σωφρόνων δέονται· νυνὶ δὲ τοὺς
μὲν φίλους ἀπήλασεν, "ἑκατὸν δὲ κύκλῳ
κεφαλαὶ κολάκων οἰμωξομένων ἐλιχμῶντο"
περὶ αὐτόν, ὡς οἱ κωμικοὶ λέγουσι· καὶ
τραχὺς ὢν πρὸς τοὺς ἐπιεικεῖς καὶ βαρὺς
αὖθις ὑπέβαλλε τοῖς πολλοῖς πρὸς χάριν
ἑαυτόν, "γερονταγωγῶν κἀναμισθαρνεῖν
διδούς," καὶ τὸ φαυλότατον καὶ τὸ νοσοῦν
μάλιστα τοῦ δήμου προσεταιριζόμενος ἐπὶ
τοὺς ἀρίστους. ὁ δὲ Θεμιστοκλῆς πάλιν
πρὸς τὸν ἀποφηνάμενον, ὡς ἄρξει καλῶς
ἴσον ἅπασι παρέχων ἑαυτόν, "μηδέποτ᾽,"
εἶπεν, "εἰς τοιοῦτον ἐγὼ καθίσαιμι θρόνον,
ἐν ᾧ πλέον οὐχ ἕξουσιν οἱ φίλοι παρ᾽ ἐμοῦ
τῶν μὴ φίλων," οὐδ᾽ οὗτος ὀρθῶς τῇ φιλίᾳ

that friendship greatly weakens and corrupts one's ability to make correct and just political decisions. He would have done better, however, if he had cast greed and contentiousness from his soul and cleansed himself of envy and malice. For cities have no need of people who lack friends and companions, but they do need people who are useful and self-controlled. But as it was, he drove his friends away, "and the heads of a hundred accursed flatterers wagged their tongues in a ring" around him, as the comic poets say.[25] He became harsh and overbearing towards those who were reasonable and fair, and he made himself subservient to the multitude in order to win their favor, "tending them like old men and giving them an income." And finally, he joined forces with the diseased and lowest element of the people

κατεπαγγελλόμενος τὴν πολιτείαν καὶ τὰ
κοινὰ καὶ δημόσια ταῖς ἰδίαις χάρισι καὶ
σπουδαῖς ὑφιέμενος. καίτοι πρός γε Σιμωνίδην
ἀξιοῦντά τι τῶν μὴ δικαίων "οὔτε ποιητής,"
ἔφη, "σπουδαῖός ἐστιν ᾄδων παρὰ μέλος οὔτ᾽
ἄρχων ἐπιεικὴς παρὰ τὸν νόμον χαριζόμενος."

Δεινὸν γὰρ ὡς ἀληθῶς καὶ σχέτλιον,
εἰ ναύτας μὲν ἐκλέγεται κυβερνήτης καὶ
κυβερνήτην ναύκληρος

against the aristocracy. Themistocles, in his turn, when someone declared to him that he would govern nobly if he treated everyone equally, said, "May I never sit upon the sort of throne that prevents me from giving more to my friends than to everyone else." But he was wrong to make his politics beholden to his friendships, and wrong as well to make public affairs and the common good subservient to private favors and interests. When Simonides, however, asked for an unjust favor, Themistocles said, "A poet who violates the meter as he sings is no good, and a civic leader who violates the law in granting a favor is unfair."

But if a ship's pilot selects his sailors and the ship's captain selects his pilot, people "who know well how to work the rudder

εὖ μὲν ἐνὶ πρύμνῃ οἰήιον, εὖ δὲ κεραίην
εἰδότας ἐντείνασθαι ἐπορνυμένου ἀνέμοιο·

καί τις ἀρχιτέκτων ὑπουργοὺς καὶ χειροτέχνας,
οἳ μὴ διαφθεροῦσιν αὐτοῦ τοὔργον ἀλλ᾽
ἄριστα συνεκπονήσουσιν· ὁ δὲ πολιτικός,
ἀριστοτέχνας τις ὢν κατὰ Πίνδαρον καὶ
δημιουργὸς εὐνομίας καὶ δίκης, οὐκ εὐθὺς
αἱρήσεται φίλους ὁμοιοπαθεῖς καὶ ὑπηρέτας
καὶ συνενθουσιῶντας αὐτῷ πρὸς τὸ καλόν,
ἀλλ᾽ ἄλλους πρὸς ἄλλην ἀεὶ χρείαν κάμπτοντας
αὐτὸν ἀδίκως καὶ βιαίως· οὐδέν τ᾽ ὀφθήσεται
διαφέρων οἰκοδόμου τινὸς ἢ τέκτονος ἀπειρίᾳ
καὶ πλημμελείᾳ γωνίαις χρωμένου καὶ κανόσι
καὶ στάθμαις, ὑφ᾽ ὧν διαστρέφεσθαι τοὔργον
ἔμελλεν· ὄργανα γὰρ οἱ φίλοι ζῶντα καὶ
φρονοῦντα τῶν πολιτικῶν ἀνδρῶν εἰσι, καὶ
οὐ δεῖ συνολισθάνειν αὐτοῖς παραβαίνουσιν,
ἀλλὰ προσέχειν ὅπως μηδ᾽ ἀγνοούντων
αὐτῶν ἐξαμαρτάνωσι. τοῦτο γὰρ καὶ Σόλωνα

on the stern and to brace the yardarm when the wind is rising," and if an architect selects the laborers and artisans who will not ruin his work but will help him to execute it in the best way, it would truly be terrible and miserable if politicians, being the finest artisans according to Pindar and the creators of well-ordered government and justice, do not from the start select friends and subordinates who share their passions and their enthusiasm for what is truly good, but instead select friends who are constantly bending them unjustly and violently to other purposes. In that case, they would appear no different from a builder or carpenter who by inexperience and error misuses squares and rules and plumb lines, thereby ensuring that his final product will be misaligned. For friends are the living and thinking tools of politicians, who must

κατήσχυνε καὶ διέβαλε πρὸς τοὺς πολίτας·
ἐπεὶ γὰρ ἐν νῷ λαβὼν τὰ ὀφλήματα κουφίσαι
καὶ τὴν σεισάχθειαν (τοῦτο δ᾽ ἦν ὑποκόρισμα
χρεῶν ἀποκοπῆς) εἰσενεγκεῖν ἐκοινώσατο
τοῖς φίλοις· οἱ δ᾽ ἔργον ἀδικώτατον ἔπραξαν·
ἐδανείσαντο γὰρ ὑποφθάσαντες ἀργύριον
πολὺ καὶ μετ᾽ ὀλίγον χρόνον εἰς φῶς τοῦ
νόμου προαχθέντος οἱ μὲν ἐφάνησαν οἰκίας τε
λαμπρὰς καὶ γῆν συνεωνημένοι πολλὴν ἐξ ὧν
ἐδανείσαντο χρημάτων, ὁ δὲ Σόλων αἰτίαν ἔσχε
συναδικεῖν ἠδικημένος.

not be tripped up along with their friends as they misstep, but who must rather be on their guard not to commit errors even when their friends go wrong. Getting caught up in his friends' transgressions is precisely what caused shame even to Solon and damaged his reputation among the citizens. For when he had decided to lighten debts and to propose the "shaking-off" (which was what he called the cancellation of debt), he informed his friends, who committed a most unjust act. Moving quickly, they borrowed great sums of money, and when the law was unveiled a short time later, his friends were revealed to have purchased elaborate houses and large tracts of land with the money they had borrowed. And Solon, though he himself was harmed by their actions, was blamed for supporting them in their injustice.

Ἐπεὶ δὲ "πάσαις κορυδαλλίσι" κατὰ Σιμωνίδην
"χρὴ λόφον ἐγγενέσθαι" καὶ πᾶσα πολιτεία
φέρει τινὰς ἔχθρας καὶ διαφοράς, οὐχ ἥκιστα
προσήκει καὶ περὶ τούτων ἐσκέφθαι τὸν
πολιτικόν. οἱ μὲν οὖν πολλοὶ τὸν Θεμιστοκλέα
καὶ τὸν Ἀριστείδην ἐπαινοῦσιν ἐπὶ τῶν
ὅρων τὴν ἔχθραν ἀποτιθεμένους, ὁσάκις ἐπὶ
πρεσβείαν ἢ στρατηγίαν ἐξίοιεν, εἶτα πάλιν
ἀναλαμβάνοντας. ἐνίοις δὲ καὶ τὸ Κρητίνου
τοῦ Μάγνητος ὑπερφυῶς ἀρέσκει· Ἑρμείᾳ
γὰρ ἀντιπολιτευόμενος ἀνδρὶ οὐ δυνατῷ
μὲν φιλοτίμῳ δὲ καὶ λαμπρῷ τὴν ψυχήν,
ἐπεὶ κατέσχεν ὁ Μιθριδατικὸς πόλεμος, τὴν
πόλιν ὁρῶν κινδυνεύουσαν ἐκέλευσε τὸν
Ἑρμείαν τὴν ἀρχὴν παραλαβόντα χρῆσθαι
τοῖς πράγμασιν, αὐτοῦ μεταστάντος· εἰ δὲ
βούλεται στρατηγεῖν ἐκεῖνον, αὐτὸν ἐκποδὼν

COOPERATION AMONG POLITICIANS
AND CITIZENS

"All larks must have a crest," as Simonides says, and all political activity brings some enmity and disagreement. This being the case, the politician is quite right to give this matter some thought. Now most people praise Themistocles and Aristides, who used to set aside their mutual hostility at the border whenever they would go abroad on an embassy or military campaign, then take it up again when they returned. And some give very high marks to Cretinas of Magnesia, who was the political opponent of Hermeias, a man who was out of power but nonetheless possessed an ambitious and brilliant soul. When the war against Mithridates was pressing them and Cretinas saw that their city was in danger, he bid

ἀπελθεῖν, ὡς μὴ φιλοτιμούμενοι πρὸς ἀλλήλους
ἀπολέσειαν τὴν πόλιν. ἤρεσεν ἡ πρόκλησις
τῷ Ἑρμείᾳ, καὶ φήσας ἑαυτοῦ πολεμικώτερον
εἶναι τὸν Κρητίναν ὑπεξῆλθε μετὰ παίδων
καὶ γυναικός. ὁ δὲ Κρητίνας ἐκεῖνόν τε
προύπεμψε, τῶν ἰδίων χρημάτων ἐπιδοὺς ὅσα
φεύγουσιν ἦν ἢ πολιορκουμένοις χρησιμώτερα,
καὶ τὴν πόλιν ἄριστα στρατηγήσας παρ᾽
οὐδὲν ἐλθοῦσαν ἀπολέσθαι περιεποίησεν
ἀνελπίστως. εἰ γὰρ εὐγενὲς καὶ φρονήματος
μεγάλου τὸ ἀναφωνῆσαι "φιλῶ τέκν᾽, ἀλλὰ
πατρίδ᾽ ἐμὴν μᾶλλον φιλῶ," πῶς οὐκ ἐκείνοις
γε προχειρότερον εἰπεῖν ἑκάστῳ "μισῶ τὸν
δεῖνα καὶ βούλομαι ποιῆσαι κακῶς, ἀλλὰ
πατρίδ᾽ ἐμὴν μᾶλλον φιλῶ"; τὸ γὰρ μὴ θέλειν
διαλυθῆναι πρὸς ἐχθρόν, ὧν ἕνεκα δεῖ καὶ
φίλον προέσθαι, δεινῶς ἄγριον καὶ θηριῶδες.
οὐ μὴν ἀλλὰ βέλτιον οἱ περὶ Φωκίωνα
καὶ Κάτωνα, μηδ᾽ ὅλως ἔχθραν τινὰ πρὸς
πολιτικὰς τιθέμενοι διαφοράς, ἀλλὰ δεινοὶ καὶ

Hermeias to take charge and manage affairs while he went abroad, or if Hermeias preferred, he offered to assume command while Hermeias got himself out of the way. His purpose was to keep their rivalry from destroying the city. The proposal pleased Hermeias, and claiming that Cretinas was more skilled at making war than he was, he withdrew from the city along with his wife and children. Cretinas gave him an escort and furnished him with whatever he had in his own estate that was more useful to refugees than to people under siege. And then he nobly commanded the city, which came very near to destruction, and saved it though there had been little hope. Now if the declaration, "I love my children, but I love my country more," is noble and the product of a great spirit, was it not even easier for both Cretinas and Hermeias to

ἀπαραίτητοι μόνον ἐν τοῖς δημοσίοις ἀγῶσιν
ὄντες μὴ προέσθαι τὸ συμφέρον, ἐν δὲ τοῖς
ἰδίοις ἀμηνίτως καὶ φιλανθρώπως χρώμενοι
τοῖς ἐκεῖ διαφερομένοις.

Δεῖ γὰρ ἐχθρὸν μηδένα πολίτην νομίζειν,
ἂν μή τις, οἷος Ἀριστίων ἢ Νάβις ἢ Κατιλίνας,
νόσημα καὶ ἀπόστημα πόλεως ἐγγένηται·
τοὺς δ᾽ ἄλλως ἀπάδοντας ὥσπερ ἁρμονικὸν
ἐπιτείνοντα καὶ χαλῶντα πράως εἰς τὸ ἐμμελὲς
ἄγειν, μὴ τοῖς ἁμαρτάνουσι σὺν ὀργῇ καὶ

say, "I hate that man and wish to do him harm, but I love my country more"? For an unwillingness to be reconciled to our personal enemies in situations that cause us to forsake even our loved ones is terribly savage and brutal. But Phocion and Cato[26] were even better, for they brought no enmity at all to their political disagreements. Rather, they were stubborn and immovable in political wrangling only when it came to protecting the public welfare, but when they had personal disagreements with their political opponents, they handled them humanely and calmly.

You must not, in fact, consider any citizen to be your personal enemy, unless someone, like Aristion or Nabis or Catiline has appeared, who is a disease or an open sore for the city.[27] But those people with whom you are otherwise out of tune you

πρὸς ὕβριν ἐπιφυόμενον, ἀλλ᾽ ὡς Ὅμηρος
ἠθικώτερον· "ὦ πέπον, ἦ τ᾽ ἐφάμην σε περὶ
φρένας ἔμμεναι ἄλλων" καὶ "οἶσθα καὶ ἄλλον
μῦθον ἀμείνονα τοῦδε νοῆσαι." ἂν τέ τι χρηστὸν
εἴπωσιν ἢ πράξωσι, μὴ τιμαῖς ἀχθόμενον
αὐτῶν μηδὲ λόγων εὐφήμων ἐπὶ καλοῖς ἔργοις
φειδόμενον· οὕτω γὰρ ὅ τε ψόγος ὅπου δεῖ
πίστιν ἕξει, καὶ πρὸς τὴν κακίαν διαβαλοῦμεν
αὐτοὺς αὔξοντες τὴν ἀρετὴν καὶ ταῦτα
παραβάλλοντες ἐκείνοις ὡς ἄξια καὶ πρέποντα
μᾶλλον. ἐγὼ δὲ καὶ μαρτυρεῖν ἀξιῶ τὰ δίκαια
καὶ τοῖς διαφόροις τὸν πολιτικὸν ἄνδρα καὶ
βοηθεῖν κρινομένοις πρὸς τοὺς συκοφάντας
καὶ ταῖς διαβολαῖς ἀπιστεῖν, ἂν ὦσιν ἀλλότριαι
τῆς προαιρέσεως αὐτῶν· ὥσπερ ὁ Νέρων
ἐκεῖνος ὀλίγον ἔμπροσθεν ἢ κτεῖναι τὸν
Θρασέαν μάλιστα μισῶν καὶ φοβούμενος, ὅμως
ἐγκαλοῦντός τινος ὡς κακῶς κεκριμένου καὶ
ἀδίκως, "ἐβουλόμην ἄν," ἔφη, "Θρασέαν οὕτως
ἐμὲ φιλεῖν, ὡς δικαστὴς ἄριστός ἐστιν."

must gently adjust, as a musician tightens and loosens strings, and bring them back into tune, rather than angrily and insolently attacking them when they are making mistakes. And you must treat them rather tactfully, in the manner of Homer, saying for example, "My friend, I thought that you were wiser than the rest"[28] and "You know how to come with up a speech better than this one."[29] And if they should say or do something good, you must not be irritated by the honors they receive or be sparing in your compliments of their good works. For thus your criticism, whenever you must make it, will be trusted, and you will divert people from making trouble by building up their virtue and demonstrating to them the sorts of deeds that are more valuable and appropriate. I personally think that politicians should testify to the just actions

Πολιτείας δ᾿ οἱ μὲν εἰς ἅπαν ἐνδύονται μέρος, ὥσπερ ὁ Κάτων, οὐδεμιᾶς ἀξιοῦντες εἰς δύναμιν ἀπολείπεσθαι φροντίδος οὐδ᾿

even of those people with whom they are at odds politically, and they should assist them when they go to trial against false accusers and disbelieve slanders made against them, if the slanders are contrary to their actual conduct. This is how even the infamous Nero behaved not long before he put Thrasea to death: although he especially hated and feared him, nonetheless when someone was accusing Thrasea of judging a court case unfairly and unjustly, Nero supported him, saying, "I wish Thrasea were as excellent a friend to me as he is a judge."

A LEADER SHOULD DO ANYTHING,
BUT NOT EVERYTHING

Now some people, such as Cato, involve themselves in every aspect of government, in the belief that good citizens, to the best

ἐπιμελείας τὸν ἀγαθὸν πολίτην· καὶ τὸν
Ἐπαμεινώνδαν ἐπαινοῦσιν, ὅτι φθόνῳ καὶ
πρὸς ὕβριν ἀποδειχθεὶς τέλμαρχος ὑπὸ τῶν
Θηβαίων οὐκ ἠμέλησεν, ἀλλ᾿ εἰπὼν ὡς οὐ
μόνον ἀρχὴ ἄνδρα δείκνυσιν ἀλλὰ καὶ ἀρχὴν
ἀνήρ, εἰς μέγα καὶ σεμνὸν ἀξίωμα προήγαγε
τὴν τελμαρχίαν, οὐδὲν οὖσαν πρότερον ἀλλ᾿
ἢ περὶ τοὺς στενωποὺς ἐκβολῆς κοπρίων καὶ
ῥευμάτων ἀποτροπῆς ἐπιμέλειάν τινα. κἀγὼ δ᾿
ἀμέλει παρέχω γέλωτα τοῖς παρεπιδημοῦσιν,
ὁρώμενος ἐν δημοσίῳ περὶ τὰ τοιαῦτα
πολλάκις· ἀλλὰ βοηθεῖ μοι τὸ τοῦ Ἀντισθένους
μνημονευόμενον· θαυμάσαντος γάρ τινος, εἰ
δι᾿ ἀγορᾶς αὐτὸς φέρει τάριχος, "ἐμαυτῷ γ᾿,"
εἶπεν· ἐγὼ δ᾿ ἀνάπαλιν πρὸς τοὺς ἐγκαλοῦντας,
εἰ κεράμῳ παρέστηκα διαμετρουμένῳ καὶ
φυράμασι καὶ λίθοις παρακομιζομένοις, "οὐκ
ἐμαυτῷ γε," φημί, "ταῦτ᾿ οἰκοδομῶν ἀλλὰ
τῇ πατρίδι." καὶ γὰρ εἰς ἄλλα πολλὰ μικρὸς
ἄν τις εἴη καὶ γλίσχρος αὑτῷ διοικῶν καὶ δι᾿

of their ability, never abandon their concern and care for the state. And people praise Epaminondas because he did not neglect his duty even when the Thebans appointed him to an insignificant office out of envy and to insult him. On the contrary, he declared that not only does an office bring distinction to a man, but a man also brings distinction to an office. Then he proceeded to transform that insignificant office into a great and respected honor, even though previously it had involved nothing more than overseeing the clearing of dung and the diverting of water from the streets. And no doubt even I myself provide a good laugh to people visiting our town, when they see me out in public performing similar duties, as I often do. But in this situation Antisthenes's memorable remark comes to my aid. For when someone expressed surprise

αὐτὸν πραγματευόμενος· εἰ δὲ δημοσίᾳ καὶ
διὰ τὴν πόλιν, οὐκ ἀγεννής, ἀλλὰ μεῖζον τὸ
μέχρι μικρῶν ἐπιμελὲς καὶ πρόθυμον. ἕτεροι
δὲ σεμνότερον οἴονται καὶ μεγαλοπρεπέστερον
εἶναι τὸ τοῦ Περικλέους· ὧν καὶ Κριτόλαός
ἐστιν ὁ Περιπατητικὸς ἀξιῶν, ὥσπερ ἡ
Σαλαμινία ναῦς Ἀθήνησι καὶ ἡ Πάραλος οὐκ
ἐπὶ πᾶν ἔργον ἀλλ᾽ ἐπὶ τὰς ἀναγκαίας καὶ
μεγάλας κατεσπῶντο πράξεις, οὕτως ἑαυτῷ
πρὸς τὰ κυριώτατα καὶ μέγιστα χρῆσθαι, ὡς ὁ
τοῦ κόσμου βασιλεύς,

τῶν ἄγαν γὰρ ἅπτεται
θεός, τὰ μικρὰ δ᾽ εἰς τύχην ἀνεὶς ἐᾷ

κατὰ τὸν Εὐριπίδην.

that he was personally carrying his salted
fish through the marketplace, he said, "Of
course I am, since it's for me."[30] Conversely,
when people reproach me for being on the
job while tiles are being measured or cement and stones are being delivered, I say
to them, "Look, I'm not building these
things for myself, but for my native city."
And so it is with many other small projects:
people would be petty and parsimonious if
they oversaw these projects for themselves
and carried them out on their own behalf,
but when they undertake them as a public
service and on behalf of the city, they are
not at all undignified. Indeed, the care and
eagerness they devote to small matters becomes even more significant. Others, however, believe that the attitude of Pericles
was more honorable and appropriate to his
high stature. Among them is Critolaus, the

Οὐδὲ γὰρ τοῦ Θεαγένους τὸ φιλότιμον ἄγαν
καὶ φιλόνεικον ἐπαινοῦμεν, ὃς οὐ μόνον τὴν
περίοδον νενικηκὼς ἀλλὰ καὶ πολλοὺς ἀγῶνας,
οὐ παγκρατίῳ μόνον ἀλλὰ καὶ πυγμῇ καὶ
δολίχῳ, τέλος ἥρῳα δειπνῶν ἐπιταφίου τινός,
ὥσπερ εἰώθει, προτεθείσης ἅπασι τῆς μερίδος,
ἀναπηδήσας διεπαγκρατίασεν, ὡς οὐδένα νικᾶν
δέον αὐτοῦ παρόντος· ὅθεν ἤθροισε χιλίους
καὶ διακοσίους στεφάνους, ὧν συρφετὸν ἄν τις

Peripatetic philosopher, who thinks that, just as the Athenians' state ships *Salaminia* and *Paralus* were not launched for ordinary tasks but were reserved for essential and great missions, so political leaders should apply themselves only to the most important and greatest matters, following the example of the king of the universe: "For god lays hold of the great affairs but lets the small ones be, leaving them to chance," as Euripides says.

I do not agree. Neither, however, do I approve of the excessive love of honor and contentiousness of Theagenes, a man who was victorious at the four great athletic festivals[31] and in many other competitions, and who won not only in the pancratium[32] but also in boxing and the long race. After all this, he was attending a festival held at the shrine of a certain hero, and after the

ἡγήσαιτο τοὺς πλείστους. οὐδὲν οὖν τούτου
διαφέρουσιν οἱ πρὸς πᾶσαν ἀποδυόμενοι
πολιτικὴν πρᾶξιν, ἀλλὰ μεμπτούς τε ταχὺ
ποιοῦσιν ἑαυτοὺς τοῖς πολλοῖς, ἐπαχθεῖς τε
γίγνονται καὶ κατορθοῦντες ἐπίφθονοι, κἂν
σφαλῶσιν, ἐπίχαρτοι, καὶ τὸ θαυμαζόμενον
αὐτῶν ἐν ἀρχῇ τῆς ἐπιμελείας εἰς χλευασμὸν
ὑπονοστεῖ καὶ γέλωτα.

Τῇ μὲν γὰρ εὐνοίᾳ καὶ κηδεμονίᾳ δεῖ
μηδενὸς ἀφεστάναι τῶν κοινῶν, ἀλλὰ πᾶσι
προσέχειν καὶ γιγνώσκειν ἕκαστα, μηδ᾽
ὥσπερ ἐν πλοίῳ σκεῦος ἱερὸν ἀποκεῖσθαι
τὰς ἐσχάτας περιμένοντα χρείας τῆς πόλεως

feast had been served to everyone as usual, he leapt up to begin the pancratium, believing that no one else ought to be victorious if he was in the contest. As a result, he collected twelve-hundred victory crowns, most of which you would consider to be essentially worthless. Those who strip[33] for every leadership opportunity are no different from Theagenes: they swiftly make themselves contemptible to the people; they become oppressive and envied when they succeed, and they bring joy to others when they fail; and the very attributes that earned them admiration when they first took office become the source of mockery and ridicule.

And so, we must not stand aloof from any public duty, but out of goodwill and concern we must be attentive and knowledgeable about everything. And we must not stow ourselves away, like the "sacred

καὶ τύχας· ἀλλ᾽ ὡς οἱ κυβερνῆται τὰ μὲν ταῖς
χερσὶ δι᾽ αὑτῶν πράττουσι, τὰ δ᾽ ὀργάνοις
ἑτέροις δι᾽ ἑτέρων ἄπωθεν καθήμενοι
περιάγουσι καὶ στρέφουσι, χρῶνται δὲ καὶ
ναύταις καὶ πρῳρεῦσι καὶ κελευσταῖς, καὶ
τούτων ἐνίους ἀνακαλούμενοι πολλάκις εἰς
πρύμναν ἐγχειρίζουσι τὸ πηδάλιον· οὕτω τῷ
πολιτικῷ προσήκει παραχωρεῖν μὲν ἑτέροις
ἄρχειν καὶ προσκαλεῖσθαι πρὸς τὸ βῆμα
μετ᾽ εὐμενείας καὶ φιλανθρωπίας, κινεῖν δὲ
μὴ πάντα τὰ τῆς πόλεως τοῖς αὑτοῦ λόγοις
καὶ ψηφίσμασιν ἢ πράξεσιν, ἀλλ᾽ ἔχοντα
πιστοὺς καὶ ἀγαθοὺς ἄνδρας ἕκαστον ἑκάστῃ
χρείᾳ κατὰ τὸ οἰκεῖον προσαρμόττειν· ὡς
Περικλῆς Μενίππῳ μὲν ἐχρῆτο πρὸς τὰς
στρατηγίας, δι᾽ Ἐφιάλτου δὲ τὴν ἐξ Ἀρείου
πάγου βουλὴν ἐταπείνωσε, διὰ δὲ Χαρίνου
τὸ κατὰ Μεγαρέων ἐκύρωσε ψήφισμα,
Λάμπωνα δὲ Θουρίων οἰκιστὴν ἐξέπεμψεν.
οὐ γὰρ μόνον, τῆς δυνάμεως εἰς πολλοὺς

anchor" on a ship,[34] waiting for our city to experience an extreme need or misfortune. Rather, consider the ships' pilots. They manage the tiller with their own hands, but they also turn and rotate other devices by means of tackle handled by the crew, while they themselves sit at a distance. Thus, they rely on sailors, bosuns, and their lookouts on the bow, and they often summon some of these crew members to the stern and entrust them with the tiller. In the same way, it is proper that politicians yield to others with goodwill and kindness, allowing them to govern and be summoned to the speaker's platform. And they must not accomplish all the public's business by their own speeches, decrees, and actions, but having under them assistants who are trustworthy and of good character, they should assign each one to

διανέμεσθαι δοκούσης, ἧττον ἐνοχλεῖ τῶν
φθόνων τὸ μέγεθος, ἀλλὰ καὶ τὰ τῶν χρειῶν
ἐπιτελεῖται μᾶλλον. ὡς γὰρ ὁ τῆς χειρὸς
εἰς τοὺς δακτύλους μερισμὸς οὐκ ἀσθενῆ
πεποίηκεν ἀλλὰ τεχνικὴν καὶ ὀργανικὴν αὐτῆς
τὴν χρῆσιν, οὕτως ὁ πραγμάτων ἑτέροις ἐν
πολιτείᾳ μεταδιδοὺς ἐνεργοτέραν ποιεῖ τῇ
κοινωνίᾳ τὴν πρᾶξιν· ὁ δ᾽ ἀπληστίᾳ δόξης ἢ
δυνάμεως πᾶσαν αὐτῷ τὴν πόλιν ἀνατιθεὶς καὶ
πρὸς ὃ μὴ πέφυκε μηδ᾽ ἤσκηται προσάγων
αὐτόν, ὡς Κλέων πρὸς τὸ στρατηγεῖν,
Φιλοποίμην δὲ πρὸς τὸ ναυαρχεῖν, Ἀννίβας
δὲ πρὸς τὸ δημηγορεῖν, οὐκ ἔχει παραίτησιν
ἁμαρτάνων ἀλλὰ προσακούει τὸ τοῦ
Εὐριπίδου "τέκτων γὰρ ὢν ἔπρασσες οὐ
ξυλουργικά" λέγειν ἀπίθανος ὢν ἐπρέσβευες
ἢ ῥᾴθυμος ὢν ᾠκονόμεις, ψήφων ἄπειρος
ἐταμίευες ἢ γέρων καὶ ἀσθενὴς ἐστρατήγεις.
Περικλῆς δὲ καὶ πρὸς Κίμωνα διενείματο
τὴν δύναμιν, αὐτὸς μὲν ἄρχειν ἐν ἄστει, τὸν

the task for which they are best suited. Thus, Pericles employed Menippus in the generalship, checked the power of the Areopagus council through the agency of Ephialtes, passed the decree punishing the city of Megara through Charinus, and sent out Lampon to found the colony at Thurii. When power appears to be distributed among many people, not only are we less troubled by an accumulation of envy, but we are also more capable of accomplishing what must be done. For just as the division of the hand into fingers does not render it weak but instead makes it a usable and practical instrument, so those who share political power with others make the work of government more effective by their cooperation. By contrast, there are some who, out of an insatiable desire for glory or power, take full responsibility for the city

δὲ πληρώσαντα τὰς ναῦς τοῖς βαρβάροις
πολεμεῖν· ἦν γὰρ ὁ μὲν πρὸς πολιτείαν ὁ δὲ
πρὸς πόλεμον εὐφυέστερος.

upon themselves and apply themselves to tasks for which they are neither naturally talented nor trained, as Cleon did when he became general, or Philopoemen as admiral, or Hannibal when he addressed the assembly. Such people have no excuse when they fail, but they must moreover endure the criticism that we read in Euripides, "You're a carpenter, but you didn't work with wood." We might similarly criticize someone by saying, "You're an unpersuasive speaker, but you were leading an embassy," "You're careless, but you became an administrator," "You're inexperienced in accounting, but you were acting as treasurer," or "You're old and infirm, but you were leading an army." Pericles, however, shared power even with Cimon, governing in Athens while his rival recruited crews for the city's ships and made war abroad,

Ἐπεὶ δὲ παντὶ δήμῳ τὸ κακόηθες καὶ
φιλαίτιον ἔνεστι πρὸς τοὺς πολιτευομένους
καὶ πολλὰ τῶν χρησίμων, ἂν μὴ στάσιν ἔχῃ
μηδ᾽ ἀντιλογίαν, ὑπονοοῦσι πράττεσθαι
συνωμοτικῶς, καὶ τοῦτο διαβάλλει μάλιστα
τὰς ἑταιρείας καὶ φιλίας, ἀληθινὴν μὲν ἔχθραν
ἢ διαφορὰν οὐδεμίαν ἑαυτοῖς ὑπολειπτέον,
ὡς ὁ τῶν Χίων δημαγωγὸς Ὀνομάδημος οὐκ
εἴα τῇ στάσει κρατήσας πάντας ἐκβάλλειν
τοὺς ὑπεναντίους "ὅπως," ἔφη, "μὴ πρὸς τοὺς
φίλους ἀρξώμεθα διαφέρεσθαι, τῶν ἐχθρῶν
παντάπασιν ἀπαλλαγέντες." τοῦτο μὲν γὰρ
εὔηθες· ἀλλ᾽ ὅταν ὑπόπτως ἔχωσιν οἱ πολλοὶ
πρός τι πρᾶγμα καὶ μέγα καὶ σωτήριον, οὐ
δεῖ πάντας ὥσπερ ἀπὸ συντάξεως ἥκοντας
τὴν αὐτὴν λέγειν γνώμην, ἀλλὰ καὶ δύο καὶ
τρεῖς διαστάντας ἀντιλέγειν ἠρέμα τῶν φίλων,
εἶθ᾽ ὥσπερ ἐξελεγχομένους μετατίθεσθαι·

for Pericles was more naturally suited to politics, while Cimon was better in war.

The people in every city can be malicious and inclined to find fault with their political leaders. Moreover, unless they observe some partisanship or opposition, the people suspect many good policies of being implemented by conspiracy, which leads especially to criticism of their leaders' political connections and friendships. Now, politicians must not allow any real hostility or disagreements between themselves to persist, as Onomademus the demagogue of Chios did. After emerging victorious from a factional fight, he would not allow his party to drive all its enemies from the city, "So that we don't begin to fight with our friends," he explained, "once we've rid ourselves entirely of our enemies." That approach is simple-minded.

συνεφέλκονται γὰρ οὕτω τὸν δῆμον, ὑπὸ τοῦ
συμφέροντος ἄγεσθαι δόξαντες. ἐν μέντοι τοῖς
ἐλάττοσι καὶ πρὸς μέγα μηδὲν διήκουσιν οὐ
χεῖρόν ἐστι καὶ ἀληθῶς ἐὰν διαφέρεσθαι τοὺς
φίλους, ἕκαστον ἰδίῳ λογισμῷ χρώμενον, ὅπως
περὶ τὰ κυριώτατα καὶ μέγιστα φαίνωνται
πρὸς τὸ βέλτιστον οὐκ ἐκ παρασκευῆς
ὁμοφρονοῦντες.

But whenever the people are suspicious of some important and beneficial proposal, do not allow every politician to come forward and speak the same opinion, as if by prior agreement. Instead, two or three of your friends should openly disagree and speak calmly in opposition, and then, acting as though their position has been refuted, they should change sides. For by this stratagem, your friends will bring the people along with them, because they appear to have been won over by what is advantageous to the city. In less important matters, however, there is no harm in allowing your friends to rely on their own reasoning and to genuinely disagree, so that when it comes to the most important issues, they may appear to reach consensus about the best course of action without any prearrangement.

Φύσει μὲν οὖν ἄρχων ἀεὶ πόλεως ὁ
πολιτικὸς ὥσπερ ἡγεμὼν ἐν μελίτταις, καὶ
τοῦτο χρὴ διανοούμενον ἔχειν τὰ δημόσια
διὰ χειρός· ἃς δ᾽ ὀνομάζουσιν ἐξουσίας καὶ
χειροτονοῦσιν ἀρχὰς μήτ᾽ ἄγαν διώκειν καὶ
πολλάκις, οὐ γὰρ σεμνὸν οὐδὲ δημοτικὸν
ἡ φιλαρχία· μήτ᾽ ἀπωθεῖσθαι, τοῦ δήμου
κατὰ νόμον διδόντος καὶ καλοῦντος· ἀλλὰ
κἂν ταπεινότεραι τῆς δόξης ὦσι, δέχεσθαι
καὶ συμφιλοτιμεῖσθαι· δίκαιον γὰρ ὑπὸ τῶν
μειζόνων κοσμουμένους ἀρχῶν ἀντικοσμεῖν
τὰς ἐλάττονας, καὶ τῶν μὲν βαρυτέρων οἷον
στρατηγίας Ἀθήνησι καὶ πρυτανείας ἐν Ῥόδῳ
καὶ βοιωταρχίας παρ᾽ ἡμῖν, ὑφίεσθαί τι καὶ
παρενδιδόναι μετριάζοντα ταῖς δὲ μικροτέραις
ἀξίωμα προστιθέναι καὶ ὄγκον, ὅπως μήτε περὶ
ταύτας εὐκαταφρόνητοι μήτ᾽ ἐπίφθονοι περὶ
ἐκείνας ὦμεν.

It is natural, then, that politicians always provide leadership in a city, just as the queen is leader among bees, and bearing this in mind, politicians must manage public affairs. Even so, they should pursue neither aggressively nor excessively those offices that confer power and are won by election, for there is nothing honorable or democratic in the love of holding office. But they should not refuse an appointment, either, if the people are calling them to serve and bestowing power lawfully. And they should accept and eagerly serve even in positions that are beneath their dignity, for politicians who enjoy renown because they have held the greater offices are obligated in turn to elevate the stature of the lesser offices by holding them, too. And with regard to the most impressive positions, such as the generalship at Athens, membership on the city

Εἰσιόντα δ' εἰς ἅπασαν ἀρχὴν οὐ μόνον ἐκείνους δεῖ προχειρίζεσθαι τοὺς λογισμούς, οὓς ὁ Περικλῆς αὑτὸν ὑπεμίμνησκεν ἀναλαμβάνων τὴν χλαμύδα, "πρόσεχε, Περίκλεις· ἐλευθέρων ἄρχεις, Ἑλλήνων ἄρχεις, πολιτῶν Ἀθηναίων"· ἀλλὰ κἀκεῖνο λέγειν πρὸς ἑαυτόν, "ἀρχόμενος ἄρχεις, ὑποτεταγμένης πόλεως ἀνθυπάτοις, ἐπιτρόποις Καίσαρος· 'οὐ ταῦτα λόγχη πεδιάς,' οὐδ' αἱ παλαιαὶ Σάρδεις οὐδ' ἡ Λυδῶν ἐκείνη δύναμις"· εὐσταλεστέραν δεῖ τὴν χλαμύδα

council at Rhodes, and leadership of our allied Boeotian cities, politicians are likewise obligated to show moderation, giving way sometimes and yielding to others, while in turn adding honor and distinction to the lesser positions. In this way, we may avoid being either despised or envied.

KNOW YOUR PLACE AND YOUR POWER

As you begin every term of office, you must bear in mind the sentiment that Pericles used to repeat to himself whenever he put on the general's cloak: "Be mindful, O Pericles, that you are leading free people; you are leading Greeks and citizens of Athens." Not only that, but say this to yourself as well: "You are a governor, but you yourself are also governed; you lead a city that is subject to the proconsul, who

ποιεῖν, καὶ βλέπειν ἀπὸ τοῦ στρατηγίου πρὸς
τὸ βῆμα, καὶ τῷ στεφάνῳ μὴ πολὺ φρονεῖν
μηδὲ πιστεύειν, ὁρῶντα τοὺς καλτίους ἐπάνω
τῆς κεφαλῆς· ἀλλὰ μιμεῖσθαι τοὺς ὑποκριτάς,
πάθος μὲν ἴδιον καὶ ἦθος καὶ ἀξίωμα τῷ ἀγῶνι
προστιθέντας, τοῦ δ᾽ ὑποβολέως ἀκούοντας καὶ
μὴ παρεκβαίνοντας τοὺς ῥυθμοὺς καὶ τὰ μέτρα
τῆς διδομένης ἐξουσίας ὑπὸ τῶν κρατούντων.
ἡ γὰρ ἔκπτωσις οὐ φέρει συριγμὸν οὐδὲ
χλευασμὸν οὐδὲ κλωγμόν, ἀλλὰ πολλοῖς μὲν
ἐπέβη "δεινὸς κολαστὴς πέλεκυς αὐχένος
τομεύς," ὡς τοῖς περὶ Παρδάλαν τὸν ὑμέτερον
ἐκλαθομένοις τῶν ὅρων· ὁ δέ τις ἐκριφεὶς εἰς
νῆσον γέγονε κατὰ τὸν Σόλωνα

Φολεγάνδριος ἢ Σικινήτης,
ἀντί γ᾽ Ἀθηναίου πατρίδ᾽ ἀμειψάμενος.

is the representative of Caesar. 'There
are no spears upon the plain;'[35] Sardis of
old is gone, and so is that famous Lydian
army."[36] You must wear a cloak suited to
your circumstances; you must turn your
gaze away from the general's headquarters
and look instead to the speaker's platform;
and you must not think too highly of or
place too much trust in your crown, since
you can see the proconsul's boots above
your head. Instead, you should imitate the
actors: they pour their own emotion, character, and dignity into their performances,
but they nonetheless obey the prompter
that feeds them lines and do not violate the
rhythms and meters of their parts, which
are assigned to them by those who run the
show.[37] For a transgression while in office
does not result merely in hissing, mockery,
or boos, but "the dreadful punisher, the axe

Τὰ μὲν γὰρ μικρὰ παιδία τῶν πατέρων
ὁρῶντες ἐπιχειροῦντα τὰς κρηπῖδας ὑποδεῖσθαι
καὶ τοὺς στεφάνους περιτίθεσθαι μετὰ παιδιᾶς
γελῶμεν, οἱ δ᾽ ἄρχοντες ἐν ταῖς πόλεσιν
ἀνοήτως τὰ τῶν προγόνων ἔργα καὶ φρονήματα
καὶ πράξεις ἀσυμμέτρους τοῖς παροῦσι καιροῖς
καὶ πράγμασιν οὔσας μιμεῖσθαι κελεύοντες
ἐξαίρουσι τὰ πλήθη, γέλωτά τε ποιοῦντες
οὐκέτι γέλωτος ἄξια πάσχουσιν, ἂν μὴ πάνυ
καταφρονηθῶσι. πολλὰ γὰρ ἔστιν ἄλλα τῶν
πρότερον Ἑλλήνων διεξιόντα τοῖς νῦν ἠθοποιεῖν
καὶ σωφρονίζειν, ὡς Ἀθήνησιν ὑπομιμνήσκοντα

that cuts the neck" has fallen upon many political leaders, as it fell upon your fellow citizen Pardalas when he neglected to observe his limits. And another man, after he was banished to an island, became, in the words of Solon, "a Pholegandrian or Sicinetan, no longer an Athenian, after he changed his homeland."

When we observe small children playfully attempting to wear their fathers' boots and to place crowns upon their heads, we laugh. But when our civic leaders foolishly excite the people by encouraging them to imitate those actions, high spirits, and achievements of our ancestors which are ill-suited to our modern times and circumstances, they do something ridiculous but suffer consequences that are no joke, unless they get off easy by being merely despised. For the Greeks of former times have many

μὴ τῶν πολεμικῶν, ἀλλ᾽ οἷόν ἐστι τὸ ψήφισμα
τὸ τῆς ἀμνηστίας ἐπὶ τοῖς τριάκοντα· καὶ τὸ
ζημιῶσαι Φρύνιχον τραγῳδίᾳ διδάξαντα τὴν
Μιλήτου ἅλωσιν· καὶ ὅτι, Θήβας Κασάνδρου
κτίζοντος, ἐστεφανηφόρησαν· τὸν δ᾽ ἐν Ἄργει
πυθόμενοι σκυταλισμόν, ἐν ᾧ πεντακοσίους
καὶ χιλίους ἀνῃρήκεσαν ἐξ αὑτῶν οἱ Ἀργεῖοι,
περιενεγκεῖν καθάρσιον περὶ τὴν ἐκκλησίαν
ἐκέλευσαν· ἐν δὲ τοῖς Ἁρπαλείοις τὰς οἰκίας
ἐρευνῶντες μόνην τὴν τοῦ γεγαμηκότος
νεωστὶ παρῆλθον. ταῦτα γὰρ καὶ νῦν ἔξεστι
ζηλοῦντας ἐξομοιοῦσθαι τοῖς προγόνοις· τὸν
δὲ Μαραθῶνα καὶ τὸν Εὐρυμέδοντα καὶ τὰς
Πλαταιάς, καὶ ὅσα τῶν παραδειγμάτων οἰδεῖν
ποιεῖ καὶ φρυάττεσθαι διακενῆς τοὺς πολλούς,
ἀπολιπόντας ἐν ταῖς σχολαῖς τῶν σοφιστῶν.

other accomplishments which political leaders may recount to shape the character of their contemporaries and teach them self-control. Politicians should remind the people of Athens, for example, not of great victories in battle, but they should recall the decree of amnesty passed in the case of the thirty tyrants,[38] or the punishment of Phrynichus for recreating the capture of Miletus in a tragedy,[39] or how celebratory crowns were worn after Cassander rebuilt the city of Thebes.[40] Or, when the Athenians learned about the death by clubbing that occurred in Argos, in which the Argives murdered 1,500 citizens, how they ordered a purification to be conducted all around the assembly, or how in the Harpalus affair they searched every house but one, that of a newly married couple.[41] For by imitating actions such as these, modern Athenians

Οὐ μόνον δὲ δεῖ παρέχειν αὑτόν τε καὶ τὴν
πατρίδα πρὸς τοὺς ἡγεμόνας ἀναίτιον, ἀλλὰ
καὶ φίλον ἔχειν ἀεί τινα τῶν ἄνω δυνατωτάτων,
ὥσπερ ἕρμα τῆς πολιτείας βέβαιον· αὐτοὶ γάρ
εἰσι Ῥωμαῖοι πρὸς τὰς πολιτικὰς σπουδὰς
προθυμότατοι τοῖς φίλοις· καὶ καρπὸν ἐκ
φιλίας ἡγεμονικῆς λαμβάνοντας, οἷον ἔλαβε
Πολύβιος καὶ Παναίτιος τῇ Σκιπίωνος
εὐνοίᾳ πρὸς αὐτοὺς μεγάλα τὰς πατρίδας
ὠφελήσαντες, εἰς εὐδαιμονίαν δημοσίαν
ἐξενέγκασθαι καλόν. Ἄρειόν τε Καῖσαρ,
ὅτε τὴν Ἀλεξάνδρειαν εἷλε, διὰ χειρὸς

can make themselves like their ancestors. But as for the great battles at Marathon, the Eurymedon River, and Platea, and any other accomplishments from the past that would cause the people to swell with pride and become arrogant to no purpose, politicians should leave them to the professors and their schools.

Not only must you ensure that both you and your native city are beyond reproach in the eyes of our Roman rulers, but you should always have a friend among those very powerful higher-ups, someone to provide steady support for your political activity. The Romans, in fact, are quite enthusiastic in promoting their friends' political interests. Moreover, the advantage you receive from your friendship with a Roman leader may nobly contribute to your city's prosperity, just as Polybius and Panaetius

ἔχων καὶ μόνῳ προσομιλῶν τῶν συνήθων
συνεισήλασεν, εἶτα τοῖς Ἀλεξανδρεῦσι τὰ
ἔσχατα προσδοκῶσι καὶ δεομένοις ἔφη
διαλλάττεσθαι διά τε τὸ μέγεθος τῆς πόλεως
καὶ διὰ τὸν οἰκιστὴν Ἀλέξανδρον, "καὶ τρίτον,"
ἔφη, "τῷ φίλῳ μου τούτῳ χαριζόμενος." ἆρά
γ᾽ ἄξιον τῇ χάριτι ταύτῃ παραβαλεῖν τὰς
πολυταλάντους ἐπιτροπὰς καὶ διοικήσεις τῶν
ἐπαρχιῶν, ἃς διώκοντες οἱ πολλοὶ γηράσκουσι
πρὸς ἀλλοτρίαις θύραις, τὰ οἴκοι προλιπόντες·
ἢ τὸν Εὐριπίδην ἐπανορθωτέον ᾄδοντα καὶ
λέγοντα, ὡς εἴπερ ἀγρυπνεῖν χρὴ καὶ φοιτᾶν
ἐπ᾽ αὔλειον ἑτέρου καὶ ὑποβάλλειν ἑαυτὸν
ἡγεμονικῇ συνηθείᾳ, πατρίδος πέρι κάλλιστον
ἐπὶ ταῦτα χωρεῖν, τὰ δ᾽ ἄλλα τὰς ἐπὶ τοῖς ἴσοις
καὶ δικαίοις φιλίας ἀσπάζεσθαι καὶ φυλάττειν;

bestowed great benefits upon their cities as a result of the goodwill that Scipio
showed to them. Or consider the case of
Augustus and Arius. After Augustus captured Alexandria, he entered the city with
Arius as his escort and conversed with him
alone among his companions.[42] And then,
when the Alexandrians were expecting to
be treated harshly and were entreating Augustus to spare them, he announced that he
would make peace with them on account
of their city's great renown and in honor
of its founder, Alexander, "and thirdly," he
added, "as a favor to my friend here." This
sort of favor is incomparable, superior even
to those lucrative governorships or the
administration of provinces, which most
people grow old pursuing at the doors of
others[43] while they neglect affairs at home.
Or perhaps we should revise the verses of

Ποιοῦντα μέντοι καὶ παρέχοντα τοῖς
κρατοῦσιν εὐπειθῆ τὴν πατρίδα δεῖ μὴ
προσεκταπεινοῦν, μηδὲ τοῦ σκέλους δεδεμένου
προσυποβάλλειν καὶ τὸν τράχηλον, ὥσπερ
ἔνιοι, καὶ μικρὰ καὶ μείζω φέροντες ἐπὶ τοὺς
ἡγεμόνας ἐξονειδίζουσι τὴν δουλείαν, μᾶλλον
δ' ὅλως τὴν πολιτείαν ἀναιροῦσι, κατάπληγα
καὶ περιδεᾶ καὶ πάντων ἄκυρον ποιοῦντες.
ὥσπερ γὰρ οἱ χωρὶς ἰατροῦ μήτε δειπνεῖν μήτε
λούεσθαι συνεθισθέντες οὐδ' ὅσον ἡ φύσις
δίδωσι χρῶνται τῷ ὑγιαίνειν, οὕτως οἱ παντὶ
δόγματι καὶ συνεδρίῳ καὶ χάριτι καὶ διοικήσει
προσάγοντες ἡγεμονικὴν κρίσιν ἀναγκάζουσιν

Euripides: if we must stay up all night, pay court to others, and subject ourselves to the company of our leaders, it is most noble to submit to such things on behalf of our city, but in all other cases, we should welcome and foster friendships that we form on the basis of equality and justice.[44]

Although we must make our cities obedient to those in authority, we must not humiliate them in the process: just because our cities' legs have been bound, we need not offer up their necks in addition. Some civic leaders do this, however, by referring matters great and small to Roman governors and so bringing the reproach of servitude upon their city. Or rather, they utterly destroy their political systems, making them hesitant, fearful, and entirely powerless. For just as some people have developed the habit of neither dining nor bathing without

ἑαυτῶν μᾶλλον ἢ βούλονται δεσπότας εἶναι
τοὺς ἡγουμένους. αἰτία δὲ τούτου μάλιστα
πλεονεξία καὶ φιλονεικία τῶν πρώτων· ἢ γὰρ
ἐν οἷς βλάπτουσι τοὺς ἐλάττονας ἐκβιάζονται
φεύγειν τὴν πόλιν ἢ περὶ ὧν διαφέρονται πρὸς
ἀλλήλους οὐκ ἀξιοῦντες ἐν τοῖς πολίταις ἔχειν
ἔλαττον ἐπάγονται τοὺς κρείττονας· ἐκ τούτου
δὲ καὶ βουλὴ καὶ δῆμος καὶ δικαστήρια καὶ
ἀρχὴ πᾶσα τὴν ἐξουσίαν ἀπόλλυσι.

Δεῖ δὲ τοὺς μὲν ἰδιώτας ἰσότητι, τοὺς δὲ
δυνατοὺς ἀνθυπείξει πραΰνοντα κατέχειν
ἐν τῇ πολιτείᾳ καὶ διαλύειν τὰ πράγματα,
πολιτικήν τινα ποιούμενον αὐτῶν ὥσπερ

the advice of a doctor, and thus they do not enjoy even the level of health that nature gives freely, so some politicians seek the Romans' judgment about every decree, council meeting, civic honor, or administrative action. In doing so, they compel their governors to become their masters, even against their will. The cause of this behavior is primarily the greed and contentiousness of the leading citizens, who either attack the weaker citizens and force them to flee the city, or who bring in the Roman authorities when they are fighting with each other and cannot tolerate losing. As a result, the senate, assembly, courts, and every civic office lose their power.

A good civic leader must keep everyone engaged in the political process, pacifying private citizens by ensuring equality and powerful citizens by allowing cooperation.

νοσημάτων ἀπορρήτων ἰατρείαν, αὐτόν τε
μᾶλλον ἡττᾶσθαι βουλόμενον ἐν τοῖς πολίταις
ἢ νικᾶν ὕβρει καὶ καταλύσει τῶν οἴκοι δικαίων,
τῶν τ' ἄλλων ἑκάστου δεόμενον καὶ διδάσκοντα
τὴν φιλονεικίαν ὅσον ἐστὶ κακόν· νῦν δ' ὅπως
μὴ πολίταις καὶ φυλέταις οἴκοι καὶ γείτοσι
καὶ συνάρχουσιν ἀνθυπείξωσι μετὰ τιμῆς καὶ
χάριτος, ἐπὶ ῥητόρων θύρας καὶ πραγματικῶν
χεῖρας ἐκφέρουσι σὺν πολλῇ βλάβῃ καὶ
αἰσχύνῃ τὰς διαφοράς. οἱ μὲν γὰρ ἰατροὶ τῶν
νοσημάτων ὅσα μὴ δύνανται παντάπασιν
ἀνελεῖν ἔξω τρέπουσιν εἰς τὴν ἐπιφάνειαν τοῦ
σώματος· ὁ δὲ πολιτικός, ἂν μὴ δύνηται τὴν
πόλιν ἀπράγμονα παντελῶς διαφυλάττειν,
ἐν αὐτῇ γε πειράσεται τὸ ταρασσόμενον
αὐτῆς καὶ στασιάζον ἀποκρύπτων ἰᾶσθαι
καὶ διοικεῖν, ὡς ἂν ἥκιστα τῶν ἐκτὸς ἰατρῶν
καὶ φαρμάκων δέοιτο. ἡ μὲν γὰρ προαίρεσις
ἔστω τοῦ πολιτικοῦ τῆς ἀσφαλείας ἐχομένη
καὶ φεύγουσα τὸ ταρακτικὸν τῆς κενῆς δόξης

Moreover, they must resolve difficult issues by applying a sort of political therapy to them as though they were terrible diseases. In the political give-and-take, civic leaders must prefer to lose rather than to win by violence and by terminating their fellow citizens' rights, and they must ask others to think likewise by teaching them how destructive political rivalries can be. But in reality, to avoid yielding honorably and gracefully to their fellow citizens, to the members of their local tribes,[45] to their neighbors, or to their colleagues in office, politicians take their disagreements straight to the doors of public advocates and put them in the hands of lawyers, to their own detriment and disgrace. When doctors are unable to cure a disease completely, they draw it outward to the surface of the patient's body. But when good politicians are

καὶ μανικόν, ὡς εἴρηται· τῇ μέντοι διαθέσει
φρόνημα καὶ

        μένος πολυθαρσὲς ἐνέστω
  ἄτρομον, οἷόν τ᾽ ἄνδρας ἐσέρχεται, οἳ περὶ
   πάτρης
  ἀνδράσι δυσμενέεσσι

καὶ πράγμασι δυσκόλοις καὶ καιροῖς
ἀντερείδουσι καὶ διαμάχονται. δεῖ γὰρ οὐ
ποιεῖν χειμῶνας αὐτὸν ἀλλὰ μὴ προλείπειν
ἐπιπεσόντων, οὐδὲ κινεῖν τὴν πόλιν ἐπισφαλῶς,
σφαλλομένῃ δὲ καὶ κινδυνευούσῃ βοηθεῖν,
ὥσπερ ἄγκυραν ἱερὰν ἀράμενον ἐξ αὐτοῦ τὴν
παρρησίαν ἐπὶ τοῖς μεγίστοις.

unable to maintain their cities entirely untroubled, they will attempt to conceal whatever elements are causing disturbance and
partisanship, and then to treat and manage
them in a way that requires as little external
doctoring and medicine as possible. For
political leaders should make a conscious
choice to promote stability and to avoid
the madness and turmoil that arise from the
vain pursuit of glory, as I have said. There
should be boldness in the leaders' disposition, however, and "let there be a confident,
fearless strength, such as comes upon men
who face hostile adversaries in defense of
their country,"[46] and who do battle in difficult circumstances and trying times. For
politicians must not create storms themselves, but neither should they abandon
their cities when storms fall upon them.
They must not be the cause of instability,

Ἱερὸν δὲ χρῆμα καὶ μέγα πᾶσαν ἀρχὴν οὖσαν
καὶ ἄρχοντα δεῖ μάλιστα τιμᾶν, τιμὴ δ' ἀρχῆς
ὁμοφροσύνη καὶ φιλία πρὸς συνάρχοντας
πολὺ μᾶλλον ἢ στέφανοι καὶ χλαμὺς
περιπόρφυρος. οἱ δὲ τὸ συστρατεύσασθαι
καὶ συνεφηβεῦσαι φιλίας ἀρχὴν τιθέμενοι,
τὸ δὲ συστρατηγεῖν καὶ συνάρχειν ἔχθρας
αἰτίαν λαμβάνοντες, ἓν τῶν τριῶν κακῶν οὐ
διαπεφεύγασιν· ἢ γὰρ ἴσους ἡγούμενοι τοὺς
συνάρχοντας αὐτοὶ στασιάζουσιν ἢ κρείττονας
φθονοῦσιν ἢ ταπεινοτέρους καταφρονοῦσι. δεῖ
δὲ καὶ θεραπεύειν τὸν κρείττονα καὶ κοσμεῖν

but when their cities have become unstable and imperiled, they must come to their aid by speaking freely and directly, as though dropping that "sacred anchor," in the direst of circumstances.

TREAT OTHERS WITH RESPECT

Above all, we must honor every public office, treating it as a great and sacred thing. We must honor every officeholder, too, knowing that concord and friendship towards our colleagues pay much greater honor to a public office than do crowns and purple cloaks. But those who make serving in the army and training together as youths the start of their friendships, but then make sharing a generalship or an elected office the cause for enmity, cannot escape one of three evils. For they either believe their colleagues

τὸν ἥττονα καὶ τιμᾶν τὸν ὅμοιον, ἀσπάζεσθαι
δὲ καὶ φιλεῖν ἄπαντας, ὡς οὐ διὰ τραπέζης
οὐδὲ κώθωνος οὐδ' ἐφ' ἑστίας, ἀλλὰ κοινῇ καὶ
δημοσίᾳ ψήφῳ φίλους γεγονότας καὶ τρόπον
τινὰ πατρῴαν τὴν ἀπὸ τῆς πατρίδος εὔνοιαν
ἔχοντας. ὁ γοῦν Σκιπίων ἤκουσεν ἐν Ῥώμῃ
κακῶς, ὅτι φίλους ἑστιῶν ἐπὶ τῇ καθιερώσει
τοῦ Ἡρακλείου τὸν συνάρχοντα Μόμμιον
οὐ παρέλαβε· καὶ γάρ, εἰ τἆλλα μὴ φίλους
ἐνόμιζον ἑαυτούς, ἐν τοῖς γε τοιούτοις ἠξίουν
τιμᾶν καὶ φιλοφρονεῖσθαι διὰ τὴν ἀρχήν. ὅπου
τοίνυν ἀνδρὶ τἆλλα θαυμασίῳ τῷ Σκιπίωνι
μικρὸν οὕτω φιλανθρώπευμα παραλειφθὲν
ὑπεροψίας ἤνεγκε δόξαν, ἦπου κολούων ἄν
τις ἀξίωμα συνάρχοντος ἢ πράξεσιν ἐχούσαις
φιλοτιμίαν ἐπηρεάζων ἢ πάντα συλλήβδην
ἀνατιθεὶς ἅμα καὶ περιάγων ὑπ' αὐθαδείας εἰς
ἑαυτὸν ἐκείνου δ' ἀφαιρούμενος, ἐπιεικὴς ἂν
φανείη καὶ μέτριος; μέμνημαι νέον ἐμαυτὸν
ἔτι πρεσβευτὴν μεθ' ἑτέρου πεμφθέντα πρὸς

to be their equals and so they fight against them; or they believe them to be superior and so they envy them; or they believe them inferior and so they despise them. We must, however, pay court to the colleague who is superior, make the inferior better, and honor the equal. We must, moreover, welcome and be friendly to everyone, on the ground that we have become their friends not at dinner, over drinks, or in our home, but through the popular vote, and that our mutual goodwill is a sort of inheritance from our native cities. Indeed, Scipio Aemilianus was criticized at Rome because he gave a feast for his friends at the dedication of the temple to Hercules, but he neglected to invite his colleague Mummius.[47] For even if in other respects they did not consider themselves friends, in situations like the dedication they used to think it right to honor each other and

ἀνθύπατον, ἀπολειφθέντος δέ πως ἐκείνου,
μόνον ἐντυχόντα καὶ διαπραξάμενον· ὡς οὖν
ἔμελλον ἐπανελθὼν ἀποπρεσβεύειν, ἀναστὰς
ὁ πατὴρ κατ᾽ ἰδίαν ἐκέλευσε μὴ λέγειν
"ᾠχόμην" ἀλλ᾽ "ᾠχόμεθα," μηδ᾽ "εἶπον" ἀλλ᾽
"εἴπομεν," καὶ τἄλλα συνεφαπτόμενον οὕτω
καὶ κοινούμενον ἀπαγγέλλειν. οὐ γὰρ μόνον
ἐπιεικὲς τὸ τοιοῦτον καὶ φιλάνθρωπόν ἐστιν,
ἀλλὰ καὶ τὸ λυποῦν τὸν φθόνον ἀφαιρεῖ
τῆς δόξης. ὅθεν οἱ μεγάλοι καὶ δαίμονα καὶ
τύχην τοῖς κατορθώμασι συνεπιγράφουσιν,
ὡς Τιμολέων ὁ τὰς ἐν Σικελίᾳ καταλύσας
τυραννίδας Αὐτοματίας ἱερὸν ἱδρύσατο·
καὶ Πύθων ἐπὶ τῷ Κότυν ἀποκτεῖναι
θαυμαζόμενος καὶ τιμώμενος ὑπὸ τῶν
Ἀθηναίων "ὁ θεός," ἔφη, "ταῦτ᾽ ἔπραξε, τὴν
χεῖρα παρ᾽ ἐμοῦ χρησάμενος." Θεόπομπος
δ᾽ ὁ βασιλεὺς τῶν Λακεδαιμονίων πρὸς τὸν
εἰπόντα σῴζεσθαι τὴν Σπάρτην διὰ τοὺς

be courteous on account of the shared office. Therefore, seeing that Scipio, who was admired in all other respects, earned the reputation for being contemptuous by neglecting such a small act of kindness, should we expect other politicians to be seen as fair and moderate when they impede the dignity of their colleagues, spitefully oppose their opportunities to act on their ambition, and in short arrogantly assign and attract all political duties to themselves while taking them away from others? I remember that when I myself was still a young man, I was sent with someone else on an embassy to the proconsul. Somehow the other person was left behind, and so I alone met with the proconsul and completed the mission. When I returned and was about to make my report, my father approached me and spoke

βασιλεῖς ἀρχικοὺς ὄντας "μᾶλλον," ἔφη, "διὰ
τοὺς πολλοὺς πειθαρχικοὺς ὄντας."

with me privately, bidding me not to say, "I went" but "we went," and not "I said" but "we said," and so in all other respects to give my colleague a share of the accomplishment. For not only is such an act fair and humane, but it also takes away the thing that causes grief, namely, the envy of someone else's glory. For this very reason, accomplished people give some credit for their success to the gods and to luck, as when Timoleon dedicated a temple to the goddess of chance after destroying the tyrannies in Sicily. Python, when the Athenians were marveling at him and honoring him for killing Cotys, said, "God did it, through the agency of my hand." And when someone said that Sparta was preserved because its kings were skilled in leading, Theopompus, king of the Lacedaemonians, replied, "No, because the people are skilled in obeying."

Ὅπου μέντοι μέγα δεῖ τι περανθῆναι καὶ
χρήσιμον ἀγῶνος δὲ πολλοῦ καὶ σπουδῆς
δεόμενον, ἐνταῦθα πειρῶ τῶν φίλων αἱρεῖσθαι
τοὺς κρατίστους ἢ τῶν κρατίστων τοὺς
πραοτάτους· ἥκιστα γὰρ ἀντιπράξουσιν οὗτοι
καὶ μάλιστα συνεργήσουσι, τὸ φρονεῖν ἄνευ
τοῦ φιλονεικεῖν ἔχοντες. οὐ μὴν ἀλλὰ καὶ
τῆς ἑαυτοῦ φύσεως ἔμπειρον ὄντα δεῖ πρὸς ὃ
χείρων ἑτέρου πέφυκας αἱρεῖσθαι τοὺς μᾶλλον
δυναμένους ἀντὶ τῶν ὁμοίων, ὡς ὁ Διομήδης
ἐπὶ τὴν κατασκοπὴν μεθ᾽ ἑαυτοῦ τὸν φρόνιμον
εἵλετο, τοὺς ἀνδρείους παρελθών. καὶ γὰρ αἱ
πράξεις μᾶλλον ἰσορροποῦσι καὶ τὸ φιλόνεικον
οὐκ ἐγγίγνεται πρὸς ἀλλήλους τοῖς ἀφ᾽ ἑτέρων
ἀρετῶν καὶ δυνάμεων φιλοτιμουμένοις.
λάμβανε δὴ καὶ δίκης συνεργὸν καὶ πρεσβείας
κοινωνόν, ἂν λέγειν μὴ δυνατὸς ᾖς, τὸν
ῥητορικόν, ὡς Πελοπίδας Ἐπαμεινώνδαν·
κἂν ᾖς ἀπίθανος πρὸς ὁμιλίαν τῷ πλήθει καὶ
ὑψηλός, ὡς Καλλικρατίδας, τὸν εὔχαριν καὶ

But whenever some great and useful deed must be accomplished, one that requires a mighty struggle and much effort, you should attempt in those situations to select your most powerful friends, or rather to select the most amenable among those that are most powerful. For those sorts of people will least of all work against you and will be especially cooperative, since they possess wisdom that is not mixed up with contentiousness. Moreover, you must understand your own nature. When you are faced with a task that you are not best suited to accomplish, select as your colleagues those who are more capable rather than those who are like you, as Diomedes did when he selected the cleverest man to accompany him on his spying mission and passed over men who were brave.[48] For in this way political actions are more balanced,

θεραπευτικόν· κἂν ἀσθενὴς καὶ δύσεργος
τὸ σῶμα, τὸν φιλόπονον καὶ ῥωμαλέον, ὡς
Νικίας Λάμαχον. οὕτω γὰρ ἂν ἦν ὁ Γηρυόνης
ζηλωτὸς ἔχων σκέλη πολλὰ καὶ χεῖρας
καὶ ὀφθαλμούς, εἰ πάντα μιᾷ ψυχῇ διώκει.
τοῖς δὲ πολιτικοῖς ἔξεστι μὴ σώματα μηδὲ
χρήματα μόνον, ἀλλὰ καὶ τύχας καὶ δυνάμεις
καὶ ἀρετάς, ἂν ὁμονοῶσιν, εἰς μίαν χρείαν
συντιθέντας εὐδοκιμεῖν μᾶλλον ἄλλου περὶ
τὴν αὐτὴν πρᾶξιν· οὐχ ὥσπερ οἱ Ἀργοναῦται
τὸν Ἡρακλέα καταλιπόντες ἠναγκάζοντο
διὰ τῆς γυναικωνίτιδος καταδόμενοι καὶ
φαρμακευόμενοι σῴζειν ἑαυτοὺς καὶ κλέπτειν
τὸ νάκος.

and contentiousness does not arise among ambitious people who have different virtues and abilities. And so, if you are not an accomplished speaker, select someone trained in rhetoric to be your colleague in a lawsuit or your partner on an embassy, just as Pelopidas chose Epaminondas; if you are unpersuasive and haughty when addressing the people, as Callicratidas was, select a partner who is gracious and courteous; and if your body is weak and ill-suited for exertion, select a partner who is industrious and strong, as Nicias selected Lamachus. For thus we would envy Geryon's many legs, hands, and eyes, if he were controlling them all with a single soul.[49] But politicians, if they are of one mind, by pooling not only their persons and their resources but also their luck, capabilities, and virtues for a single purpose, can be more highly esteemed

Χρυσὸν μὲν εἰς ἔνια τῶν ἱερῶν εἰσιόντες ἔξω
καταλείπουσι, σίδηρον δ᾽ ὡς ἁπλῶς εἰπεῖν
εἰς οὐδὲν συνεισφέρουσιν. ἐπεὶ δὲ κοινόν
ἐστιν ἱερὸν τὸ βῆμα Βουλαίου τε Διὸς καὶ
Πολιέως καὶ Θέμιδος καὶ Δίκης, αὐτόθεν
μὲν ἤδη φιλοπλουτίαν καὶ φιλοχρηματίαν,
ὥσπερ σίδηρον μεστὸν ἰοῦ καὶ νόσημα
τῆς ψυχῆς, ἀποδυσάμενος εἰς ἀγορὰς
καπήλων ἢ δανειστῶν ἀπόρριψον, "αὐτὸς
δ᾽ ἀπονόσφι τραπέσθαι" τὸν ἀπὸ δημοσίων

for a combined effort than for an individual accomplishment. This is contrary to the example of the Argonauts, who abandoned Hercules and then were compelled to save themselves and steal the golden fleece via the women's quarters, with the aid of spells and potions.[50]

THE REWARD OF POLITICS

People entering some temples leave their gold outside, but no one, to put it simply, brings iron into any temple. Since the speaker's platform is the temple common to Zeus of the Council and Protector of the City, and to Law and to Justice, right there on the spot strip away from yourself greed and avarice, as you would strip off iron covered in rust or a disease of the soul. Cast these vices away into the marketplace of

χρηματιζόμενον ἡγούμενος ἀφ᾽ ἱερῶν κλέπτειν,
ἀπὸ τάφων, ἀπὸ φίλων, ἐκ προδοσίας, ἀπὸ
ψευδομαρτυρίας, σύμβουλον ἄπιστον εἶναι,
δικαστὴν ἐπίορκον, ἄρχοντα δωροδόκον,
οὐδεμιᾶς ἁπλῶς καθαρὸν ἀδικίας. ὅθεν οὐ δεῖ
πολλὰ περὶ τούτων λέγειν.

Ἡ δὲ φιλοτιμία, καίπερ οὖσα σοβαρωτέρα
τῆς φιλοκερδείας, οὐκ ἐλάττονας ἔχει
κῆρας ἐν πολιτείᾳ· καὶ γὰρ τὸ τολμᾶν αὐτῇ
πρόσεστι μᾶλλον· ἐμφύεται γὰρ οὐκ ἀργαῖς
οὐδὲ ταπειναῖς ἀλλ᾽ ἐρρωμέναις μάλιστα
καὶ νεανικαῖς προαιρέσεσι, καὶ τὸ παρὰ τῶν
ὄχλων ῥόθιον πολλάκις συνεξαῖρον αὐτὴν καὶ
συνεξωθοῦν τοῖς ἐπαίνοις ἀκατάσχετον ποιεῖ
καὶ δυσμεταχείριστον. ὥσπερ οὖν ὁ Πλάτων

the retailers and moneylenders, "and turn yourself away from them,"[51] in the belief that politicians who make money doing the public's business steal from temples, from tombs, and from friends; that they profit from treachery and from bearing false witness; that they are untrustworthy advisors, lying jurors, and corrupt leaders; that they are sullied—to put it simply—with every form of injustice. And therefore, I need not say much about that.

Now the love of honor, although it is a more impressive quality than the love of profit, is no less ruinous to a political system. For a love of honor makes people bolder and more reckless; it is a natural component not of sluggish and humble policies, but of those that are especially vigorous and impetuous; and the wave of praise that surges from the mob often

ἀκουστέον εἶναι τοῖς νέοις ἔλεγεν ἐκ παίδων
εὐθύς, ὡς οὔτε περικεῖσθαι χρυσὸν αὐτοῖς
ἔξωθεν οὔτε κεκτῆσθαι θέμις, οἰκεῖον ἐν τῇ
ψυχῇ συμμεμιγμένον ἔχοντας, αἰνιττόμενος
οἶμαι τὴν ἐκ γένους διατείνουσαν εἰς τὰς
φύσεις αὐτῶν ἀρετήν· οὕτω παραμυθώμεθα
τὴν φιλοτιμίαν, λέγοντες ἐν ἑαυτοῖς ἔχειν
χρυσὸν ἀδιάφθορον καὶ ἀκήρατον καὶ ἄχραντον
ὑπὸ φθόνου καὶ μώμου τιμήν, ἅμα λογισμῷ
καὶ παραθεωρήσει τῶν πεπραγμένων ἡμῖν
καὶ πεπολιτευμένων αὐξανόμενον· διὸ μὴ
δεῖσθαι γραφομένων τιμῶν ἢ πλαττομένων ἢ
χαλκοτυπουμένων, ἐν αἷς καὶ τὸ εὐδοκιμοῦν
ἀλλότριόν ἐστιν· ἐπαινεῖται γὰρ οὐχ ᾧ γέγονεν
ἀλλ᾽ ὑφ᾽ οὗ γέγονεν ὡς ὁ σαλπικτὴς καὶ ὁ
δορυφόρος. ὁ δὲ Κάτων, ἤδη τότε τῆς Ῥώμης
καταπιμπλαμένης ἀνδριάντων, οὐκ ἐῶν αὑτοῦ
γενέσθαι "μᾶλλον," ἔφη, "βούλομαι πυνθάνεσθαί
τινας, διὰ τί μου ἀνδριὰς οὐ κεῖται ἢ διὰ τί
κεῖται." καὶ γὰρ φθόνον ἔχει τὰ τοιαῦτα καὶ

helps to elevate and inflate one's love of honor, rendering it uncontrollable and unmanageable. Plato used to say that young people must be taught from childhood that it is not right to wear gold on their bodies or to possess it, since they have their own personal gold intermixed into their soul, hinting (I think) at the virtue that is part of human nature and received at birth.[52] In the same way, let us hold our love of honor in check by referring to honor as gold that we possess within ourselves, uncorrupted, uncontaminated, and undefiled by envy or reproach, and at the same time increased by the counting up and examining of our deeds and political accomplishments. Thus, we have no need of honors that are painted, sculpted, or wrought in bronze, which in fact enhance the reputation of someone else, since they inspire admiration not

νομίζουσιν οἱ πολλοὶ τοῖς μὴ λαβοῦσιν αὐτοὶ
χάριν ὀφείλειν, τοὺς δὲ λαβόντας αὐτοῖς
καὶ βαρεῖς εἶναι, οἷον ἐπὶ μισθῷ τὰς χρείας
ἀπαιτοῦντας. ὥσπερ οὖν ὁ παραπλεύσας τὴν
Σύρτιν εἶτ᾽ ἀνατραπεὶς περὶ τὸν πορθμὸν
οὐδὲν μέγα πεποίηκεν οὐδὲ σεμνόν, οὕτως ὁ
τὸ ταμιεῖον φυλαξάμενος καὶ τὸ δημοσιώνιον
ἁλοὺς δὲ περὶ τὴν προεδρίαν ἢ τὸ πρυτανεῖον,
ὑψηλῷ μὲν προσέπταικεν ἀκρωτηρίῳ
βαπτίζεται δ᾽ ὁμοίως.

for the person *for whom* they were made but *by whom* they were made, as with the Trumpeter and the Discus Thrower.[53] And so Cato the Elder, at a time when Rome was already filled with statues, would not allow one to be made of himself, saying, "I would prefer to have people asking why there is no statue of me rather than asking why there is one." For material honors arouse envy, and the people believe that they owe a favor to politicians who have not received them, while they view those politicians who have received them as overbearing, as though they were seeking public service in return for payment. Just as the person who sails past Syrtis[54] but then capsizes crossing the sea has done nothing great or noble, so the politician who has supervised the treasury and public revenue but then fails to measure up in the presidency or the town hall

ΠΟΛΙΤΙΚΑ ΠΑΡΑΓΓΕΛΜΑΤΑ

Ἄριστος μὲν οὖν ὁ μηδενὸς δεόμενος τῶν τοιούτων ἀλλὰ φεύγων καὶ παραιτούμενος· ἂν δ᾽ ᾖ μὴ ῥᾴδιον δήμου τινὰ χάριν ἀπώσασθαι καὶ φιλοφροσύνην πρὸς τοῦτο ῥυέντος, ὥσπερ οὐκ ἀργυρίτην οὐδὲ δωρίτην ἀγῶνα πολιτείας ἀγωνιζομένοις ἀλλ᾽ ἱερὸν ὡς ἀληθῶς καὶ στεφανίτην, ἐπιγραφή τις ἀρκεῖ καὶ πινάκιον καὶ ψήφισμα καὶ θαλλός, ὡς Ἐπιμενίδης ἔλαβεν ἐξ ἀκροπόλεως καθήρας τὴν πόλιν. Ἀναξαγόρας δὲ τὰς διδομένας ἀφεὶς τιμὰς ᾐτήσατο τὴν ἡμέραν ἐκείνην, καθ᾽ ἣν ἂν τελευτήσῃ, τοὺς παῖδας ἀφιέναι παίζειν καὶ σχολάζειν ἀπὸ τῶν μαθημάτων. οὐ γὰρ μισθὸν εἶναι δεῖ τῆς πράξεως ἀλλὰ σύμβολον τὴν τιμήν, ἵνα καὶ διαμένῃ πολὺν χρόνον. τῶν δὲ Δημητρίου τοῦ Φαληρέως τριακοσίων ἀνδριάντων οὐδεὶς ἔσχεν ἰὸν οὐδὲ πίνον, ἀλλὰ πάντες ἔτι ζῶντος προανηρέθησαν· τοὺς

not only strikes against a high promontory but likewise ends up sinking.[55]

The best politician, then, has no need of material honors, but even avoids and refuses them. But if some favor or kindness cannot easily be declined because the people are eager to bestow it, then for politicians who compete not for money or gifts but because the political contest is truly sacred and awards a crown,[56] an inscription is sufficient, or a brief notice, a decree, or a palm-branch, such as Epimenides received from the Acropolis after he purified the city. Anaxagoras declined the honors that were offered to him: he asked instead that children be allowed to play and take a holiday from their lessons to celebrate the day of his death. For an honor must not be a payment for the service performed but a symbol, so that it may last a long time. Consider the

δὲ Δημάδου κατεχώνευσαν εἰς ἀμίδας· καὶ
πολλαὶ τοιαῦτα τιμαὶ πεπόνθασιν οὐ μοχθηρίᾳ
τοῦ λαβόντος μόνον ἀλλὰ καὶ μεγέθει τοῦ
δοθέντος δυσχερανθεῖσαι. διὸ κάλλιστον καὶ
βεβαιότατον εὐτέλεια τιμῆς φυλακτήριον, αἱ
δὲ μεγάλαι καὶ ὑπέρογκοι καὶ βάρος ἔχουσαι
παραπλησίως τοῖς ἀσυμμέτροις ἀνδριᾶσι ταχὺ
περιτρέπονται.

three hundred statues of Demetrius of Pha-
lerum: not one ever saw rust or tarnish, but
they were all toppled in his own lifetime.
As for the statues of Demades, they were
melted down to make chamberpots. And
many material honors have suffered similar
fates, after people came to be annoyed not
only by the depravity of the recipient but
also by the magnitude of the gift. And so,
thrift is the finest and most stable safeguard
of honor, whereas magnificent, inflated,
and weighty rewards are swiftly toppled,
just like badly proportioned statues.

SHOULD AN OLD MAN
ENGAGE IN POLITICS?

Plutarch conceived of an "old man" as someone over fifty years old who had spent twenty to thirty years in service to the state. He claims that he himself was senior when he wrote the essay, and he addresses it to a certain Euphanes, whom he describes as being of the same age and as having followed a similar political career, though in Athens instead of Chaeronea. The essay is divided into two parts. In the first, which I have entitled "The Value of the Senior Politician," Plutarch addresses the question of whether an aged leader ought to retire. His answer is unequivocally "no," and in giving it, he argues for the great benefit to be gained from older people. They bring experience, wisdom, and level heads to policy making, and having already earned their reputations, they lack the ambition, impetuousness, and contentiousness that drive the young. In the second part, entitled "The Role of the Senior Politician," Plutarch more fully develops the image of the elder as teacher and mentor. The advice that he claims the older generation may impart to the younger is in fact quite similar to the advice that he himself gives to the young Menemachus in *How to Be a Good Leader*. Plutarch also explains that the skills and experience possessed by senior leaders cannot be acquired in any other way than through constant and life-long political activity. Moreover, dedicated politicians commit all aspects and phases of their lives to serving their cities and the people, working on their behalf even when they are not holding office.

This essay has many correspondences with Cicero's *How to Grow Old*, which is framed as a dialogue between Cato the Elder and two younger men, Scipio Aemilianus and Gaius Laelius. Plutarch draws on the experiences of all three of these Roman politicians as he makes his arguments in the present essay. He seems to have felt that Cato in particular was an excellent example for how leaders ought to conduct themselves during the final phase of their careers.

■ ■ ■

ΕΙ ΠΡΕΣΒΥΤΕΡΩΙ ΠΟΛΙΤΕΥΤΕΟΝ

1. Ὅτι μέν, ὦ Εὔφανες, ἐπαινέτης ὢν Πινδάρου
πολλάκις ἔχεις διὰ στόματος ὡς εἰρημένον εὖ
καὶ πιθανῶς ὑπ᾽ αὐτοῦ

τιθεμένων ἀγώνων πρόφασις
ἀρετὰν ἐς αἰπὺν ἔβαλε σκότον,

οὐκ ἀγνοοῦμεν. ἐπειδὴ δὲ πλείστας αἱ πρὸς
τοὺς πολιτικοὺς ἀγῶνας ἀποκνήσεις καὶ
μαλακίαι προφάσεις ἔχουσαι τελευταίαν
ὥσπερ τὴν "ἀφ᾽ ἱερᾶς" ἐπάγουσιν ἡμῖν τὸ
γῆρας, καὶ μάλιστα δὴ τούτῳ τὸ φιλότιμον
ἀμβλύνειν καὶ δυσωπεῖν δοκοῦσαι πείθουσιν
εἶναί τινα πρέπουσαν οὐκ ἀθλητικῆς μόνον
ἀλλὰ καὶ πολιτικῆς περιόδου κατάλυσιν·

1. I am well aware, O Euphanes, that you admire Pindar and so are often repeating something that he has articulated well and persuasively: "When the contests are being set, a pretext casts one's courage into utter darkness."[1] Now with respect to political contests, our hesitations and weaknesses find abundant pretexts, and as a final excuse they bring up our old age, just as though they were making "the sacred move."[2] And with this move they seem to blunt and shame our ambition, convincing us that there is some proper finale not only for athletes but also for politicians. This being so, I think that I should explain for you what I regularly conclude for myself about

οἴομαι δεῖν ἃ πρὸς ἐμαυτὸν ἑκάστοτε
λογίζομαι καὶ πρὸς σὲ διελθεῖν περὶ τῆς
πρεσβυτικῆς πολιτείας· ὅπως μηδέτερος
ἀπολείψει τὴν μακρὰν συνοδίαν μέχρι δεῦρο
κοινῇ προερχομένην μηδὲ τὸν πολιτικὸν
βίον ὥσπερ ἡλικιώτην καὶ συνήθη φίλον
ἀπορρίψας μεταβαλεῖται πρὸς ἄλλον
ἀσυνήθη καὶ χρόνον οὐκ ἔχοντα συνήθη
γενέσθαι καὶ οἰκεῖον, ἀλλ᾽ ἐμμενοῦμεν οἷς ἀπ᾽
ἀρχῆς προειλόμεθα, ταὐτὸ τοῦ ζῆν καὶ τοῦ
καλῶς ζῆν ποιησάμενοι πέρας· εἴ γε δὴ μὴ
μέλλοιμεν ἐν βραχεῖ τῷ λειπομένῳ τὸν πολὺν
ἐλέγχειν χρόνον, ὡς ἐπ᾽ οὐδενὶ καλῷ μάτην
ἀνηλωμένον.

Οὐ γὰρ ἡ τυραννίς, ὥς τις εἶπε Διονυσίῳ,
καλὸν ἐντάφιον· ἀλλ᾽ ἐκείνῳ γε τὴν μοναρχίαν
μετὰ τῆς ἀδικίας τό γε μὴ παύσασθαι
συμφορὰν τελεωτέραν ἐποίησε. καὶ καλῶς
Διογένης ὕστερον ἐν Κορίνθῳ τὸν υἱὸν
αὐτοῦ θεασάμενος ἰδιώτην ἐκ τυράννου

being involved in politics in old age. I do not want us to abandon our long companionship on the journey that we have made together till now, nor to cast aside our political life, which is like an old and familiar friend, and switch to a new, unfamiliar life that will be too short to become familiar and friendly. My hope instead is that we will remain true to the life we chose in the beginning, when we decided that "living" and "living nobly" were one and the same goal. Unless, of course, we intend to prove in the short period of our life which remains that we lived the longer part in vain and ignobly.

THE VALUE OF THE
SENIOR POLITICIAN

Contrary to what someone once said to Dionysius, tyranny does not in fact make

γεγενημένον "ὡς ἀναξίως," ἔφη, "Διονύσιε,
σεαυτοῦ πράττεις· οὐ γὰρ ἐνταῦθά σε μεθ᾽
ἡμῶν ἔδει ζῆν ἐλευθέρως καὶ ἀδεῶς, ἀλλ᾽
ἐκεῖ τοῖς τυραννείοις ἐγκατῳκοδομημένον
ὥσπερ ὁ πατὴρ ἄχρι γήρως ἐγκαταβιῶσαι."
πολιτεία δὲ δημοκρατικὴ καὶ νόμιμος
ἀνδρὸς εἰθισμένου παρέχειν αὐτὸν οὐχ
ἧττον ἀρχόμενον ὠφελίμως ἢ ἄρχοντα
καλὸν ἐντάφιον ὡς ἀληθῶς τὴν ἀπὸ τοῦ
βίου δόξαν τῷ θανάτῳ προστίθησι· τοῦτο
γὰρ "ἔσχατον δύεται κατὰ γᾶς" ὥς φησι
Σιμωνίδης, πλὴν ὧν προαποθνήσκει τὸ
φιλάνθρωπον καὶ φιλόκαλον καὶ προαπαυδᾷ
τῆς τῶν ἀναγκαίων ἐπιθυμίας ὁ τῶν καλῶν
ζῆλος, ὡς τὰ πρακτικὰ μέρη καὶ θεῖα τῆς
ψυχῆς ἐξιτηλότερα τῶν παθητικῶν καὶ
σωματικῶν ἐχούσης· ὅπερ οὐδὲ λέγειν
καλὸν οὐδ᾽ ἀποδέχεσθαι τῶν λεγόντων, ὡς
κερδαίνοντες μόνον οὐ κοπιῶμεν· ἀλλὰ καὶ
τὸ τοῦ Θουκυδίδου παράγειν ἐπὶ τὸ βέλτιον,

for a noble funeral shroud. But Dionysius also combined his long reign as tyrant with injustice, which made his disaster even more complete. And later, when Diogenes saw Dionysius's son in Corinth, living as a private citizen after also having been a tyrant himself, rightly did the philosopher say to him, "How unworthy of your stature is the fortune you're experiencing, Dionysius! For you ought not to live here among us, free and without fear, but like your father you ought to live on into old age back home, hidden away in the tyrant's palace." However, when people are accustomed to make themselves useful to the state as private citizens no less than when they hold office, the reputation they earn in life through their democratic and law-abiding political activity becomes the reputation they enjoy in death. This is

μὴ τὸ φιλότιμον ἀγήρων μόνον ἡγουμένους,
ἀλλὰ μᾶλλον τὸ κοινωνικὸν καὶ πολιτικόν,
ὃ καὶ μύρμηξιν ἄχρι τέλους παραμένει
καὶ μελίτταις· οὐδεὶς γὰρ πώποτ᾽ εἶδεν
ὑπὸ γήρως κηφῆνα γενομένην μέλιτταν,
ὥσπερ ἔνιοι τοὺς πολιτικοὺς ἀξιοῦσιν, ὅταν
παρακμάσωσιν, οἴκοι σιτουμένους καθῆσθαι
καὶ ἀποκεῖσθαι, καθάπερ ἰῷ σίδηρον ὑπ᾽
ἀργίας τὴν πρακτικὴν ἀρετὴν σβεννυμένην
περιορῶντας. ὁ γὰρ Κάτων ἔλεγεν, ὅτι
πολλὰς ἰδίας ἔχοντι τῷ γήρᾳ κῆρας οὐ δεῖ τὴν
ἀπὸ τῆς κακίας ἑκόντας ἐπάγειν αἰσχύνην·
πολλῶν δὲ κακιῶν οὐδεμιᾶς ἧττον ἀπραξία
καὶ δειλία καὶ μαλακία καταισχύνουσιν
ἄνδρα πρεσβύτην, ἐκ πολιτικῶν ἀρχείων
καταδυόμενον εἰς οἰκουρίαν γυναικῶν ἢ κατ᾽
ἀγρὸν ἐφορῶντα καλαμητρίδας καὶ θεριστάς·
"ὁ δ᾽ Οἰδίπους ποῦ καὶ τὰ κλείν᾽ αἰνίγματα;"

Τὸ μὲν γὰρ ἐν γήρᾳ πολιτείας ἄρχεσθαι
καὶ μὴ πρότερον, ὥσπερ Ἐπιμενίδην

the reputation that makes for a genuinely noble funeral shroud, because it "last of all, sinks down into the earth," as Simonides says. But there is no such reputation for those whose love of humanity and love of goodness die before they do, or whose zeal for true beauty and goodness fails before their desire for basic bodily needs, just as in the soul the practical and divine elements are more fleeting than the emotional and physical elements.[3] Nor is it right to say, or to agree when others say it, that only while earning a profit do we fail to grow tired in our efforts. We should instead improve on the saying of Thucydides, believing not only that "love of honor is ageless,"[4] but also that community and politics, which even among ants and bees endure to the end, are ageless as well. For no one has ever seen a honey bee that has become a drone

λέγουσι κατακοιμηθέντα νεανίαν ἐξεγρέσθαι
γέροντα μετὰ πεντήκοντα ἔτη· εἶτα τὴν
οὕτω μακρὰν καὶ συμβεβιωκυῖαν ἡσυχίαν
ἀποθέμενον ἐμβαλεῖν ἑαυτὸν εἰς ἀγῶνας καὶ
ἀσχολίας, ἀήθη καὶ ἀγύμναστον ὄντα καὶ
μήτε πράγμασιν ἐνωμιληκότα πολιτικοῖς
μήτ' ἀνθρώποις, ἴσως ἂν αἰτιωμένῳ τινὶ
παράσχοι τὸ τῆς Πυθίας εἰπεῖν "ὄψ' ἦλθες"
ἀρχὴν καὶ δημαγωγίαν διζήμενος, καὶ παρ'
ὥραν στρατηγίου κόπτεις θύραν, ὥσπερ τις
ἀτεχνότερος ὢν νύκτωρ ἐπίκωμος ἀφιγμένος,
ἢ ξένος οὐ τόπον οὐδὲ χώραν ἀλλὰ βίον,
οὗ μὴ πεπείρασαι, μεταλλάττων. τὸ γὰρ
"πόλις ἄνδρα διδάσκει" κατὰ Σιμωνίδην
ἀληθές ἐστιν ἐπὶ τῶν ἔτι χρόνον ἐχόντων
μεταδιδαχθῆναι καὶ μεταμαθεῖν μάθημα,
διὰ πολλῶν ἀγώνων καὶ πραγμάτων μόλις
ἐκπονούμενον, ἄνπερ ἐν καιρῷ φύσεως
ἐπιλάβηται καὶ πόνον ἐνεγκεῖν καὶ
δυσημερίαν εὐκόλως δυναμένης. ταῦτα δόξει

due to old age, in the way that some people believe it is best for politicians, once past their prime, to sit at home taking their meals and to remain out of the way, watching their practical expertise become dull through disuse, as an iron tool is blunted by rust. For Cato the Elder used to say that we ought not willingly add to old age, which has many of its own problems, the shame of misbehavior. And of the many forms of misbehavior, idleness and cowardice and moral weakness bring more shame than any other to an old person who is descending from public service to women's work in the home, or who oversees the reapers and the threshers in the field. We may rightly ask that person, "What has become of Oedipus and his famous riddles?"[5]

In contrast to those who retire early, what about those who commence their political

τις μὴ κακῶς λέγεσθαι πρὸς τὸν ἀρχόμενον ἐν
γήρᾳ πολιτείας.

careers in old age rather than early in life, as they say Epimenides slept away his youth and awoke as an old man fifty years later? These people set aside the quiet life that they have lived for so long and throw themselves into competitions and offices, being unaccustomed, unpracticed, and unconversant with the business of politics and the people involved. This scenario could allow some critic to say, as the Pythia did, "You've come too late" seeking office and public leadership; you are knocking at the door to the general's headquarters in the wrong season of life. You are like a party guest who is quite ignorant of social norms and so arrives late at night, or like a foreigner, but not one who changes location or country, but one who exchanges a known way of life for one that is completely unfamiliar. For the saying of Simonides, "The city teaches

2. Καίτοι τοὐναντίον ὁρῶμεν ὑπὸ τῶν
νοῦν ἐχόντων τὰ μειράκια καὶ τοὺς νέους
ἀποτρεπομένους τοῦ τὰ κοινὰ πράττειν· καὶ
μαρτυροῦσιν οἱ νόμοι διὰ τοῦ κήρυκος ἐν ταῖς
ἐκκλησίαις οὐκ Ἀλκιβιάδας οὐδὲ Πυθέας
ἀνιστάντες ἐπὶ τὸ βῆμα πρώτους, ἀλλὰ τοὺς
ὑπὲρ πεντήκοντ᾽ ἔτη γεγονότας, λέγειν
καὶ συμβουλεύειν παρακαλοῦντες· οὐ γὰρ
τοιούτους ἀήθεια τόλμης καὶ τριβῆς ἔνδεια

the man," is true in the case of those who still have time to be retrained and to learn a new lesson. Even this education is barely accomplished via many political contests and public affairs, if the city, at just the right moment, lays hold of a nature that is able to withstand toil and misery with ease.[6] This advice will strike a chord with those who are just beginning a political career in old age.

2. On the other hand, however, we also observe that youths and people just starting out are turned away from public affairs by those who are sensible. The laws testify to this through the heralds at the assemblies, since they do not set the likes of Alcibiades and Pytheas upon the speaker's platform first,[7] but rather they summon those who are more than fifty years old to speak and

καλεῖ πρὸς τροπαῖον κατ᾽ ἀντιστασιωτῶν.
ὁ δὲ Κάτων μετ᾽ ὀγδοήκοντ᾽ ἔτη δίκην
ἀπολογούμενος ἔφη χαλεπὸν εἶναι βεβιωκότα
μετ᾽ ἄλλων ἐν ἄλλοις ἀπολογεῖσθαι. Καίσαρος
δὲ τοῦ καταλύσαντος Ἀντώνιον οὔτι μικρῷ
βασιλικώτερα καὶ δημωφελέστερα γενέσθαι
πολιτεύματα πρὸς τῇ τελευτῇ πάντες
ὁμολογοῦσιν· αὐτὸς δὲ τοὺς νέους ἔθεσι καὶ
νόμοις αὐστηρῶς σωφρονίζων, ὡς ἐθορύβησαν,
"ἀκούσατ᾽," εἶπε, "νέοι γέροντος οὗ νέου
γέροντες ἤκουον." ἡ δὲ Περικλέους πολιτεία
τὸ μέγιστον ἐν γήρᾳ κράτος ἔσχεν, ὅτε καὶ τὸν
πόλεμον ἄρασθαι τοὺς Ἀθηναίους ἔπεισε· καὶ
προθυμουμένων οὐ κατὰ καιρὸν μάχεσθαι πρὸς
ἑξακισμυρίους ὁπλίτας, ἐνέστη καὶ διεκώλυσε,
μονονοὺ τὰ ὅπλα τοῦ δήμου καὶ τὰς κλεῖς τῶν
πυλῶν ἀποσφραγισάμενος. ἀλλὰ μὴν ἅ γε
Ξενοφῶν περὶ Ἀγησιλάου γέγραφεν, αὐτοῖς
ὀνόμασιν ἄξιόν ἐστι παραθέσθαι· "ποίας γάρ,"
φησί, "νεότητος οὐ κρεῖττον τὸ ἐκείνου γῆρας

give advice. This is because older politicians have plenty of experience and are no strangers to daring deeds, and so they are not tempted to score victories over their political opponents, as younger people are. Now Cato the Elder, when he was on trial at more than eighty years old, said that it was difficult, having lived his life with one generation, to defend himself before another. And everyone agrees that Caesar (that is Augustus, the one who defeated Antony) made his administration quite a bit more kinglike and advantageous to the people near the end of his life. Augustus himself was taming the youth severely by means of habits and laws, and when they raised an uproar he said, "Listen, young men, to an old man, to whom old men used to listen when he was young." The political leadership of Pericles was most

ἐφάνη; τίς μὲν γὰρ τοῖς ἐχθροῖς ἀκμάζων οὕτω
φοβερὸς ἦν, ὡς Ἀγησίλαος τὸ μήκιστον τοῦ
αἰῶνος ἔχων; τίνος δ᾽ ἐκποδὼν γενομένου
μᾶλλον ἥσθησαν οἱ πολέμιοι ἢ Ἀγησιλάου,
καίπερ γηραιοῦ τελευτήσαντος; τίς δὲ
συμμάχοις θάρσος παρέσχεν ἢ Ἀγησίλαος,
καίπερ ἤδη πρὸς τῷ τέρματι τοῦ βίου ὤν; τίνα
δὲ νέον οἱ φίλοι πλέον ἐπόθησαν ἢ Ἀγησίλαον
γηραιὸν ἀποθανόντα;"

powerful in his old age, when he convinced the Athenians to undertake even the war.[8] And when the Athenians were eager to do battle against sixty thousand hoplites at an inopportune moment, he stood in their way and prevented them, all but sealing up the people's weapons and the keys to the city's gates. But what Xenophon has written about Agesilaus is worth quoting verbatim:[9] "To what youth was that man's old age not clearly superior? Who in their prime was as fearsome to his political enemies as Agesilaus was at the very end of his life? Whom were his military enemies gladder to have out of the way than Agesilaus, even though he died quite old? Who but Agesilaus gave courage to the allies, even when he was already near the end of his life? What young man was more missed by his friends than Agesilaus although he died an old man?"

3. Εἶτ᾽ ἐκείνους μὲν τηλικαῦτα πράττειν
ὁ χρόνος οὐκ ἐκώλυεν, ἡμεῖς δ᾽ οἱ νῦν
τρυφῶντες ἐν πολιτείαις, μὴ τυραννίδα
μὴ πόλεμόν τινα μὴ πολιορκίαν ἐχούσαις,
ἀπολέμους δ᾽ ἁμίλλας καὶ φιλοτιμίας νόμῳ
τὰ πολλὰ καὶ λόγῳ μετὰ δίκης περαινομένας
ἀποδειλιῶμεν; οὐ μόνον στρατηγῶν τῶν
τότε καὶ δημαγωγῶν, ἀλλὰ καὶ ποιητῶν καὶ
σοφιστῶν καὶ ὑποκριτῶν ὁμολογοῦντες εἶναι
κακίους· εἴγε Σιμωνίδης μὲν ἐν γήρᾳ χοροῖς
ἐνίκα, ὡς τοὐπίγραμμα δηλοῖ τοῖς τελευταίοις
ἔπεσιν·

  ἀμφὶ διδασκαλίῃ δὲ Σιμωνίδῃ ἕσπετο
    κῦδος
  ὀγδωκονταέτει παιδὶ Λεωπρέπεος.

Σοφοκλῆς δὲ λέγεται μὲν ὑπὸ παίδων
παρανοίας δίκην φεύγων ἀναγνῶναι τὴν ἐν
Οἰδίποδι τῷ ἐπὶ Κολωνῷ πάροδον, ᾗ ἐστιν ἀρχὴ

3. Old age did not keep those leaders from performing such great deeds. But as for us who live easily nowadays in political systems that include neither tyranny nor any war or siege, should we exhibit fear when facing peaceful conflicts and rivalries that are for the most part settled justly by means of law and debate? If we do, we are admitting that we are inferior not only to the generals and popular leaders of the past, but even to the poets and teachers and actors. Indeed, Simonides won a choral contest in old age, as this epigram demonstrates with its closing lines: "For his training of the chorus, glory followed Simonides, the eighty-year-old son of Leoprepes." And Sophocles, they say, in order to acquit himself against the charge of dementia brought by his children, read aloud the first choral song from his

εὐίππου, ξένε, τᾶσδε χώρας
ἵκου τὰ κράτιστα γᾶς ἔπαυλα,
τὸν ἀργῆτα Κολωνόν, ἔνθ᾽
ἁ λίγεια μινύρεται
θαμίζουσα μάλιστ᾽ ἀηδὼν
χλωραῖς ὑπὸ βάσσαις.

θαυμαστοῦ δὲ τοῦ μέλους φανέντος, ὥσπερ
ἐκ θεάτρου τοῦ δικαστηρίου προπεμφθῆναι
μετὰ κρότου καὶ βοῆς τῶν παρόντων.
τουτὶ δ᾽ ὁμολογουμένως Σοφοκλέους ἐστὶ
τοὐπιγραμμάτιον

    ᾠδὴν Ἡροδότῳ τεῦξεν Σοφοκλῆς ἐτέων ὢν
    πέντ᾽ ἐπὶ πεντήκοντα.

Φιλήμονα δὲ τὸν κωμικὸν καὶ Ἄλεξιν ἐπὶ τῆς
σκηνῆς ἀγωνιζομένους καὶ στεφανουμένους ὁ
θάνατος κατέλαβε. Πῶλον δὲ τὸν τραγῳδὸν
Ἐρατοσθένης καὶ Φιλόχορος ἱστοροῦσιν

Oedipus at Colonus, which begins as follows: "You have arrived, stranger, at the land's mightiest houses in this country famed for horses, shining Colonus, where the sweet-voiced nightingale comes most often to sing, down in the green glens."[10] The song was so obviously magnificent that Sophocles, they say, was escorted from the court, as if from a theater, to the applause and cheers of those in attendance. And everyone agrees that Sophocles wrote this brief epigram: "At the age of fifty-five, Sophocles wrote a song for Herodotus." Death snatched Philemon the comic poet and Alexis, too, as they were performing on stage and receiving crowns. And Eratosthenes and Philochorus report that Polus the tragic actor, at seventy years of age, performed in eight tragedies over four days just before he died.

ἑβδομήκοντ' ἔτη γεγενημένον ὀκτὼ τραγῳδίας
ἐν τέτταρσιν ἡμέραις διαγωνίσασθαι μικρὸν
ἔμπροσθεν τῆς τελευτῆς.

4. Ἆρ' οὖν οὐκ αἰσχρόν ἐστι τῶν ἀπὸ
σκηνῆς γερόντων τοὺς ἀπὸ τοῦ βήματος
ἀγεννεστέρους ὁρᾶσθαι, καὶ τῶν ἱερῶν ὡς
ἀληθῶς ἐξισταμένους ἀγώνων ἀποτίθεσθαι
τὸ πολιτικὸν πρόσωπον, οὐκ οἶδ' ὁποῖον
ἀντιμεταλαμβάνοντας; καὶ γὰρ τὸ τῆς
γεωργίας ἐκ βασιλικοῦ ταπεινόν· ὅπου
γὰρ ὁ Δημοσθένης φησὶν ἀνάξια πάσχειν
τὴν Πάραλον, ἱερὰν οὖσαν τριήρη, ξύλα
καὶ χάρακας καὶ βοσκήματα τῷ Μειδίᾳ
παρακομίζουσαν, ἢ που πολιτικὸς ἀνὴρ
ἀγωνοθεσίας καὶ βοιωταρχίας καὶ τὰς ἐν
Ἀμφικτύοσι προεδρίας ἀπολιπών, εἶθ'
ὁρώμενος ἐν ἀλφίτων καὶ στεμφύλων
διαμετρήσει καὶ πόκοις προβάτων οὐ
παντάπασι δόξει τοῦτο δὴ τὸ καλούμενον

4. Is it not a shame, then, that the old people who appear on the stage are viewed as more noble than those who appear on the speaker's platform, and who, after withdrawing from the contests that are truly sacred, set aside their political role and take up instead something inconceivable? For the role of a farmer is humble after playing a king.[11] Demosthenes says that the *Paralus* was treated unworthily because it was a sacred ship, but Meidias nonetheless used it to transport wood and vine props and feed for animals.[12] On the same basis, will not politicians appear to one and all to have put themselves voluntarily "out to pasture," as they say, if they abandon directorships of

"ἵππου γῆρας" ἐπάγεσθαι, μηδενὸς
ἀναγκάζοντος; ἐργασίας γε μὴν βαναύσου καὶ
ἀγοραίας ἅπτεσθαι μετὰ πολιτείαν ὅμοιόν ἐστι
τῷ γυναικὸς ἐλευθέρας καὶ σώφρονος ἔνδυμα
περισπάσαντα καὶ περίζωμα δόντα συνέχειν
ἐπὶ καπηλείου· καὶ γὰρ τῆς πολιτικῆς ἀρετῆς
οὕτως ἀπόλλυται τὸ ἀξίωμα καὶ τὸ μέγεθος
πρός τινας οἰκονομίας καὶ χρηματισμοὺς
ἀγομένης.

Ἂν δ', ὅπερ λοιπόν ἐστι, ῥαστώνας καὶ
ἀπολαύσεις τὰς ἡδυπαθείας καὶ τὰς τρυφὰς
ὀνομάζοντες ἐν ταύταις μαραινόμενον ἡσυχῇ
παρακαλῶσι γηράσκειν τὸν πολιτικόν, οὐκ
οἶδα ποτέρα δυεῖν εἰκόνων αἰσχρῶν πρέπειν
δόξει μᾶλλον ὁ βίος αὐτοῦ· πότερον ἀφροδίσια
ναύταις ἄγουσι πάντα τὸν λοιπὸν ἤδη χρόνον
οὐκ ἐν λιμένι τὴν ναῦν ἔχουσιν ἀλλ' ἔτι
πλέουσαν ἀπολείπουσιν· ἢ καθάπερ ἔνιοι
τὸν Ἡρακλέα παίζοντες οὐκ εὖ γράφουσιν
ἐν Ὀμφάλης κροκωτοφόρον ἐνδιδόντα

games, leadership of the Boeotian cities, and presidencies of Amphictyonic Councils, but then are later observed distributing barley and crushed olives and shearing sheep? To take on menial and common work after practicing politics is like stripping away the dress of a free and modest woman, replacing it with an apron, and then forcing her to work in a tavern. For in this way, the dignity and stature of one's political virtue is ruined when it is transferred to managing the household and moneymaking.

But if—and this is the only option that remains—one gives the names "relaxation and enjoyment" to "high living and luxury" and then invites politicians to grow old in that environment as they fade quietly away, I do not know which of these two shameful pictures describes that life better. Maybe it is that of the sailors who abandon their

Λυδαῖς θεραπαινίσι ῥιπίζειν καὶ παραπλέκειν ἑαυτόν, οὕτω τὸν πολιτικὸν ἐκδύσαντες τὴν λεοντὴν καὶ κατακλίναντες εὐωχήσομεν ἀεὶ καταψαλλόμενον καὶ καταυλούμενον, οὐδὲ τῇ τοῦ Πομπηίου Μάγνου φωνῇ διατραπέντες τῇ πρὸς Λεύκολλον αὐτὸν μὲν εἰς λουτρὰ καὶ δεῖπνα καὶ συνουσίας μεθημερινὰς καὶ πολὺν ἄλυν καὶ κατασκευὰς οἰκοδομημάτων νεοπρεπεῖς μετὰ τὰς στρατείας καὶ πολιτείας ἀφεικότα, τῷ δὲ Πομπηίῳ φιλαρχίαν ἐγκαλοῦντα καὶ φιλοτιμίαν παρ᾽ ἡλικίαν· ἔφη γὰρ ὁ Πομπήιος ἀωρότερον εἶναι γέροντι τὸ τρυφᾶν ἢ τὸ ἄρχειν· ἐπεὶ δὲ νοσοῦντι συνέταξε κίχλην ὁ ἰατρός, ἦν δὲ δυσπόριστον καὶ παρ᾽ ὥραν, ἔφη δέ τις εἶναι παρὰ Λευκόλλῳ πολλὰς τρεφομένας, οὐκ ἔπεμψεν οὐδ᾽ ἔλαβεν εἰπών, "οὐκοῦν, εἰ μὴ Λεύκολλος ἐτρύφα, Πομπήιος οὐκ ἂν ἔζησε;"

ship still under sail and before they even reach port, and then spend the whole rest of their lives indulging in sexual pleasures. Or, as some artists playfully and inaccurately represent Hercules at the court of Omphale—wearing a saffron robe and submitting to the Lydian maidservants, fanning himself and curling his hair—shall we likewise entertain politicians extravagantly after stripping them of their lion skins and making them recline at the table to forever enjoy music and be charmed by the *aulos*?[13] And in doing so, shall we be undeterred by Pompey the Great's admonishment of Lucullus? Now Lucullus, after his military and political career, gave himself up to baths, dinners, sex in the daytime, prolonged tedium, and the construction of buildings such as a young man would undertake, while he criticized Pompey for

5. Καὶ γὰρ εἰ ζητεῖ πάντως ἡ φύσις τὸ ἡδὺ
καὶ τὸ χαίρειν, τὸ μὲν σῶμα τῶν γερόντων
ἀπείρηκε πρὸς πάσας, πλὴν ὀλίγων τῶν
ἀναγκαίων, τὰς ἡδονάς, καὶ οὐχ "ἡ Ἀφροδίτη
τοῖς γέρουσιν ἄχθεται" μόνον, ὡς Εὐριπίδης

a love of holding office and a love of honor that he said were inappropriate for his age. Pompey, in response, said that it was in fact more unseasonable for an old man to indulge in luxurious living than to continue serving in government. And further, when a doctor prescribed that Pompey should eat a thrush when he was sick, but the bird was out of season and hard to procure, someone told him that many thrushes were being raised on Lucullus's estate. He did not send for one, however, but instead he exclaimed, "So, Pompey would not survive if Lucullus were not a hedonist?"

5. Even if our human nature seeks pleasure and joy by all means, the bodies of old people have given up on all pleasures, except those few that are necessary. And not only "is Aphrodite exasperated by the elderly,"

φησίν, ἀλλὰ καὶ τὰς περὶ πόσιν καὶ βρῶσιν
ἐπιθυμίας ἀπημβλυμμένας τὰ πολλὰ καὶ
νωδὰς κατέχοντες μόλις οἷον ἐπιθήγουσι καὶ
χαράττουσιν· ἐν δὲ τῇ ψυχῇ παρασκευαστέον
ἡδονὰς οὐκ ἀγεννεῖς οὐδ' ἀνελευθέρους, ὡς
Σιμωνίδης ἔλεγε πρὸς τοὺς ἐγκαλοῦντας αὐτῷ
φιλαργυρίαν, ὅτι τῶν ἄλλων ἀπεστερημένος διὰ
τὸ γῆρας ἡδονῶν ὑπὸ μιᾶς ἔτι γηροβοσκεῖται
τῆς ἀπὸ τοῦ κερδαίνειν. ἀλλ' ἡ πολιτεία
καλλίστας μὲν ἡδονὰς ἔχει καὶ μεγίστας, αἷς
καὶ τοὺς θεοὺς εἰκός ἐστιν ἢ μόναις ἢ μάλιστα
χαίρειν· αὗται δ' εἰσίν, ἃς τὸ εὖ ποιεῖν καὶ
καλόν τι πράττειν ἀναδίδωσιν. εἰ γὰρ Νικίας
ὁ ζωγράφος οὕτως ἔχαιρε τοῖς τῆς τέχνης
ἔργοις, ὥστε τοὺς οἰκέτας ἐρωτᾶν πολλάκις,
εἰ λέλουται καὶ ἠρίστηκεν· Ἀρχιμήδην δὲ
τῇ σανίδι προσκείμενον ἀποσπῶντες βίᾳ
καὶ ἀποδύοντες ἤλειφον οἱ θεράποντες, ὁ
δ' ἐπὶ τοῦ σώματος ἀληλιμμένου διέγραφε
τὰ σχήματα· Κάνος δ' ὁ αὐλητής, ὃν καὶ σὺ

as Euripides says, but old people possess desires for food and drink that are for the most part dull and toothless, and only barely do they whet and sharpen them, so to speak.[14] But we must cultivate pleasures in our souls that are neither ignoble nor servile, unlike Simonides, who used to say to those who were charging him with avarice that after being deprived by old age of all other pleasures, he was still nourished in his declining years by a single one, that of turning a profit. But participation in politics provides the finest and greatest of pleasures, in which alone, or above all others, even the gods probably rejoice. These are the pleasures imparted by doing something well and accomplishing a noble deed. Now Nicias the painter took such joy in working at his art that he was often asking his servants whether he had bathed or eaten

γιγνώσκεις, ἔλεγεν ἀγνοεῖν τοὺς ἀνθρώπους,
ὅσῳ μᾶλλον αὐτὸν αὐλῶν ἢ ἑτέρους εὐφραίνει·
λαμβάνειν γὰρ ἂν μισθὸν οὐ διδόναι τοὺς
ἀκούειν ἐθέλοντας· ἆρ᾽ οὐκ ἐπινοοῦμεν,
ἡλίκας ἡδονὰς αἱ ἀρεταὶ τοῖς χρωμένοις ἀπὸ
τῶν καλῶν πράξεων καὶ τῶν κοινωνικῶν
ἔργων καὶ φιλανθρώπων παρασκευάζουσιν,
οὐ κνῶσαι οὐδὲ θρύπτουσαι, ὥσπερ αἱ εἰς
σάρκα λεῖαι καὶ προσηνεῖς γινόμεναι κινήσεις;
ἀλλ᾽ αὗται μὲν οἰστρώδες καὶ ἀβέβαιον καὶ
μεμιγμένον σφυγμῷ τὸ γαργαλίζον ἔχουσιν,
αἱ δ᾽ ἐπὶ τοῖς καλοῖς ἔργοις, οἵων δημιουργὸς ὁ
πολιτευόμενος ὀρθῶς ἐστιν, οὐ ταῖς Εὐριπίδου
χρυσαῖς πτέρυξιν, ἀλλὰ τοῖς Πλατωνικοῖς
ἐκείνοις καὶ οὐρανίοις πτεροῖς ὅμοια τὴν
ψυχὴν μέγεθος καὶ φρόνημα μετὰ γήθους
λαμβάνουσαν ἀναφέρουσιν.

lunch. When Archimedes was absorbed in his writing tablet, his servants used to drag him away by force to strip and anoint him, while he kept drawing his plans in the oil on his body.[15] And Canus the *aulos* player, whom you know, too, used to say that people were ignorant of how much more he enjoyed his music than they did. For if they knew, his audiences would charge him rather than pay him to perform. In light of these examples, do we not perceive how exercising one's virtues generates such great pleasures, which arise from noble deeds and communal and philanthropic works? And do we not perceive how we experience these pleasures without the gnawing and corruption that accompany the smooth and soft pleasures of the flesh? For pleasures of the flesh consist of a tickling that is frenzied, irregular, and mingled with throbbing,

6. Ὑπομίμνησκε δὲ σεαυτὸν ὧν πολλάκις
ἀκήκοας· ὁ μὲν γὰρ Ἐπαμεινώνδας ἐρωτηθεὶς
τί ἥδιστον αὐτῷ γέγονεν, ἀπεκρίνατο τὸ τοῦ
πατρὸς ἔτι ζῶντος καὶ τῆς μητρὸς νικῆσαι
τὴν ἐν Λεύκτροις μάχην. ὁ δὲ Σύλλας, ὅτε
τῶν ἐμφυλίων πολέμων τὴν Ἰταλίαν καθήρας
προσέμιξε τῇ Ῥώμῃ πρῶτον, οὐδὲ μικρὸν ἐν
τῇ νυκτὶ κατέδαρθεν, ὑπὸ γήθους καὶ χαρᾶς
μεγάλης ὥσπερ πνεύματος ἀναφερόμενος τὴν
ψυχήν· καὶ ταῦτα περὶ αὐτοῦ γέγραφεν ἐν τοῖς
ὑπομνήμασιν. ἄκουσμα μὲν γὰρ ἔστω μηδὲν
ἥδιον ἐπαίνου κατὰ τὸν Ξενοφῶντα, θέαμα δὲ

while pleasures based on noble works—of the sort created by one who rightly engages in politics—elevate the soul as it acquires stature and purpose, together with joy. We should compare these noble works not to the golden wings of Euripides, but to those heavenly wings described by Plato.[16]

6. Remind yourself of the examples you have often heard. When Epaminondas was asked what pleased him most, he answered that it was to have won the battle at Leuctra while his father and mother were still alive. And when Sulla first arrived at Rome after having cleansed Italy of civil war, he slept not a bit that night because he was carried away in his soul by great delight and joy as though by the wind; he has even written this about himself in his commentaries. Now I concede that nothing we hear is

καὶ μνημόνευμα καὶ διανόημα τῶν ὄντων οὐδὲν
ἔστιν ὃ τοσαύτην φέρει χάριν, ὅσην πράξεων
ἰδίων ἐν ἀρχαῖς καὶ πολιτείαις ὥσπερ ἐν τόποις
λαμπροῖς καὶ δημοσίοις ἀναθεώρησις. οὐ μὴν
ἀλλὰ καὶ χάρις εὐμενὴς συμμαρτυροῦσα τοῖς
ἔργοις καὶ συναμιλλώμενος ἔπαινος, εὐνοίας
δικαίας ἡγεμών, οἷόν τι φῶς καὶ γάνωμα τῷ
χαίροντι τῆς ἀρετῆς προστίθησι· καὶ δεῖ μὴ
περιορᾶν ὥσπερ ἀθλητικὸν στέφανον ἐν γήρᾳ
ξηρὰν γενομένην τὴν δόξαν, ἀλλὰ καινὸν ἀεί τι
καὶ πρόσφατον ἐπιφέροντα τὴν τῶν παλαιῶν
χάριν ἐγείρειν καὶ ποιεῖν ἀμείνω καὶ μόνιμον·
ὥσπερ οἱ τεχνῖται, οἷς ἐπέκειτο φροντίζειν σῶον
εἶναι τὸ Δηλιακὸν πλοῖον, ἀντὶ τῶν πονούντων
ξύλων ἐμβάλλοντες ἄλλα καὶ συμπηγνύντες
ἀίδιον ἐκ τῶν τότε χρόνων καὶ ἄφθαρτον
ἐδόκουν διαφυλάττειν.

Ἔστι δὲ καὶ δόξης καὶ φλογὸς οὐ
χαλεπὴ σωτηρία καὶ τήρησις ἀλλὰ μικρῶν
ὑπεκκαυμάτων δεομένη, κατασβεσθὲν δὲ καὶ

more pleasant than praise, as Xenophon says, but there is no sight nor recollection nor thought of anything which brings as much gratification as reflecting on the deeds you have performed in highly visible and public spaces, that is to say, while holding office and practicing politics. What is more, a kindly gratitude that bears witness to your deeds and is accompanied by praise leads the way for justly earned goodwill, and it adds a sort of shine and brilliance to the joy of your virtue. And we must not disregard our reputation when, like the athlete's crown, it has become dry in old age, but we must always add to it something new and fresh. Thus, we revive the gratitude expressed for those former deeds and make our reputation stronger and permanent. In this we are like the craftsmen who have been assigned

ὑποψυχθὲν οὐδέτερον ἄν τις ἀπραγμόνως
πάλιν ἐξάψειεν. ὡς δὲ Λάμπις ὁ ναύκληρος
ἐρωτηθεὶς πῶς ἐκτήσατο τὸν πλοῦτον "οὐ
χαλεπῶς," ἔφη, "τὸν μέγαν, τὸν δὲ βραχὺν
ἐπιπόνως καὶ βραδέως"· οὕτω τῆς πολιτικῆς
δόξης καὶ δυνάμεως ἐν ἀρχῇ τυχεῖν οὐ ῥᾴδιόν
ἐστι, τὸ δὲ συναυξῆσαι καὶ διαφυλάξαι
μεγάλην γενομένην ἀπὸ τῶν τυχόντων
ἕτοιμον. οὔτε γὰρ φίλος ὅταν γένηται πολλὰς
λειτουργίας ἐπιζητεῖ καὶ μεγάλας, ἵνα μένῃ
φίλος, μικροῖς δὲ σημείοις τὸ ἐνδελεχὲς ἀεὶ
διαφυλάττει τὴν εὔνοιαν· ἥ τε δήμου φιλία
καὶ πίστις οὐκ ἀεὶ δεομένη χορηγοῦντος οὐδὲ
προδικοῦντος οὐδ' ἄρχοντος αὐτῇ τῇ προθυμίᾳ
συνέχεται καὶ τῷ μὴ προαπολείποντι μηδ'
ἀπαγορεύοντι τῆς ἐπιμελείας καὶ φροντίδος.
οὐδὲ γὰρ αἱ στρατεῖαι παρατάξεις ἀεὶ καὶ
μάχας καὶ πολιορκίας ἔχουσιν, ἀλλὰ καὶ θυσίας
ἔστιν ὅτε καὶ συνουσίας διὰ μέσου καὶ σχολὴν
ἄφθονον ἐν παιδιαῖς καὶ φλυαρίαις δέχονται.

to care for the integrity of the Delian ship: by inserting and fitting new wood in place of that which has worn out, they seem to preserve the ship eternal and undecayed from days gone by.[17]

It happens that the preservation and safekeeping of both reputation and fire is quite simple and requires little kindling, but neither reputation nor fire, once extinguished and cooled, may be reignited without effort. Thus, when Lampis the ship-owner was asked how he acquired his wealth, he replied, "The greater part came quite easily, but the first, smaller part took time and effort." And so, in the beginning it is difficult to acquire one's reputation and power in politics, but once they have become great, it is easy to protect and increase them by means of ordinary deeds. A friendship, once established, does not

πόθεν γε δὴ τὴν πολιτείαν φοβητέον, ὡς
ἀπαραμύθητον καὶ πολύπονον καὶ βαρεῖαν,
ὅπου καὶ θέατρα καὶ πομπαὶ καὶ νεμήσεις καὶ
"χοροὶ καὶ Μοῖσα καὶ Ἀγλαΐα" καὶ θεοῦ τινος
ἀεὶ τιμῇ τὰς ὀφρῦς λύουσα παντὸς ἀρχείου
καὶ συνεδρίου πολλαπλάσιον τὸ ἐπιτερπὲς καὶ
κεχαρισμένον ἀποδίδωσιν;

require many great services in order to be maintained, but small gestures frequently made will preserve the friends' goodwill. Nor do the friendship and trust of the people always require that you sponsor choruses or appear in court or hold office, but they are maintained by your very eagerness, and by not quitting or walking away from your commission and responsibility. Military campaigns do not entail only marshalling troops, fighting battles, and laying siege, but they also consist sometimes of sacrifices and parties between battles and plenty of free time spent in play and triviality. Why, then, must practicing politics be feared as though it were comfortless, toilsome, and a burden, when the theaters and parades and distributions of land and "choruses and the Muse and Aglaea"[18] and the honor always being paid to some god

7. Ὁ τοίνυν μέγιστον κακὸν ἔχουσιν αἱ
πολιτεῖαι, τὸν φθόνον, ἥκιστα διερείδεται
πρὸς τὸ γῆρας· "κύνες γὰρ καὶ βαΰζουσιν
ὃν ἂν μὴ γινώσκωσι" καθ᾽ Ἡράκλειτον, καὶ
πρὸς τὸν ἀρχόμενον ὥσπερ ἐν θύραις τοῦ
βήματος μάχεται καὶ πάροδον οὐ δίδωσι· τὴν
δὲ σύντροφον καὶ συνήθη δόξαν οὐκ ἀγρίως
οὐδὲ χαλεπῶς ἀλλὰ πράως ἀνέχεται. διὸ τὸν
φθόνον ἔνιοι τῷ καπνῷ παρεικάζουσι· πολὺς
γὰρ ἐν τοῖς ἀρχομένοις διὰ τὸ φλέγεσθαι
προεκπίπτων, ὅταν ἐκλάμψωσιν, ἀφανίζεται.
καὶ ταῖς μὲν ἄλλαις ὑπεροχαῖς προσμάχονται
καὶ διαμφισβητοῦσιν ἀρετῆς καὶ γένους καὶ
φιλοτιμίας, ὡς ἀφαιροῦντες αὐτῶν ὅσον ἄλλοις
ὑφίενται· τὸ δ᾽ ἀπὸ τοῦ χρόνου πρωτεῖον, ὃ
καλεῖται κυρίως πρεσβεῖον, ἀζηλοτύπητόν

bring cheer to every town hall and council chamber, and repay politicians many times over with delight and pleasure?[19]

7. Envy, however, which is the greatest evil in political life, hardly comes into conflict with old age. "For dogs bark at those they don't know," as Heraclitus says, and so envy does battle with the ones getting their start on the speaker's platform (knocking at the door, so to speak) and does not allow them to pass. It accepts the familiar and well-known reputation, however, not with savageness or anger, but mildly. Wherefore some liken envy to smoke, for though it pours forth abundantly in front of those starting out because they are just kindling their careers, it dissipates once they are in full flame. Now on the one hand, people attack every other form of superiority and

ἐστι καὶ παραχωρούμενον· οὐδεμιᾷ γὰρ οὕτω
τιμῇ συμβέβηκε τὸν τιμῶντα μᾶλλον ἢ τὸν
τιμώμενον κοσμεῖν, ὡς τῇ τῶν γερόντων.
ἔτι τὴν μὲν ἀπὸ τοῦ πλούτου δύναμιν ἢ
λόγου δεινότητος ἢ σοφίας οὐ πάντες αὑτοῖς
γενήσεσθαι προσδοκῶσιν, ἐφ' ἣν δὲ προάγει
τὸ γῆρας αἰδῶ καὶ δόξαν οὐδεὶς ἀπελπίζει
τῶν πολιτευομένων. οὐδὲν οὖν διαφέρει
κυβερνήτου πρὸς ἐναντίον κῦμα καὶ πνεῦμα
πλεύσαντος ἐπισφαλῶς, εὐδίας δὲ καὶ
εὐαερίας γενομένης ὁρμίσασθαι ζητοῦντος, ὁ
τῷ φθόνῳ διαναυμαχήσας πολὺν χρόνον, εἶτα
παυσαμένου καὶ στορεσθέντος, ἀνακρουόμενος
ἐκ τῆς πολιτείας καὶ προϊέμενος ἅμα ταῖς
πράξεσι τὰς κοινωνίας καὶ τὰς ἑταιρείας.
ὅσῳ γὰρ χρόνος γέγονε πλείων, καὶ φίλους
πλείονας καὶ συναγωνιστὰς πεποίηκεν, οὓς
οὔτε συνεξάγειν ἑαυτῷ πάντας ἐνδέχεται
καθάπερ διδασκάλῳ χορὸν οὔτ' ἐγκαταλείπειν
δίκαιον· ἀλλ' ὥσπερ τὰ παλαιὰ δένδρα

argue especially over virtue, birth, and ambition, as though they would deprive themselves of whatever distinctions they allowed to someone else. But on the other hand, the primacy that is earned over time, which is properly called "the privilege of age," is not begrudged but is rather conceded. For in fact no other honor besides that paid to our elders adorns the one who gives it more than the one who receives it. Moreover, not everyone expects to acquire the authority that comes from wealth or clever speaking or wisdom, but there is no one engaged in politics who does not hope for the reverence and reputation that old age delivers. There is no difference, then, between the ship's pilot who, after sailing dangerously against an opposing sea and wind, seeks a safe anchorage once fair weather and a favorable wind have returned,[20] and the politician who,

τὴν μακρὰν πολιτείαν οὐ ῥᾴδιόν ἐστιν
ἀνασπάσαι πολύρριζον οὖσαν καὶ πράγμασιν
ἐμπεπλεγμένην, ἃ πλείονας παρέχει ταραχὰς
καὶ σπαραγμοὺς ἀπερχομένοις ἢ μένουσιν.
εἰ δέ τι καὶ περίεστι φθόνου λείψανον ἢ
φιλονεικίας πρὸς τοὺς γέροντας ἐκ τῶν
πολιτικῶν ἀγώνων, κατασβεστέον τοῦτο τῇ
δυνάμει μᾶλλον ἢ δοτέον τὰ νῶτα, γυμνοὺς καὶ
ἀόπλους ἀπιόντας· οὐ γὰρ οὕτως ἀγωνιζομένοις
φθονοῦντες ὡς ἀπειπαμένοις καταφρονήσαντες
ἐπιτίθενται.

after maintaining a sea battle against envy over a long career, backs-water away from political life and abandons partnerships, clubs, and all other activity once envy has ceased and been made calm. For the longer your career, the more friends and colleagues you make. But you cannot escort them all off with you, as a music director can lead off the chorus, nor is it right to leave them behind. But just as with aged trees, it is not easy to dig up a long political career, which has branching roots and has become inter-twined with one's other affairs. This creates more upheaval and rending for those who withdraw than for those who remain active. And if there survives some remnant of envy or contentiousness against our elders as a result of their political contests, they must snuff this out with their authority, not turn their backs and walk away, unprotected and

8. Μαρτυρεῖ δὲ καὶ τὸ λεχθὲν ὑπ᾽
Ἐπαμεινώνδα τοῦ μεγάλου πρὸς τοὺς
Θηβαίους, ὅτε χειμῶνος ὄντος οἱ Ἀρκάδες
παρεκάλουν αὐτοὺς ἐν ταῖς οἰκίαις διαιτᾶσθαι
παρελθόντας εἰς τὴν πόλιν· οὐ γὰρ εἴασεν,
ἀλλὰ "νῦν μέν," ἔφη, "θαυμάζουσιν ὑμᾶς καὶ
θεῶνται πρὸς τὰ ὅπλα γυμναζομένους καὶ
παλαίοντας· ἂν δὲ πρὸς τῷ πυρὶ καθημένους
ὁρῶσι τὸν κύαμον κάπτοντας, οὐδὲν αὐτῶν
ἡγήσονται διαφέρειν." οὕτω δὴ σεμνόν ἐστι
θέαμα πρεσβύτης λέγων τι καὶ πράττων
καὶ τιμώμενος, ὁ δ᾽ ἐν κλίνῃ διημερεύων
ἢ καθήμενος ἐν γωνίᾳ στοᾶς φλυαρῶν καὶ
ἀπομυττόμενος εὐκαταφρόνητος. τοῦτο δ᾽
ἀμέλει καὶ Ὅμηρος διδάσκει τοὺς ὀρθῶς

unarmed. For others do not, out of envy, attack them for continuing to fight, but out of contempt, they attack them for having renounced politics.

8. Evidence for this is what the great Epaminondas said to the Thebans when they were passing through Arcadia in the midst of winter. The Arcadians invited the Theban soldiers into their city to stay in their homes, but Epaminondas would not allow it. "Now they marvel at you and look on as you train in arms and wrestle," he said, "but if they see you sitting around the fire and eating beans, they will believe that you are no different from them." Thus, elders, when saying or doing something or being honored, are a noble sight, while old people who pass the day on the couch or sit in the corner of a portico,[21] talking nonsense and

ἀκούοντας· ὁ μὲν γὰρ Νέστωρ στρατευόμενος
ἐν Τροίᾳ σεμνὸς ἦν καὶ πολυτίμητος, ὁ
δὲ Πηλεὺς καὶ ὁ Λαέρτης οἰκουροῦντες
ἀπερρίφησαν καὶ κατεφρονήθησαν. οὐδὲ γὰρ
ἡ τοῦ φρονεῖν ἕξις ὁμοίως παραμένει τοῖς
μεθεῖσιν αὐτούς, ἀλλ᾽ ὑπ᾽ ἀργίας ἐξανιεμένη
καὶ ἀναλυομένη κατὰ μικρὸν ἀεί τινα ποθεῖ
φροντίδος μελέτην, τὸ λογιστικὸν καὶ
πρακτικὸν ἐγειρούσης καὶ διακαθαιρούσης·

λάμπει γὰρ ἐν χρείαισιν, ὥσπερ εὐπρεπὴς
χαλκός.

Οὐ γὰρ τόσον σώματος ἀσθένεια κακὸν
πρόσεστι ταῖς πολιτείαις τῶν παρ᾽ ἡλικίαν
ἐπὶ τὸ βῆμα καὶ τὸ στρατήγιον βαδιζόντων,
ὅσον ἔχουσιν ἀγαθὸν τὴν εὐλάβειαν καὶ
τὴν φρόνησιν, καὶ τὸ μὴ φερόμενον, ἄλλοτε
μὲν δι᾽ ἐσφαλμένα ὅτε δ᾽ ὑπὸ δόξης κενῆς,
προσπίπτειν πρὸς τὰ κοινὰ καὶ συνεφέλκεσθαι

wiping their nose, are contemptible. Homer, of course, teaches this to those who hear him correctly: Nestor, who went out on the campaign to Troy, was noble and held in high regard, while Peleus and Laertes,[22] who remained at home, were disparaged and held in contempt. For the habit of thinking does not persist in those who otherwise neglect themselves, but diluted and dissolved little by little through disuse, it constantly yearns for some exercise of the mind, which rouses and purges the logical and practical elements of the soul: "For it shines when being used, like fine-looking bronze."[23]

Even if political activity suffers because of the bodily weakness of those who ascend the speaker's platform or enter the general's headquarters at an advanced age, the harm is not as great as the benefit conferred by the elders' discretion and practical wisdom.

τὸν ὄχλον, ὥσπερ θάλατταν ὑπὸ πνευμάτων
ἐκταραττόμενον, ἀλλὰ πράως τε χρῆσθαι καὶ
μετρίως τοῖς ἐντυγχάνουσιν. ὅθεν αἱ πόλεις,
ὅταν πταίσωσιν ἢ φοβηθῶσι, πρεσβυτέρων
ποθοῦσιν ἀρχὴν ἀνθρώπων· καὶ πολλάκις
ἐξ ἀγροῦ κατάγουσαι γέροντα μὴ δεόμενον
μηδὲ βουλόμενον ἠνάγκασαν ὥσπερ οἴακων
ἐφαψάμενον εἰς ἀσφαλὲς καταστῆσαι τὰ
πράγματα, παρωσάμεναί τε στρατηγοὺς
καὶ δημαγωγοὺς βοᾶν μέγα καὶ λέγειν
ἀπνευστὶ καὶ νὴ Δία τοῖς πολεμίοις διαβάντας
εὖ μάχεσθαι δυναμένους· οἷον οἱ ῥήτορες
Ἀθήνησι Τιμοθέῳ καὶ Ἰφικράτει Χάρητα τὸν
Θεοχάρους ἐπαποδύοντες ἀκμάζοντα τῷ
σώματι καὶ ῥωμαλέον ἠξίουν τοιοῦτον εἶναι
τὸν τῶν Ἀθηναίων στρατηγόν, ὁ δὲ Τιμόθεος
"οὐ μὰ τοὺς θεούς," εἶπεν, "ἀλλὰ τοιοῦτον μὲν
εἶναι τὸν μέλλοντα τῷ στρατηγῷ τὰ στρώματα
κομίζειν, τὸν δὲ στρατηγὸν 'ἅμα πρόσω καὶ
ὀπίσω' τῶν πραγμάτων ὁρῶντα καὶ μηδενὶ

Nor are elders prone, as young people are, to being carried away—sometimes to cover a mistake, sometimes to build a hollow reputation—and then to jump into public affairs and drag the mob along with them, stirred up like a sea in high winds. Instead, older politicians manage circumstances mildly and with moderation. This is why cities, when in a crisis or frightened, long for the leadership of their elders. Oftentimes they will even bring an old man back from his farm, though he is not asking or wishing to be restored, and compel him to take the helm, so to speak, and stabilize their affairs, while in the meantime they have pushed aside generals and popular leaders who are able to shout loudly, to speak without taking a breath, and—by Zeus!—to plant their feet firmly and do battle with the enemy. For example, the speakers in the assembly

πάθει τοὺς περὶ τῶν συμφερόντων λογισμοὺς
ἐπιταραττόμενον." ὁ γὰρ Σοφοκλῆς ἄσμενος
ἔφη τὰ ἀφροδίσια γεγηρακὼς ἀποπεφευγέναι
καθάπερ ἄγριον καὶ λυσσῶντα δεσπότην·
ἐν δὲ ταῖς πολιτείαις οὐχ ἕνα δεῖ δεσπότην,
ἔρωτα παίδων ἢ γυναικῶν, ἀποφεύγειν, ἀλλὰ
πολλοὺς μανικωτέρους τούτου, φιλονεικίαν,
φιλοδοξίαν, τὴν τοῦ πρῶτον εἶναι καὶ μέγιστον
ἐπιθυμίαν, γονιμώτατον φθόνου νόσημα καὶ
ζηλοτυπίας καὶ διχοστασίας· ὧν τὰ μὲν ἀνίησι
καὶ παραμβλύνει, τὰ δ᾽ ὅλως ἀποσβέννυσι
καὶ καταψύχει τὸ γῆρας, οὐ τοσοῦτον τῆς
πρακτικῆς ὁρμῆς παραιρούμενον, ὅσον τῶν
ἀκράτων καὶ διαπύρων ἀπερύκει παθῶν,
ὥστε νήφοντα καὶ καθεστηκότα τὸν λογισμὸν
ἐπάγειν ταῖς φροντίσιν.

at Athens were once promoting Chares, son of Theochares, as a rival to Timotheus and Iphicrates, because he was vigorous and flourishing in bodily strength. They thought that a strong man like that was worthy to be the Athenians' general, but Timotheus protested, "No, by the gods! That is the sort of man who should carry the general's bedding! The real general is the one who sees 'both beyond and behind' political affairs and, when deciding upon a course of action, remains untroubled by any passion." For Sophocles said that in growing old he gladly escaped sexual pleasures, as though he had escaped a savage and rabid master. But in politics we must escape not a single master (that is, the desire for youths or women), but many masters even more maniacal than this: contentiousness, love of glory, the desire to be first and greatest,

9. Οὐ μὴν ἀλλ᾽ ἔστω καὶ δοκείτω διατρεπτικὸς
εἶναι λόγος πρὸς τὸν ἀρχόμενον ἐν πολιαῖς
νεανιεύεσθαι λεγόμενος καὶ καθαπτόμενος
ἐκ μακρᾶς οἰκουρίας ὥσπερ νοσηλείας
ἐξανισταμένου καὶ κινουμένου γέροντος
ἐπὶ στρατηγίαν ἢ πραγματείαν, "μέν᾽, ὦ
ταλαίπωρ᾽, ἀτρέμα σοῖς ἐν δεμνίοις"· ὁ δὲ
τὸν ἐμβεβιωκότα πολιτικαῖς πράξεσι καὶ
διηγωνισμένον οὐκ ἐῶν ἐπὶ τὴν δᾷδα καὶ
τὴν κορωνίδα τοῦ βίου προελθεῖν, ἀλλ᾽

and the sickness that produces envy, jealousy, and dissention in abundance. Old age slackens and blunts some of these desires, while it snuffs out entirely and cools others, not so much by denying people their impulse to act as by separating them from the uncontrolled and fiery passions, so that they may apply a sober and stable reasoning to their thinking.

9. Even so, let the following warning be considered dissuasive—and may it actually be dissuasive—when spoken to a grey-hair who begins to swagger like a youth, or when used to chastise an old person who is arising from a long spell at home as if from a convalescence and is entering upon a generalship or some other official duty: "Lie still, poor soul, in your bed."[24] But as for the warning that prevents people who have

ἀνακαλούμενος καὶ κελεύων ὥσπερ ἐξ ὁδοῦ
μακρᾶς μεταβαλέσθαι, παντάπασιν ἀγνώμων
καὶ μηδὲν ἐκείνῳ προσεοικώς ἐστιν. ὥσπερ
γὰρ ὁ γαμεῖν παρασκευαζόμενον γέροντ᾽
ἐστεφανωμένον καὶ μυριζόμενον ἀποτρέπων
καὶ λέγων τὰ πρὸς τὸν Φιλοκτήτην

  τίς δ᾽ ἄν σε νύμφη, τίς δὲ παρθένος νέα
  δέξαιτ᾽ ἄν; εὖ γοῦν ὡς γαμεῖν ἔχεις τάλας

οὐκ ἄτοπός ἐστι· καὶ γὰρ αὐτοὶ πολλὰ τοιαῦτα
παίζουσιν εἰς ἑαυτούς, "γαμῶ γέρων, εὖ οἶδα,
καὶ τοῖς γείτοσιν"· ὁ δὲ τὸν πάλαι συνοικοῦντα
καὶ συμβιοῦντα πολὺν χρόνον ἀμέμπτως
οἰόμενος δεῖν ἀφεῖναι διὰ τὸ γῆρας τὴν γυναῖκα
καὶ ζῆν καθ᾽ ἑαυτὸν ἢ παλλακίδιον ἀντὶ τῆς
γαμετῆς ἐπισπάσασθαι, σκαιότητος ὑπερβολὴν
οὐκ ἀπολέλοιπεν· οὕτως ἔχει τινὰ λόγον τὸ
προσιόντα δήμῳ πρεσβύτην, ἢ Χλίδωνα τὸν
γεωργὸν ἢ Λάμπωνα τὸν ναύκληρον ἢ τινα

spent a lifetime contending in politics from continuing until the finale of their lives, and instead recalls them and orders them to change course as after a long journey, this warning is entirely hard-hearted and wholly inappropriate. Now, when an old man is preparing to marry, having put on his wedding crown and smelling of perfume, the one who dissuades him and speaks the advice given to Philoctetes—"Who would be your bride? What youthful maiden would take you? You wretch, aren't you a great catch!"—is not out of line. For even old men say many such things in jest about themselves, such as, "I'm marrying as an old man, I well know, and for the neighbors' benefit, too."[25] But when a man has long shared his home and life contentedly over many years, if someone thinks he ought to send away his wife on account of old age

τῶν ἐκ τοῦ κήπου φιλοσόφων, νουθετῆσαι καὶ
κατασχεῖν ἐπὶ τῆς συνήθους ἀπραγμοσύνης·
ὁ δὲ Φωκίωνος ἢ Κάτωνος ἢ Περικλέους
ἐπιλαβόμενος καὶ λέγων "ὦ ξέν' Ἀθηναῖε ἢ
Ῥωμαῖε, 'ἀζαλέῳ γήρᾳ κρᾶτ' ἀνθίζων κήδει,'
γραψάμενος ἀπόλειψιν τῇ πολιτείᾳ καὶ
τὰς περὶ τὸ βῆμα καὶ τὸ στρατήγιον ἀφεὶς
διατριβὰς καὶ τὰς φροντίδας εἰς ἀγρὸν ἐπείγου
σὺν ἀμφιπόλῳ τῇ γεωργίᾳ συνεσόμενος ἢ πρὸς
οἰκονομίᾳ τινὶ καὶ λογισμοῖς διαθησόμενος τὸν
λοιπὸν χρόνον," ἄδικα πείθει καὶ ἀχάριστα
πράττειν τὸν πολιτικόν.

and then live alone or replace his lawful spouse with a mistress, that person knows no limit of perversity. Thus, it makes some sense to admonish people such as Chlidon the farmer, Lampon the ship-owner, or one of the philosophers of the garden,[26] who appear before the assembly for the first time in old age, and to restrict them to their usual apolitical life. But one is unjustly deceptive and does the politician a disservice if he lays hold of a Phocion, a Cato, or a Pericles and says, "O Athenian or Roman friend, now that 'you've adorned your head with withered old age as for your funeral,' divorce yourself from politics and stop worrying about the speaker's platform and the general's headquarters! Then get yourself to the country to live with farming as your handmaid or to devote your remaining years to house-holding and budgets."

10. Τί οὖν; φήσαι τις ἄν, οὐκ ἀκούομεν ἐν
κωμῳδίᾳ στρατιώτου λέγοντος "λευκή με
θρὶξ ἀπόμισθον ἐντεῦθεν ποιεῖ;" πάνυ μὲν οὖν,
ὦ ἑταῖρε· τοὺς γὰρ Ἄρεος θεράποντας ἡβᾶν
πρέπει καὶ ἀκμάζειν, οἷα δὴ "πόλεμον πολέμοιό
τε μέρμερα ἔργα" διέποντας, ἐν οἷς τοῦ γέροντος
κἂν τὸ κράνος ἀποκρύψῃ τὰς πολιάς, "ἀλλά τε
λάθρῃ γυῖα βαρύνεται" καὶ προαπολείπει τῆς
προθυμίας ἡ δύναμις· τοὺς δὲ τοῦ Βουλαίου
καὶ Ἀγοραίου καὶ Πολιέως Διὸς ὑπηρέτας
οὐ ποδῶν ἔργα καὶ χειρῶν ἀπαιτοῦμεν, ἀλλὰ
βουλῆς καὶ προνοίας καὶ λόγου, μὴ ῥαχίαν
ποιοῦντος ἐν δήμῳ καὶ ψόφον ἀλλὰ νοῦν ἔχοντος
καὶ φροντίδα πεπνυμένην καὶ ἀσφάλειαν· οἷς
ἡ γελωμένη πολιὰ καὶ ῥυτὶς ἐμπειρίας μάρτυς
ἐπιφαίνεται, καὶ πειθοῦς συνεργὸν αὐτῷ καὶ
δόξαν ἤθους προστίθησι. πειθαρχικὸν γὰρ ἡ
νεότης ἡγεμονικὸν δὲ τὸ γῆρας, καὶ μάλιστα
σῴζεται πόλις "ἔνθα βουλαὶ γερόντων, καὶ νέων
ἀνδρῶν ἀριστεύοισιν αἰχμαί"· καὶ τὸ

10. "But wait," someone might say. "Don't we hear a soldier in a comedy claim, 'My grey hair grants me a discharge from service'"? Of course, my friend. For to be young and vigorous suits the servants of Ares, since they are engaged in "war, and the destructive deeds of war."[27] In such circumstances, a helmet may conceal the old man's grey hair, "but his limbs are weighed down invisibly"[28] and his strength gives out before his enthusiasm. But from the servants of Zeus of the Council, of the Marketplace, and of the City we do not demand deeds of the feet or hands, but rather of counsel, foresight, and speech, and not speech that creates an uproar among the people or mere noise, but speech that consists of sense, wise judgment, and stability. In the context of these sorts of deeds, the derided grey hair and wrinkles appear as witnesses to experience, and they

> βουλὴν δὲ πρῶτον μεγαθύμων ἷζε γερόντων
> Νεστορέῃ παρὰ νηὶ

θαυμαστῶς ἐπαινεῖται. διὸ τὴν μὲν ἐν
Λακεδαίμονι παραζευχθεῖσαν ἀριστοκρατίαν
τοῖς βασιλεῦσιν ὁ Πύθιος "πρεσβυγενέας" ὁ δὲ
Λυκοῦργος ἄντικρυς "γέροντας" ὠνόμασεν, ἡ
δὲ Ῥωμαίων σύγκλητος ἄχρι νῦν "γερουσία"
καλεῖται. καὶ καθάπερ ὁ νόμος τὸ διάδημα καὶ
τὸν στέφανον, οὕτω τὴν πολιὰν ἡ φύσις ἔντιμον
ἡγεμονικοῦ σύμβολον ἀξιώματος ἐπιτίθησι·
καὶ τὸ "γέρας" οἶμαι καὶ τὸ "γεραίρειν" ὄνομα
σεμνὸν ἀπὸ τῶν γερόντων γενόμενον διαμένει,
οὐχ ὅτι θερμολουτοῦσι καὶ καθεύδουσι
μαλακώτερον, ἀλλ᾽ ὡς βασιλικὴν ἐχόντων
τάξιν ἐν ταῖς πόλεσι κατὰ τὴν φρόνησιν, ἧς
καθάπερ ὀψικάρπου φυτοῦ τὸ οἰκεῖον ἀγαθὸν
καὶ τέλειον ἐν γήρᾳ μόλις ἡ φύσις ἀποδίδωσι.
τὸν γοῦν βασιλέα τῶν βασιλέων εὐχόμενον τοῖς
θεοῖς "τοιοῦτοι δέκα μοι συμφράδμονες εἶεν

collaborate in making a person persuasive and impute a reputation for character. For obedience belongs to youth, while old age is made to lead. And a city is safest "where the counsels of elders and the spears of young men hold the highest distinction" and where the verses, "first he seated a council of great-hearted elders alongside Nestor's ship"[29] are especially admired. For this reason, Pythian Apollo used the name "first-borns" for the aristocratic class that is associated with the kings in Sparta, while Lycurgus openly called them "old men," and the council of Romans is to this day called the "senate."[30] And just as the law places the diadem and the crown upon a leader's head, so nature places grey hair as an honored symbol of a leader's rank. And I think *"geras"* ("gift of honor") and *"geraiein"* ("to give a gift of honor") maintain their nobility because

Ἀχαιῶν," οἷος ἦν ὁ Νέστωρ, οὐδεὶς ἐμέμψατο
τῶν "ἀρηίων" καὶ "μένεα πνεόντων Ἀχαιῶν,"
ἀλλὰ συνεχώρουν ἅπαντες οὐκ ἐν πολιτείᾳ
μόνον ἀλλὰ καὶ ἐν πολέμῳ μεγάλην ἔχειν ῥοπὴν
τὸ γῆρας·

   σοφὸν γὰρ ἓν βούλευμα τὰς πολλὰς χέρας
   νικᾷ

καὶ μία γνώμη λόγον ἔχουσα καὶ πειθὼ τὰ
κάλλιστα καὶ μέγιστα διαπράττεται τῶν
κοινῶν.

they are derived from "*gerontes*" ("old men"). They are noble not because old men take warm baths and sleep on softer bedding, but because they hold a king's rank[31] in their cities as befits their practical wisdom. Nature allows one to possess this sort of wisdom as a good and perfect thing only in old age, as though it came from a plant that bears fruit late in the season. And so not one of the "warlike" and "force-breathing Achaeans" found fault with the king of kings[32] when he prayed to the gods, "I wish I had ten counselors among the Achaeans" like Nestor, but they all agreed that old age has great influence not only in politics but also in war. "For a single wise plan defeats many hands,"[33] and a single decision based on reason, together with persuasiveness, accomplishes the noblest and greatest of public deeds.

11. Ἀλλὰ μὴν ἥ γε βασιλεία, τελεωτάτη πασῶν οὖσα καὶ μεγίστη τῶν πολιτειῶν, πλείστας φροντίδας ἔχει καὶ πόνους καὶ ἀσχολίας· τὸν γοῦν Σέλευκον ἑκάστοτε λέγειν ἔφασαν, εἰ γνοῖεν οἱ πολλοὶ τὸ γράφειν μόνον ἐπιστολὰς τοσαύτας καὶ ἀναγινώσκειν ὡς ἐργῶδές ἐστιν, ἐρριμμένον οὐκ ἂν ἀνελέσθαι διάδημα· τὸν δὲ Φίλιππον ἐν καλῷ χωρίῳ μέλλοντα καταστρατοπεδεύειν, ὡς ἤκουσεν ὅτι χόρτος οὐκ ἔστι τοῖς ὑποζυγίοις "ὦ Ἡράκλεις," εἰπεῖν, "οἷος ἡμῶν ὁ βίος, εἰ καὶ πρὸς τὸν τῶν ὄνων καιρὸν ὀφείλομεν ζῆν." ὥρα τοίνυν καὶ βασιλεῖ παραινεῖν πρεσβύτῃ γεγενημένῳ τὸ μὲν διάδημα καταθέσθαι καὶ τὴν πορφύραν, ἱμάτιον δ᾿ ἀναλαβόντα καὶ καμπύλην ἐν ἀγρῷ διατρίβειν, μὴ δοκῇ περίεργα καὶ ἄωρα πράττειν ἐν πολιαῖς βασιλεύων. εἰ δ᾿ οὐκ ἄξιον ταῦτα λέγειν περὶ Ἀγησιλάου καὶ Νομᾶ καὶ Δαρείου, μηδὲ τῆς ἐξ Ἀρείου πάγου βουλῆς Σόλωνα μηδὲ τῆς συγκλήτου

11. Now truly even monarchy, the most perfect and greatest of all constitutions, requires very great attention, toil, and official duty. It is reported, for instance, that Seleucus said repeatedly that if the people only knew how much effort he expended just to write and read all his letters, they would not even bother to pick up a crown that a king had cast aside. And we hear that when Philip was about to make his camp in a fine location but then learned that there was no place to pasture the pack animals, he exclaimed, "O Hercules, what a life I lead, if I'm obliged to live for the benefit of my asses!" There is a right time, however, to advise even a king who has become aged to set aside the crown and the purple garment, and after adopting ordinary clothes and a crooked staff, to spend his life in the country, so as not to be seen acting strangely and

Κάτωνα διὰ τὸ γῆρας ἐξάγωμεν, οὐκοῦν μηδὲ
Περικλεῖ συμβουλεύωμεν ἐγκαταλιπεῖν τὴν
δημοκρατίαν· οὐδὲ γὰρ ἄλλως λόγον ἔχει
νέον ὄντα κατασκιρτῆσαι τοῦ βήματος, εἶτ'
ἐκχέαντα τὰς μανικὰς ἐκείνας φιλοτιμίας
καὶ ὁρμὰς εἰς τὸ δημόσιον, ὅταν ἡ τὸ φρονεῖν
ἐπιφέρουσα δι' ἐμπειρίαν ἡλικία παραγένηται,
προέσθαι καὶ καταλιπεῖν ὥσπερ γυναῖκα τὴν
πολιτείαν καταχρησάμενον.

12. Ἡ μὲν γὰρ Αἰσώπειος ἀλώπηξ τὸν ἐχῖνον
οὐκ εἴα τοὺς κρότωνας αὐτῆς ἀφαιρεῖν
βουλόμενον· "ἂν γὰρ τούτους," ἔφη, "μεστοὺς
ἀπαλλάξῃς, ἕτεροι προσίασι πεινῶντες"· τὴν

unseasonably while ruling in grey hair. But if it is not proper to say this about Agesilaus and Numa and Darius, nor to lead Solon out of the council of the Areopagus or Cato the Elder from the senate on account of their age,[34] then let us not advise Pericles to abandon his democracy. For it makes no sense that we should prance upon the speaker's platform and pour our crazed ambitions and impulses into public affairs when we are young, but once old age arrives bringing wisdom through experience, we should give up and abandon politics, as one might dissolve a marriage, in the belief that there is no more to be gained from it.[35]

12. Now Aesop's fox would not allow the hedgehog to remove her ticks even though the hedgehog wished to do it: "For if you take away these full ticks," she said, "other

δὲ πολιτείαν ἀεὶ τοὺς γέροντας ἀποβάλλουσαν
ἀναπίμπλασθαι νέων ἀνάγκη διψώντων
δόξης καὶ δυνάμεως, νοῦν δὲ πολιτικὸν οὐκ
ἐχόντων· πόθεν γάρ, εἰ μηδενὸς ἔσονται
μαθηταὶ μηδὲ θεαταὶ πολιτευομένου
γέροντος; ἢ πλοίων μὲν ἄρχοντας οὐ ποιεῖ
γράμματα κυβερνητικά, μὴ πολλάκις
γενομένους ἐν πρύμνῃ θεατὰς τῶν πρὸς κῦμα
καὶ πνεῦμα καὶ νύκτα χειμέριον ἀγώνων,
"ὅτε Τυνδαριδᾶν ἀδελφῶν ἅλιον ναύταν
πόθος βάλλει," πόλιν δὲ μεταχειρίσασθαι
καὶ πεῖσαι δῆμον ἢ βουλὴν δύναιτ᾽ ἂν
ὀρθῶς νέος ἀναγνοὺς βίβλον ἢ σχολὴν περὶ
πολιτείας ἐν Λυκείῳ γραψάμενος, ἂν μὴ
παρ᾽ ἡνίαν καὶ παρ᾽ οἴακα πολλάκις στὰς
δημαγωγῶν καὶ στρατηγῶν ἀγωνιζομένων
ἐμπειρίαις ἅμα καὶ τύχαις συναποκλίνων ἐπ᾽
ἀμφότερα, μετὰ κινδύνων καὶ πραγμάτων
λάβῃ τὴν μάθησιν; οὐκ ἔστιν εἰπεῖν· ἀλλ᾽ εἰ
διὰ μηδὲν ἄλλο τῷ γέροντι παιδείας ἕνεκα

hungry ones will take their place." By ne-
cessity, the political system that continually
pushes out its elders is refilled with younger
people who thirst for glory and power but
lack political sense. For where would they
get it, if they have been neither students
nor observers of their elders as they practice politics? And if books about piloting
ships do not produce captains, unless those
captains have often stood upon the stern
to observe the struggles against wave and
wind and stormy night, "when a desire
for the sons of Tyndareus strikes the sailor
upon the sea,"[36] could a young person suc-
cessfully manage a city and persuade the
assembly or senate after reading a book or
writing an essay about the constitution in
school, without first having stood often near
the reins and rudder, pulling left and right
and sharing the experiences and fortunes

τῶν νέων καὶ διδασκαλίας πολιτευτέον
ἐστίν. ὡς γὰρ οἱ γράμματα καὶ μουσικὴν
διδάσκοντες, αὐτοὶ προανακρούονται καὶ
προαναγινώσκουσιν ὑφηγούμενοι τοῖς
μανθάνουσιν, οὕτως ὁ πολιτικὸς οὐ λέγων
μόνον οὐδ' ὑπαγορεύων ἔξωθεν ἀλλὰ πράττων
τὰ κοινὰ καὶ διοικῶν ἐπευθύνει τὸν νέον,
ἔργοις ἅμα καὶ λόγοις πλαττόμενον ἐμψύχως
καὶ κατασχηματιζόμενον. ὁ γὰρ τοῦτον
ἀσκηθεὶς τὸν τρόπον οὐκ ἐν παλαίστραις καὶ
κηρώμασιν ἀκινδύνοις εὐρύθμων σοφιστῶν,
ἀλλ' ὡς ἀληθῶς ἐν Ὀλυμπιακοῖς καὶ Πυθικοῖς
ἀγῶσιν "ἄθηλος ἵππῳ πῶλος ὣς ἅμα τρέχει"
κατὰ Σιμωνίδην, ὡς Ἀριστείδης Κλεισθένει
καὶ Κίμων Ἀριστείδῃ καὶ Φωκίων Χαβρίᾳ καὶ
Κάτων Μαξίμῳ Φαβίῳ καὶ Σύλλᾳ Πομπήιος
καὶ Φιλοποίμενι Πολύβιος· νέοι γὰρ ὄντες
πρεσβυτέροις ἐπιβάλλοντες, εἶθ' οἷον
παραβλαστάνοντες καὶ συνεξανιστάμενοι
ταῖς ἐκείνων πολιτείαις καὶ πράξεσιν,

of the popular leaders and generals as they contend in politics, and so learn a lesson amidst dangerous affairs? Of course not. But if for no other reason, elders should engage in politics for the sake of teaching and training the young. For as teachers of literature and music guide their students by playing and reading aloud as an example, so politicians, not only by speaking and dictating from the sidelines but also by engaging in and directing public affairs, guide young people, whose minds are shaped and molded by deeds and words together. For the one trained in this manner—not in the risk-free schools and wrestling rings of the graceful professors, but as though in actual Olympic and Pythian games—"runs like the newly-weaned foal alongside a horse," as Simonides says. And thus, Aristides ran alongside Cleisthenes and then Cimon

ἐμπειρίαν καὶ συνήθειαν ἐκτῶντο πρὸς τὰ
κοινὰ μετὰ δόξης καὶ δυνάμεως.

13. Ὁ μὲν οὖν Ἀκαδημαϊκὸς Αἰσχίνης,
σοφιστῶν τινων λεγόντων ὅτι προσποιεῖται
γεγονέναι Καρνεάδου μὴ γεγονὼς μαθητής,
"ἀλλὰ τότε γ᾽," εἶπεν, "ἐγὼ Καρνεάδου
διήκουον, ὅτε τὴν ῥαχίαν καὶ τὸν ψόφον
ἀφεικὼς ὁ λόγος αὐτοῦ διὰ τὸ γῆρας εἰς τὸ
χρήσιμον συνῆκτο καὶ κοινωνικόν"· τῆς δὲ
πρεσβυτικῆς πολιτείας οὐ τῷ λόγῳ μόνον
ἀλλὰ καὶ ταῖς πράξεσιν ἀπηλλαγμένης

alongside Aristides, and Phocion ran alongside Chabrias, Cato the Elder alongside Fabius Maximus, Pompey alongside Sulla, and Polybius alongside Philopoemen. For while young, these men devoted themselves to their elders. Then in a sense they sprouted and grew amidst their elders' political deeds, and so they acquired experience and familiarity with public affairs, together with glory and power.

13. Consider what Aeschines the Academic philosopher said when some sophists charged that he was pretending to have been a student of Carneades but really was not: "But I was listening to Carneades at that time when his manner of speaking had lost its crashing roar and noisiness on account of age, and was instead focused on utility and the common good." The

πανηγυρισμοῦ καὶ δοξοκοπίας, ὥσπερ τὴν ἶριν
λέγουσιν ὅταν παλαιὰ γενομένη τὸ βρομῶδες
ἀποπνεύσῃ καὶ θολερὸν εὐωδέστερον τὸ
ἀρωματικὸν ἴσχειν, οὕτως οὐδέν ἐστι δόγμα
γεροντικὸν οὐδὲ βούλευμα τεταραγμένον
ἀλλ᾽ ἐμβριθῆ πάντα καὶ καθεστῶτα. διὸ
καὶ τῶν νέων ἕνεκα δεῖ, καθάπερ εἴρηται,
πολιτεύεσθαι τὸν πρεσβύτην, ἵνα, ὃν τρόπον
φησὶ Πλάτων ἐπὶ τοῦ μιγνυμένου πρὸς ὕδωρ
ἀκράτου, μαινόμενον θεὸν ἑτέρῳ θεῷ νήφοντι
σωφρονίζεσθαι κολαζόμενον, οὕτως εὐλάβεια
γεροντικὴ κεραννυμένη πρὸς ζέουσαν ἐν
δήμῳ νεότητα, βακχεύουσαν ὑπὸ δόξης
καὶ φιλοτιμίας, ἀφαιρῇ τὸ μανικὸν καὶ λίαν
ἄκρατον.

political activity of elders, however, is free from ostentation and desire for glory in its actions as well as in its manner of speaking. For just as they say the iris, when it has become old, loses its foul, dirty scent and has a sweeter aroma, so no opinion or counsel of an elder is muddled, but all of them are weighty and well-established. Wherefore, as I have said, the elder must engage in politics for the sake of the young, so that, in the way that Plato speaks about neat wine mixed with water (namely, that a raging god is brought to his senses when a punished by a sober god),[37] so the discretion of an elder, when mixed into youth as it boils in public and is in a frenzy over glory and love of honor, takes away its madness and excessive lack of self-control.

14. Ἄνευ δὲ τούτων ἁμαρτάνουσιν οἱ οἷον
τὸ πλεῦσαι καὶ τὸ στρατεύσασθαι, τοιοῦτον
ἡγούμενοι καὶ τὸ πολιτεύσασθαι πρὸς ἄλλο
τι πραττόμενον, εἶτα καταλῆγον ἐν τῷ τυχεῖν
ἐκείνου· λειτουργία γὰρ οὐκ ἔστιν ἡ πολιτεία
τὴν χρείαν ἔχουσα πέρας, ἀλλὰ βίος ἡμέρου καὶ
πολιτικοῦ καὶ κοινωνικοῦ ζῴου καὶ πεφυκότος
ὅσον χρὴ χρόνον πολιτικῶς καὶ φιλοκάλως
καὶ φιλανθρώπως ζῆν. διὸ πολιτεύεσθαι
καθῆκόν ἐστιν οὐ πεπολιτεῦσθαι, καθάπερ
ἀληθεύειν οὐκ ἀληθεῦσαι καὶ δικαιοπραγεῖν
οὐ δικαιοπραγῆσαι καὶ φιλεῖν οὐ φιλῆσαι τὴν
πατρίδα καὶ τοὺς πολίτας. ἐπὶ ταῦτα γὰρ ἡ
φύσις ἄγει, καὶ ταύτας ὑπαγορεύει τὰς φωνὰς
τοῖς μὴ διεφθορόσι τελείως ὑπ' ἀργίας καὶ
μαλακίας· "πολλοῦ σε θνητοῖς ἄξιον τίκτει
πατήρ" καὶ "μή τι παυσώμεσθα δρῶντες εὖ
βροτούς."

14. Moreover, it is a mistake to believe that practicing politics is like sailing or going on a military campaign, as though we engage in politics to achieve some external goal and then we stop once that goal has been achieved. For politics is not a public service with a functional objective. Rather, it is a way of life for a tamed, political, and social animal,[38] one that by its nature must live its whole life interacting with its fellow citizens, pursuing what is good, and caring for humankind. Therefore, it is proper for us *to be engaged* in politics continuously and not simply *to have been engaged* in politics in the past, just as it is proper for us *to be speaking* the truth and not *to have spoken* it once, *to be acting* honestly and not simply *to have acted* honestly, and *to be loving* our country and fellow citizens, not only *to have loved* them. For nature leads us in

15. Οἱ δὲ τὰς ἀρρωστίας προβαλλόμενοι καὶ τὰς ἀδυναμίας νόσου καὶ πηρώσεως μᾶλλον ἢ γήρως κατηγοροῦσι· καὶ γὰρ νέοι πολλοὶ νοσώδεις καὶ ῥωμαλέοι γέροντες· ὥστε δεῖ μὴ τοὺς γέροντας ἀλλὰ τοὺς ἀδυνάτους ἀποτρέπειν, μηδὲ τοὺς νέους παρακαλεῖν ἀλλὰ τοὺς δυναμένους. καὶ γὰρ καὶ Ἀριδαῖος ἦν νέος γέρων δ' Ἀντίγονος, ἀλλ' ὁ μὲν ἅπασαν ὀλίγου δεῖν κατεκτήσατο τὴν Ἀσίαν, ὁ δ' ὥσπερ ἐπὶ σκηνῆς δορυφόρημα κωφὸν ἦν ὄνομα βασιλέως καὶ πρόσωπον ὑπὸ τῶν ἀεὶ κρατούντων παροινούμενον. ὥσπερ οὖν ὁ Πρόδικον τὸν σοφιστὴν ἢ Φιλήταν

this direction, and it speaks in these voices to those who are not entirely undone by idleness and moral weakness: "Your father begets you to be of much worth to mortals" and "Let us in no way stop treating mortals well."

15. Now those who use infirmities and weaknesses as excuses are really finding fault with sickness and disability rather than with old age. For many young people are sickly, and many old people are vigorous, so that we ought to reject not the old but the weak, and we ought to encourage not the young but the able. For in fact Arrhidaeus was young and Antigonus was old, but Antigonus gained control over nearly all of Asia, while Arrhidaeus, like the silent character of the bodyguard in a play, had the title and role of a king but was

τὸν ποιητὴν ἀξιῶν πολιτεύεσθαι. νέους
μὲν ἰσχνοὺς δὲ καὶ νοσώδεις καὶ τὰ πολλὰ
κλινοπετεῖς δι᾽ ἀρρωστίαν ὄντας, ἀβέλτερός
ἐστιν· οὕτως ὁ κωλύων ἄρχειν καὶ στρατηγεῖν
τοιούτους γέροντας, οἷος ἦν Φωκίων οἷος ἦν
Μασανάσσης ὁ Λίβυς οἷος Κάτων ὁ Ῥωμαῖος.
ὁ μὲν γὰρ Φωκίων, ὡρμημένων πολεμεῖν
ἀκαίρως τῶν Ἀθηναίων, παρήγγειλε τοὺς ἄχρι
ἑξήκοντ᾽ ἐτῶν ἀκολουθεῖν ὅπλα λαβόντας·
ὡς δ᾽ ἠγανάκτουν, "οὐδέν," ἔφη, "δεινόν· ἐγὼ
γὰρ ἔσομαι μεθ᾽ ὑμῶν ὁ στρατηγὸς ὑπὲρ
ὀγδοήκοντ᾽ ἔτη γεγονώς." Μασανάσσην
δ᾽ ἱστορεῖ Πολύβιος ἐνενήκοντα μὲν ἐτῶν
ἀποθανεῖν, τετράετες καταλιπόντα παιδάριον
ἐξ αὐτοῦ γεγενημένον, ὀλίγῳ δ᾽ ἔμπροσθεν
τῆς τελευτῆς μάχῃ νικήσαντα μεγάλῃ
Καρχηδονίους ὀφθῆναι τῇ ὑστεραίᾳ πρὸ τῆς
σκηνῆς ῥυπαρὸν ἄρτον ἐσθίοντα, καὶ πρὸς
τοὺς θαυμάζοντας εἰπεῖν, ὅτι τοῦτο ποιεῖ <διὰ
τὴν ἕξιν ἀεί>.

abused by the people who actually wielded power. And so, one is foolish who thinks that Prodicus the sophist or Philetas the poet should engage in politics: they were indeed young, but they were also feeble and sickly, and they spent most of their time in bed due to illness. Foolish likewise is anyone who stops old men such as Phocion, Masinissa the Libyan, or Cato the Elder in Rome from holding office or commanding an army. For when the Athenians were mobilizing for an ill-timed war, Phocion summoned all men up to sixty years old to take up arms and follow him. When they were upset by this, he said, "Not to worry, for I will accompany you as general, and I am over eighty!"[39] And Polybius reports in his history that Masinissa died at ninety years old, leaving behind a four-year-old child that he had fathered. Just a little before his

λάμπει γὰρ ἐν χρείαισιν ὥσπερ εὐπρεπὴς
χαλκός· χρόνῳ δ᾽ ἀργῆσαν ἤμυσε στέγος,

ὥς φησι Σοφοκλῆς· ὡς δ᾽ ἡμεῖς φαμεν, ἐκεῖνο
τῆς ψυχῆς τὸ γάνωμα καὶ τὸ φέγγος, ᾧ
λογιζόμεθα καὶ μνημονεύομεν καὶ φρονοῦμεν.

16. Διὸ καὶ τοὺς βασιλεῖς φασι γίγνεσθαι
βελτίονας ἐν τοῖς πολέμοις καὶ ταῖς στρατείαις
ἢ σχολὴν ἄγοντας. Ἄτταλον γοῦν τὸν
Εὐμένους ἀδελφόν, ὑπ᾽ ἀργίας μακρᾶς καὶ
εἰρήνης ἐκλυθέντα κομιδῇ, Φιλοποίμην εἷς
τῶν ἑταίρων ἐποίμαινεν ἀτεχνῶς πιαινόμενον·
ὥστε καὶ τοὺς Ῥωμαίους παίζοντας ἑκάστοτε
διαπυνθάνεσθαι παρὰ τῶν ἐξ Ἀσίας πλεόντων,

death he won a great battle against the Carthaginians, and then was seen the very next day eating a dirty piece of bread in front of his tent. To those who wondered at what he did, he said he was doing it to maintain the habit, "for when it's being used a house shines like handsome bronze, but through disuse it collapses with time," as Sophocles says. And we say the same thing about that brilliance and splendor of the soul, by which we reason and remember and are wise.

16. And this is why they say that kings become better in the midst of wars and campaigns than when they remain at leisure. Attalus the brother of Eumenes, once he had been completely mollified by a long period of inactivity and peace, was simply beguiled and fattened up by Philopoemen, one of his companions, so that even the

εἰ δύναται παρὰ τῷ Φιλοποίμενι βασιλεύς.
Λευκόλλου δὲ Ῥωμαίων οὐ πολλοὺς ἄν τις
εὕροι δεινοτέρους στρατηγούς, ὅτε τῷ πράττειν
τὸ φρονεῖν συνεῖχεν· ἐπεὶ δὲ μεθῆκεν ἑαυτὸν
εἰς βίον ἄπρακτον καὶ δίαιταν οἰκουρὸν καὶ
ἄφροντιν, ὥσπερ οἱ σπόγγοι ταῖς γαλήναις
ἐννεκρωθεὶς καὶ καταμαρανθείς, εἶτα
Καλλισθένει τινὶ τῶν ἀπελευθόρων βόσκειν
καὶ τιθασεύειν παρέχων τὸ γῆρας, ἐδόκει
καταφαρμακεύεσθαι φίλτροις ὑπ᾽ αὐτοῦ καὶ
γοητεύμασιν, ἄχρι οὗ Μάρκος ὁ ἀδελφὸς
ἀπελάσας τὸν ἄνθρωπον αὐτὸς ᾠκονόμει καὶ
ἐπαιδαγώγει τὸν λοιπὸν αὐτοῦ βίον, οὐ πολὺν
γενόμενον. ἀλλὰ Δαρεῖος ὁ Ξέρξου πατὴρ
ἔλεγεν αὐτὸς αὐτοῦ παρὰ τὰ δεινὰ γίγνεσθαι
φρονιμώτερος, ὁ δὲ Σκύθης Ἀτέας μηδὲν
οἴεσθαι τῶν ἱπποκόμων διαφέρειν ἑαυτόν, ὅτε
σχολάζοι· Διονύσιος δ᾽ ὁ πρεσβύτερος πρὸς
τὸν πυθόμενον εἰ σχολάζοι "μηδέποτ᾽," εἶπεν,
"ἐμοὶ τοῦτο συμβαίη." τόξον μὲν γάρ, ὥς φασιν,

Romans used to ask jokingly of everyone sailing out of Asia whether the king had any influence with Philopoemen.[40] And one would not find many Roman generals more clever than Lucullus, when he combined thought with action. But then he surrendered himself to an idle way of life and the carefree routine of a stay-at-home man, which caused him to wither up and die away as sponges do in calm seas, and he essentially handed his twilight years over to a certain Callisthenes, one of his freedmen,[41] to maintain and cultivate. It seemed as though Callisthenes had drugged him with potions and charms, until his brother Marcus drove the freedman away and took it upon himself to arrange and manage the rest of Lucullus's life, which in fact was not very long. But Darius the father of Xerxes used to say that he became wiser than he

ἐπιτεινόμενον ῥήγνυται, ψυχὴ δ᾽ ἀνιεμένη. καὶ γὰρ ἁρμονικοὶ τὸ κατακούειν ἡρμοσμένου καὶ γεωμέτραι τὸ ἀναλύειν καὶ ἀριθμητικοὶ τὴν ἐν τῷ λογίζεσθαι συνέχειαν ἐκλιπόντες ἅμα ταῖς ἐνεργείαις ἀμαυροῦσι ταῖς ἡλικίαις τὰς ἕξεις, καίπερ οὐ πρακτικὰς ἀλλὰ θεωρητικὰς τέχνας ἔχοντες· ἡ δὲ τῶν πολιτικῶν ἕξις, εὐβουλία καὶ φρόνησις καὶ δικαιοσύνη, πρὸς δὲ τούτοις ἐμπειρία στοχαστικὴ καιρῶν καὶ λόγων, πειθοῦς δημιουργὸς δύναμις οὖσα, τῷ λέγειν ἀεί τι καὶ πράττειν καὶ λογίζεσθαι καὶ δικάζειν συνέχεται· καὶ δεινόν, εἰ τούτων ἀποδρᾶσα περιόψεται τηλικαύτας ἀρετὰς καὶ τοσαύτας ἐκρυείσας τῆς ψυχῆς· καὶ γὰρ τὸ φιλάνθρωπον εἰκός ἐστιν ἀπομαραίνεσθαι καὶ τὸ κοινωνικὸν καὶ τὸ εὐχάριστον, ὧν οὐδεμίαν εἶναι δεῖ τελευτὴν οὐδὲ πέρας.

really was when facing dangers, and the Scythian Ateas said that he thought himself no different from the men who tended his horse when he was inactive. And when someone asked the elder Dionysius if he ever had any leisure time, he said, "I hope I never do!" For, as they say, a bow breaks when it is stretched, but a soul breaks when relaxed. Now when musicians stop listening to compositions, and geometricians stop solving problems, and arithmeticians stop their constant reckoning, the skills that they acquired through habit fade as they grow old and cease to practice them, even though they are not engaged in practical but rather in contemplative arts. But the skills that politicians acquire through habit are good counsel and wisdom and justice, and, in addition, experience, which allows them to select the right moments and

17. Εἰ γοῦν πατέρα τὸν Τιθωνὸν εἶχες,
ἀθάνατον μὲν ὄντα χρείαν δ᾽ ἔχοντα
διὰ γῆρας ἀεὶ πολλῆς ἐπιμελείας, οὐκ
ἂν οἶμαί σε φυγεῖν οὐδ᾽ ἀπείπασθαι τὸ
θεραπεύειν καὶ προσαγορεύειν καὶ βοηθεῖν
ὡς λελειτουργηκότα πολὺν χρόνον· ἡ δὲ
πατρὶς καὶ μητρὶς ὡς Κρῆτες καλοῦσι,
πρεσβύτερα καὶ μείζονα δίκαια γονέων

words. This experience, in turn, gives them the ability to be persuasive. These skills are maintained by constantly speaking, acting, reasoning, and judging about some matter, and it is a terrible thing if, having abandoned such activities, one allows such great and numerous virtues to seep out of the soul. Indeed, one's concern for others, sense of community, and graciousness are all liable to waste away, even though there ought to be no end or limit to them.

17. Now Tithonus was immortal but constantly required a great deal of attention on account of his old age.[42] If he were your father, I do not think that you would leave him or decline to care for, speak to, or help him on the ground that you had already been attending to him for a long time. But your fatherland (or as the Cretans say,

ἔχουσα, πολυχρόνιος μέν ἐστιν οὐ μὴν ἀγήρως
οὐδ᾿ αὐτάρκης, ἀλλ᾿ ἀεὶ πολυωρίας δεομένη
καὶ βοηθείας καὶ φροντίδος ἐπισπᾶται καὶ
κατέχει τὸν πολιτικὸν "εἰανοῦ ἁπτομένη καί
τ᾿ ἐσσύμενον κατερύκει." καὶ μὴν οἶσθά με
τῷ Πυθίῳ λειτουργοῦντα πολλὰς Πυθιάδας·
ἀλλ᾿ οὐκ ἂν εἴποις "ἱκανά σοι, ὦ Πλούταρχε,
τέθυται καὶ πεπόμπευται καὶ κεχόρευται,
νῦν δ᾿ ὥρα πρεσβύτερον ὄντα τὸν στέφανον
ἀποθέσθαι καὶ τὸ χρηστήριον ἀπολιπεῖν διὰ
τὸ γῆρας." οὐκοῦν μηδὲ σεαυτὸν οἴου δεῖν, τῶν
πολιτικῶν ἱερῶν ἔξαρχον ὄντα καὶ προφήτην,
ἀφεῖναι τὰς τοῦ Πολιέως καὶ Ἀγοραίου τιμὰς
Διός, ἔκπαλαι κατωργιασμένον αὐταῖς.

your motherland), which is older and has greater rights than your parents, though it may be long-lived is neither ageless nor self-sufficient. Rather, it is always in need of attention, help, and care, and it draws in and holds the politician, "laying hold of his cloak and holding him back as he rushes along."[43] And you know that I have been serving the Pythian god[44] for many Pythiads, but you would not say to me, "There have been enough sacrifices and processions and choral dances for you, Plutarch. Now that you're older, it's time to set aside the crown and leave behind the oracle on account of old age." And surely you do not think that you yourself, who preside over and act as interpreter at your city's religious rites, should forgo the honors of Zeus of the City and Marketplace, into which you were initiated so long ago.

18. Ἀλλ᾽ ἀφέντες, εἰ βούλει, τὸν ἀποσπῶντα τῆς πολιτείας λόγον ἐκεῖνο σκοπῶμεν ἤδη καὶ φιλοσοφῶμεν, ὅπως μηδὲν ἀπρεπὲς μηδὲ βαρὺ τῷ γήρᾳ προσάξωμεν ἀγώνισμα, πολλὰ μέρη τῆς πολιτείας ἐχούσης ἁρμόδια καὶ πρόσφορα τοῖς τηλικούτοις. ὥσπερ γάρ, εἰ καθῆκον ἦν ᾄδοντας διατελεῖν, ἔδει, πολλῶν τόνων καὶ τρόπων ὑποκειμένων φωνῆς, οὓς ἁρμονίας οἱ μουσικοὶ καλοῦσι, μὴ τὸν ὀξὺν ἅμα καὶ σύντονον διώκειν γέροντας γενομένους, ἀλλ᾽ ἐν ᾧ τὸ ῥᾴδιον ἔπεστι μετὰ τοῦ πρέποντος ἤθους· οὕτως, ἐπεὶ τὸ πράττειν καὶ λέγειν μᾶλλον ἀνθρώποις ἢ κύκνοις τὸ ᾄδειν ἄχρι τελευτῆς κατὰ φύσιν ἔστιν, οὐκ ἀφετέον τὴν πρᾶξιν ὥσπερ τινὰ λύραν σύντονον, ἀλλ᾽ ἀνετέον ἐπὶ τὰ κοῦφα καὶ μέτρια καὶ προσῳδὰ πρεσβύταις πολιτεύματα μεθαρμοττομένους. οὐδὲ γὰρ τὰ σώματα παντελῶς ἀκίνητα καὶ ἀγύμναστα

THE ROLE OF THE SENIOR POLITICIAN

18. But now that we have disposed of the argument for excluding our elders from politics, let us, if you wish, consider in our discussion how we may avoid assigning to old age any duties that are inappropriate or burdensome, since there are in fact many aspects of politics that are fitting and suitable for older people. Now there exist many pitches and modes of the human voice, which musicians call harmonies, and supposing it were proper to continue singing even when we have become old, we should not, then, attempt to reach the piercing and high-pitched notes, but rather we should attempt to sing those that are easy and suit our character. In the same way, since it is more natural for humans to remain active and to keep speaking until the time they

περιορῶμεν, ὅτε μὴ δυνάμεθα σκαφείοις
μηδ᾽ ἁλτῆρσι χρῆσθαι μηδὲ δισκεύειν
μηδ᾽ ὁπλομαχεῖν ὡς καὶ πρότερον, ἀλλ᾽
αἰώραις καὶ περιπάτοις, ἔνιοι δὲ καὶ σφαίρᾳ
προσπαλαίοντες ἐλαφρῶς καὶ διαλεγόμενοι
κινοῦσι τὸ πνεῦμα καὶ τὸ θερμὸν ἀναρριπίζουσι.

Μήτε δὴ τελέως ἐκπαγέντας ἑαυτοὺς καὶ
καταψυχθέντας ἀπραξίᾳ περιίδωμεν μήτ᾽ αὖ
πάλιν πᾶσαν ἀρχὴν ἐπαιρόμενοι καὶ παντὸς
ἐπιδραττόμενοι πολιτεύματος ἀναγκάζωμεν
τὸ γῆρας ἐξελεγχόμενον ἐπὶ τοιαύτας φωνὰς
καταφέρεσθαι

ὦ δεξιὰ χείρ, ὡς ποθεῖς λαβεῖν δόρυ·
ἐν δ᾽ ἀσθενείᾳ τὸν πόθον διώλεσας.

οὐδὲ γὰρ ἀκμάζων καὶ δυνάμενος ἀνὴρ
ἐπαινεῖται, πάντα συλλήβδην ἀνατιθεὶς
ἑαυτῷ τὰ κοινὰ πράγματα καὶ μηδὲν ἑτέρῳ
παριέναι βουλόμενος, ὥσπερ οἱ Στωικοὶ τὸν

die than even for swans to sing, we must not set aside our active political life as we would set aside a high-pitched lyre,[45] but we must relax our actions and adapt them to political deeds that are light, measured, and in harmony with older people. For we do not allow the body to remain completely sedentary and unexercised when we are no longer able to use a shovel or jumping weights or to throw the discus or to fight in arms as in our younger years. We turn instead to light exercise and walks, and some people, by training lightly with a ball and engaging in conversation, breathe deeply and rekindle their body heat.

And so, let us not allow ourselves to become entirely stiff and cold through inaction, but at the same time, let us not, by getting excited about every office and about being involved in every political activity,

Δία λέγουσιν, εἰς πάντα παρενείρων καὶ
πᾶσι καταμιγνὺς ἑαυτὸν ἀπληστίᾳ δόξης ἢ
φθόνῳ τῶν μεταλαμβανόντων ἀμωσγέπως
τιμῆς τινος ἐν τῇ πόλει καὶ δυνάμεως·
πρεσβύτῃ δὲ κομιδῇ, κἂν τὸ ἄδοξον ἀφέλῃς,
ἐπίπονος καὶ ταλαίπωρος ἡ πρὸς πᾶν μὲν ἀεὶ
κληρωτήριον ἀπαντῶσα φιλαρχία, παντὶ δ᾽
ἐφεδρεύουσα δικαστηρίου καιρῷ καὶ συνεδρίου
πολυπραγμοσύνη, πᾶσαν δὲ πρεσβείαν καὶ
προδικίαν ὑφαρπάζουσα φιλοτιμία. καὶ γὰρ
ταῦτα πράττειν καὶ μετ᾽ εὐνοίας βαρὺ παρ᾽
ἡλικίαν, συμβαίνει δέ γε τἀναντία· μισοῦνται
μὲν γὰρ ὑπὸ τῶν νέων, ὡς οὐ προϊέμενοι
πράξεων αὐτοῖς ἀφορμὰς μηδ᾽ εἰς μέσον
ἐῶντες προελθεῖν, ἀδοξεῖ δὲ παρὰ τοῖς ἄλλοις
τὸ φιλόπρωτον αὐτῶν καὶ φίλαρχον οὐχ
ἧττον ἢ τὸ φιλόπλουτον ἑτέρων γερόντων καὶ
φιλήδονον.

force our old age to be proved deficient and brought to the point of saying, "O my right hand, how you long to hold the spear, but in your weakness your longing has come to nothing."[46] For we do not even praise those who are in their prime and powerful if they take upon themselves practically all public business and wish to yield nothing to anyone else. In this way, they act as the Stoics say that Zeus behaves: they intrude and involve themselves in everything because of their insatiable desire for glory or their envy of anyone who in any way shares some honor or power in the city. But for the older person—even if you disregard the bad reputation earned by such an attitude—the love of holding office that asserts itself at every election, the meddlesomeness that watches for every opportunity to appear in court or at a council meeting, and the love of honor

19. Ὥσπερ οὖν τὸν Βουκέφαλον ὁ Ἀλέξανδρος πρεσβύτερον ὄντα μὴ βουλόμενος πιέζειν ἑτέροις ἐπωχεῖτο πρὸ τῆς μάχης ἵπποις, ἐφοδεύων τὴν φάλαγγα καὶ καθιστὰς εἰς τὴν τάξιν, εἶτα δοὺς τὸ σύνθημα καὶ μεταβὰς ἐπ᾽ ἐκεῖνον εὐθὺς ἐπῆγε τοῖς πολεμίοις καὶ

that grasps at every embassy and guardian-
ship, all of this is wearying and miserable.
For to do these things at an advanced age,
even with good will, is overbearing and produces the opposite of the desired outcome.
Such old people are hated by the young, on
the ground that they do not yield to them
any occasion for action or allow them any
public exposure. In addition, their fellow
citizens have contempt for their love of being first and holding office no less than they
have contempt for the love of money and
pleasure found in other old people.

19. Alexander did not wish to stress Bucephalus when the horse was older, and so
he used to ride other horses before battle
as he reviewed and arranged his troops.
Then, once he had given the signal to
fight, he would switch to Bucephalus and

διεκινδύνευεν· οὕτως ὁ πολιτικός, ἂν ἔχῃ νοῦν,
αὐτὸς αὑτὸν ἡνιοχῶν πρεσβύτην γενόμενον
ἀφέξεται τῶν οὐκ ἀναγκαίων καὶ παρήσει τοῖς
ἀκμάζουσι χρῆσθαι πρὸς τὰ μικρότερα τὴν
πόλιν, ἐν δὲ τοῖς μεγάλοις αὐτὸς ἀγωνιεῖται
προθύμως. οἱ μὲν γὰρ ἀθληταὶ τὰ σώματα
τῶν ἀναγκαίων πόνων ἄθικτα τηροῦσι καὶ
ἀκέραια πρὸς τοὺς ἀχρήστους· ἡμεῖς δὲ
τοὐναντίον, ἐῶντες τὰ μικρὰ καὶ φαῦλα,
τοῖς ἀξίοις σπουδῆς φυλάξομεν ἑαυτούς.
"νέῳ" μὲν γὰρ ἴσως "ἐπέοικε" καθ᾿ Ὅμηρον
"πάντα," καὶ δέχονται καὶ ἀγαπῶσι τὸν μὲν
μικρὰ καὶ πολλὰ πράττοντα δημοτικὸν καὶ
φιλόπονον τὸν δὲ λαμπρὰ καὶ σεμνὰ γενναῖον
καὶ μεγαλόφρονα καλοῦντες· ἔστι δ᾿ ὅπου καὶ
τὸ φιλόνεικον καὶ παράβολον ὥραν ἔχει τινὰ
καὶ χάριν ἐπιπρέπουσαν τοῖς τηλικούτοις. ὁ
πρεσβύτης δ᾿ ἀνὴρ ἐν πολιτείᾳ διακονικὰς
λειτουργίας ὑπομένων, οἷα τελῶν πράσεις
καὶ λιμένων ἐπιμελείας καὶ ἀγορᾶς, ἔτι δὲ

straightaway attack the enemy and run every risk. Sensible politicians likewise will apply the reins to themselves once they have grown older, keeping themselves out of unnecessary business and allowing the city to use those in their prime for smaller matters, while still contending eagerly in the important affairs. Now athletes keep their bodies untouched by necessary labors and strong for work that serves no practical purpose, while we elders, by contrast, will disregard the small and ordinary matters, and instead reserve ourselves for problems that deserve our attention. Perhaps "everything is appropriate to the young man," as Homer says,[47] and people welcome and adore him, calling the one who takes on many small matters "democratic" and "industrious," and the one who does splendid and honorable deeds "noble" and "high-minded." And there are

πρεσβείας καὶ ἀποδημίας πρὸς ἡγεμόνας καὶ δυνάστας ὑποτρέχων, ἐν αἷς ἀναγκαῖον οὐδὲν οὐδὲ σεμνὸν ἔνεστιν ἀλλὰ θεραπεία καὶ τὸ πρὸς χάριν, ἐμοὶ μὲν οἰκτρόν, ὦ φίλε, φαίνεται καὶ ἄζηλον, ἑτέροις δ᾽ ἴσως καὶ ἐπαχθὲς φαίνεται καὶ φορτικόν.

20. Οὐδὲ γὰρ ἐν ἀρχαῖς τὸν τηλικοῦτον ὥρα φέρεσθαι, πλὴν ὅσαι γε μέγεθός τι κέκτηνται καὶ ἀξίωμα· καθάπερ ἦν σὺ νῦν Ἀθήνησι μεταχειρίζῃ τῆς ἐξ Ἀρείου πάγου βουλῆς ἐπιστασίαν καὶ νὴ Δία τὸ πρόσχημα τῆς

situations where even contentiousness or rashness are called for and have a certain charm that suits people who are young. But older people who endure servile political duties, such as the awarding of contracts to tax collectors and the oversight of ports and the marketplace, and who moreover get themselves sent abroad on the sorts of embassies and missions that are unnecessary and lack dignity, but only involve paying court and currying favor, these people seem to me, my friend, to be pitiable and unappealing, and perhaps they also appear onerous and wearisome to others.

20. For old age is not the right time for someone to be appointed to office, except those offices that have acquired a certain stature and honor, like authority over the council of the Areopagus, which you now

Άμφικτυονίας, ἥν σοι διὰ τοῦ βίου παντὸς ἡ
πατρὶς ἀνατέθεικε "πόνον ἡδὺν κάματόν τ᾽
εὐκάματον" ἔχουσαν. δεῖ δὲ καὶ ταύτας μὴ
διώκειν τὰς τιμὰς ἀλλὰ φεύγοντας ἄρχειν, μηδ᾽
αἰτουμένους ἀλλὰ παραιτουμένους, μηδ᾽ ὡς
αὑτοῖς τὸ ἄρχειν λαμβάνοντας ἀλλ᾽ ὡς αὑτοὺς
τῷ ἄρχειν ἐπιδιδόντας. οὐ γάρ, ὡς Τιβέριος ὁ
Καῖσαρ ἔλεγε, τὸ τὴν χεῖρα τῷ ἰατρῷ προτείνειν
ὑπὲρ ἑξήκοντ᾽ ἔτη γεγονότας αἰσχρόν ἐστιν,
ἀλλὰ μᾶλλον τὸ τὴν χεῖρα τῷ δήμῳ προτείνειν
ψῆφον αἰτοῦντας ἢ φωνὴν ἀρχαιρεσιάζουσαν·
ἀγεννὲς γὰρ τοῦτο καὶ ταπεινόν· ὡς τοὐναντίον
ἔχει τινὰ σεμνότητα καὶ κόσμον, αἱρουμένης
τῆς πατρίδος καὶ καλούσης καὶ περιμενούσης,
κατιόντα μετὰ τιμῆς καὶ φιλοφροσύνης γεραρὸν
ὡς ἀληθῶς καὶ περίβλεπτον ἀσπάσασθαι καὶ
δεξιώσασθαι τὸ γέρας.

exercise at Athens, and, by Zeus, membership in the Amphictyonic Council, which your native city has conferred upon you for your whole life and which involves "a pleasant toil and labor easily endured."[48] But we elders ought not chase after even these sorts of honors. Rather, we should take up offices while at the same time trying to avoid them. We ought not be asking for them but begging ourselves off, on the principle that we do not take leadership roles for ourselves but rather we surrender ourselves to being leaders. Contrary to what Tiberius Caesar used to say, there is in fact no shame in extending your hand to the doctor when you are over sixty years old, but the shame lies in extending that hand to the people as you ask them to cast a ballot or vote in the assembly: that is ignoble and dishonorable. But the opposite approach

21. Οὕτω δέ πως καὶ λόγῳ χρηστέον
ἐν ἐκκλησίᾳ πρεσβύτην γενόμενον, μὴ
ἐπιπηδῶντα συνεχῶς τῷ βήματι μηδ᾽
ἀεὶ δίκην ἀλεκτρυόνος ἀντᾴδοντα τοῖς
φθεγγομένοις, μηδὲ τῷ συμπλέκεσθαι καὶ
διερεθίζειν ἀποχαλινοῦντα τὴν πρὸς αὑτὸν
αἰδῶ τῶν νέων μηδὲ μελέτην ἐμποιοῦντα καὶ
συνήθειαν ἀπειθείας καὶ δυσηκοΐας, ἀλλὰ
καὶ παριέντα ποτὲ καὶ διδόντα πρὸς δόξαν
ἀναχαιτίσαι καὶ θρασύνασθαι, μηδὲ παρόντα
μηδὲ πολυπραγμονοῦντα, ὅπου μὴ μέγα τὸ
κινδυνευόμενόν ἐστι πρὸς σωτηρίαν κοινὴν ἢ
τὸ καλὸν καὶ πρέπον. ἐκεῖ δὲ χρὴ καὶ μηδενὸς

possesses a certain dignity and decorum, when your native city elects you, summons you, and awaits you, and you return with honor and kindliness to welcome and greet their gift of honor,[49] which truly is honorable and universally admired.

21. This principle in some respects also applies to elders when they speak in the assembly. They should not be leaping continually upon the speaker's platform or singing like a rooster in response to the other speakers, nor should they toss away the respect of the younger people through fighting and provocation, or instill in them the regular habit of disobeying and disregarding their elders. Rather, they ought sometimes to allow others to rear up and show their spirit, and so to enhance their own reputations. They ought sometimes to

καλοῦντος ὠθεῖσθαι δρόμῳ παρὰ δύναμιν,
ἀναθέντα χειραγωγοῖς αὑτὸν ἢ φοράδην
κομιζόμενον, ὥσπερ ἱστοροῦσιν ἐν Ῥώμῃ
Κλαύδιον Ἄππιον· ἡττημένων γὰρ ὑπὸ Πύρρου
μάχῃ μεγάλῃ, πυθόμενος τὴν σύγκλητον
ἐνδέχεσθαι λόγους περὶ σπονδῶν καὶ εἰρήνης
οὐκ ἀνασχετὸν ἐποιήσατο, καίπερ ἀμφοτέρας
ἀποβεβληκὼς τὰς ὄψεις, ἀλλ' ἧκε δι' ἀγορᾶς
φερόμενος πρὸς τὸ βουλευτήριον· εἰσελθὼν
δὲ καὶ καταστὰς εἰς μέσον ἔφη πρότερον μὲν
ἄχθεσθαι τῷ τῶν ὀμμάτων στέρεσθαι, νῦν
δ' ἂν εὔξασθαι μηδ' ἀκούειν οὕτως αἰσχρὰ
καὶ ἀγεννῆ βουλευομένους καὶ πράττοντας
ἐκείνους. ἐκ δὲ τούτου τὰ μὲν καθαψάμενος
αὐτῶν τὰ δὲ διδάξας καὶ παρορμήσας, ἔπεισεν
εὐθὺς ἐπὶ τὰ ὅπλα χωρεῖν καὶ διαγωνίζεσθαι
περὶ τῆς Ἰταλίας πρὸς τὸν Πύρρον. ὁ δὲ
Σόλων, τῆς Πεισιστράτου δημαγωγίας, ὅτι
τυραννίδος ἦν μηχάνημα, φανερᾶς γενομένης,
μηδενὸς ἀμύνεσθαι μηδὲ κωλύειν τολμῶντος,

stay away and not meddle, except where the city's safety or what is right and proper is in great danger. In that situation, even with no one summoning them, elders should rush forward at a run, overcoming their infirmity by entrusting themselves to guides or even being carried on a litter, as the historians say happened with Appius Claudius in Rome. For after the Romans had been defeated by Pyrrhus in a great battle, Appius learned that the senate was entertaining arguments for a peace treaty, which he found unbearable. And so, despite having lost sight in both his eyes, he was carried through the forum and arrived at the senate house. After he entered and stood in the midst of the senators, he said that previously he had been vexed by the loss of his eyes, but now he prayed not to hear the senators deliberating and acting upon such shameful and ignoble plans. In

αὐτὸς ἐξενεγκάμενος τὰ ὅπλα καὶ πρὸ τῆς
οἰκίας θέμενος ἠξίου βοηθεῖν τοὺς πολίτας·
πέμψαντος δὲ τοῦ Πεισιστράτου πρὸς αὐτὸν
καὶ πυνθανομένου τίνι πεποιθὼς ταῦτα
πράττει, "τῷ γήρᾳ," εἶπεν.

22. Ἀλλὰ τὰ μὲν οὕτως ἀναγκαῖα καὶ τοὺς
ἀπεσβηκότας κομιδῇ γέροντας, ἂν μόνον
ἐμπνέωσιν, ἐξάπτει καὶ διανίστησιν· ἐν δὲ τοῖς
ἄλλοις ποτὲ μέν, ὥσπερ εἴρηται, παραιτούμενος
ἐμμελὴς ἔσται τὰ γλίσχρα καὶ διακονικὰ καὶ

this way, by confronting the Romans, instructing them, and urging them on, he convinced them straightaway to take up arms and to fight against Pyrrhus for the sake of Italy. And there is the example of Solon. When the demagoguery of Pisistratus had openly become a means to achieve tyranny, but no one was daring to put up a defense or obstruct him, Solon himself brought out his weapons, set them in front of his house, and asked the citizens to take action. And when Pisistratus sent a messenger to ask what gave him the confidence to take this stand, Solon replied, "My old age."

22. Now such pressing situations will inflame and arouse even old people whose fire is all but extinguished, if they are at least still breathing. In other situations, as I have said, elders will be doing the right

μείζονας ἔχοντα τοῖς πράττουσιν ἀσχολίας ἢ
δι᾽ οὓς πράττεται χρείας καὶ ὠφελείας· ἔστι
δ᾽ ὅπου περιμένων καλέσαι καὶ ποθῆσαι καὶ
μετελθεῖν οἴκοθεν τοὺς πολίτας ἀξιοπιστότερος
δεομένοις κάτεισι. τὰ δὲ πλεῖστα καὶ παρὼν
σιωπῇ τοῖς νεωτέροις λέγειν παρίησιν, οἷον
βραβεύων φιλοτιμίας πολιτικῆς ἅμιλλαν· ἐὰν
δ᾽ ὑπερβάλλῃ τὸ μέτριον, καθαπτόμενος ἠπίως
καὶ μετ᾽ εὐμενείας ἀφαιρῶν φιλονεικίας καὶ
βλασφημίας καὶ ὀργάς, ἐν δὲ ταῖς γνώμαις τὸν
ἁμαρτάνοντα παραμυθούμενος ἄνευ ψόγου καὶ
διδάσκων, ἐπαινῶν δ᾽ ἀφόβως τὸν κατορθοῦντα
καὶ νικώμενος ἑκουσίως καὶ προϊέμενος τὸ
πεῖσαι καὶ περιγενέσθαι πολλάκις ὅπως
αὐξάνωνται καὶ θαρσῶσιν, ἐνίοις δὲ καὶ
συναναπληρῶν μετ᾽ εὐφημίας τὸ ἐλλεῖπον, ὡς
ὁ Νέστωρ

οὔτις τοι τὸν μῦθον ὀνόσσεται ὅσσοι
   Ἀχαιοί,

thing if they decline duties that are trouble-some and servile and require an effort on the part of the doer that is greater than the benefit to the people on whose account the duties are being performed. In some situations, if elders wait for their fellow citizens to summon them, long for them, and come get them from home, they re-turn more trusted by the people who need them. And even when they are present, in most cases they remain silent and allow the younger people to speak, acting like judges at a contest of political ambitions. And when others go too far, the elder politician confronts them gently and, with goodwill, relieves them of their contentiousness, slander, and anger. The elder speaks sooth-ingly and, without finding fault, instructs those who are mistaken in their judgments, fearlessly praising those who get things

οὐδὲ πάλιν ἐρέει· ἀτὰρ οὐ τέλος ἵκεο
    μύθων.
ἦ μὴν καὶ νέος ἐσσί, ἐμὸς δέ κε καὶ πάις
    εἴης.

23. Τούτου δὲ πολιτικώτερον, μὴ μόνον
ἐμφανῶς μηδὲ δημοσίᾳ ὀνειδίζων ἄνευ
δηγμοῦ σφόδρα κολούοντος καὶ ταπεινοῦντος,
ἀλλὰ μᾶλλον ἰδίᾳ τοῖς εὖ πεφυκόσι πρὸς
πολιτείαν ὑποτιθέμενος καὶ συνεισηγούμενος
εὐμενῶς λόγους τε χρηστοὺς καὶ
πολιτεύματα, συνεξορμῶν πρὸς τὰ καλὰ καὶ
συνεπιλαμπρύνων τὸ φρόνημα καὶ παρέχων,

right and willingly losing political contests. Oftentimes the elder forgoes the chance to persuade and come out on top so that others may grow and gain confidence. And the elder will compensate for what is lacking in some people by offering a helpful comment, as when Nestor said, "No one of all the Achaeans will reproach your speech, nor speak against it, though you have not had the final word. Indeed, you are a young man; you could even be my own son."[50]

23. But elders are even more diplomatic than this, for not only do they reproach other politicians openly and in public without the stinging rebukes that demean and belittle, but more often they privately instruct those who have innate political talent and kindly advise them about effective speaking and public policy. Thus, elders

ὥσπερ οἱ διδάσκοντες ἱππεύειν, ἐν ἀρχῇ
χειροήθη καὶ πρᾶον ἐπιβῆναι τὸν δῆμον· εἰ
δέ τι σφαλείη, μὴ περιορῶν ἐξαθυμοῦντα
τὸν νέον, ἀλλ' ἀνιστὰς καὶ παραμυθούμενος,
ὡς Ἀριστείδης Κίμωνα καὶ Μνησίφιλος
Θεμιστοκλέα, δυσχεραινομένους καὶ κακῶς
ἀκούοντας ἐν τῇ πόλει τὸ πρῶτον ὡς ἰταμοὺς
καὶ ἀκολάστους, ἐπῆραν καὶ ἀνεθάρρυναν.
λέγεται δὲ καὶ Δημοσθένους ἐκπεσόντος ἐν τῷ
δήμῳ καὶ βαρέως φέροντος ἅψασθαι παλαιόν
τινα γέροντα τῶν ἀκηκοότων Περικλέους
καὶ εἰπεῖν, ὡς ἐκείνῳ τἀνδρὶ προσεοικὼς τὴν
φύσιν οὐ δικαίως αὐτοῦ κατέγνωκεν. οὕτω δὲ
καὶ Τιμόθεον Εὐριπίδης συριττόμενον ἐπὶ τῇ
καινοτομίᾳ καὶ παρανομεῖν εἰς τὴν μουσικὴν
δοκοῦντα θαρρεῖν ἐκέλευσεν, ὡς ὀλίγου χρόνου
τῶν θεάτρων ὑπ' αὐτῷ γενησομένων.

facilitate their moral improvement, aid in the enlightenment of their intellect, and, as riding instructors do with horses, make the people manageable and gentle when the young politician first climbs into the saddle. And when young politicians stumble in some way, the elders do not allow them to be disheartened, but they raise them up and encourage them, as Aristides did for Cimon and Mnesiphilus for Themistocles. For when the city was scorning and insulting those men early in their careers for being reckless and lacking self-control, Aristides and Mnesiphilus lifted them up and gave them courage. It is said that when Demosthenes was rejected by the assembly and was taking it hard, a very old man from the generation that had heard Pericles address the assembly approached Demosthenes and told him that he was very much like Pericles

24. Καθόλου δ' ὥσπερ ἐν Ῥώμῃ ταῖς Ἑστιάσι παρθένοις τοῦ χρόνου διώρισται τὸ μὲν μανθάνειν τὸ δὲ δρᾶν τὰ νενομισμένα τὸ δὲ τρίτον ἤδη διδάσκειν, καὶ τῶν ἐν Ἐφέσῳ περὶ τὴν Ἄρτεμιν ὁμοίως ἑκάστην Μελλιέρην τὸ πρῶτον εἶθ' Ἱέρην τὸ δὲ τρίτον Παριέρην καλοῦσιν· οὕτως ὁ τελέως πολιτικὸς ἀνὴρ τὰ μὲν πρῶτα μανθάνων ἔτι πολιτεύεται καὶ μυούμενος τὰ δ' ἔσχατα διδάσκων καὶ μυσταγωγῶν· τὸν μὲν γὰρ ἐπιστάτην ἀθλοῦσιν ἑτέροις οὐκ ἔστιν αὐτὸν ἀθλεῖν, ὁ δὲ παιδοτριβῶν νέον ἐν πράγμασι κοινοῖς

in his nature and so was condemning himself unjustly. And likewise, when Timotheus[51] was being booed for his inventiveness and was believed to be violating musical standards, Euripides urged him to take heart, saying that within a short time he would come to dominate the theaters.

24. Just as in Rome the service of the Vestal Virgins is divided into a period of training, a period of performing the rites, and a third period of teaching, and likewise each of the attendants at the temple of Artemis in Ephesus is called first "Novice Priestess," then "Priestess," and third "Retired Priestess," so full-career politicians follow the same trajectory, spending their early years learning and being initiated into politics, and then in their later years they teach and initiate others. Now those who supervise

καὶ δημοσίοις ἀγῶσι καὶ παρασκευάζων τῇ
πατρίδι "μύθων τε ῥητῆρ᾽ ἔμεναι πρηκτῆρά
τε ἔργων" ἐν οὐ μικρῷ μέρει πολιτείας οὐδὲ
φαύλῳ χρήσιμός ἐστιν, ἀλλ᾽ εἰς ὃ μάλιστα
καὶ πρῶτον ὁ Λυκοῦργος ἐντείνας ἑαυτὸν
εἴθισε τοὺς νέους παντὶ πρεσβύτῃ καθάπερ
νομοθέτῃ πειθομένους διατελεῖν. ἐπεὶ πρὸς τί
βλέψας ὁ Λύσανδρος εἶπεν, ὡς ἐν Λακεδαίμονι
κάλλιστα γηρῶσιν; ἆρ᾽ ὅτι γ᾽ ἀργεῖν ἔξεστι
μάλιστα τοῖς πρεσβυτέροις ἐκεῖ καὶ δανείζειν
ἢ κυβεύειν συγκαθεζομένους ἢ πίνειν ἐν ὥρᾳ
συνάγοντας; οὐκ ἂν εἴποις· ἀλλ᾽ ὅτι τρόπον
τινὰ πάντες οἱ τηλικοῦτοι τάξιν ἀρχόντων ἢ
τινων πατρονόμων ἢ παιδαγωγῶν ἔχοντες
οὐ τὰ κοινὰ μόνον ἐπισκοποῦσιν, ἀλλὰ καὶ
τῶν νέων ἕκαστ᾽ ἀεὶ περί τε τὰ γυμνάσια
καὶ παιδιὰς καὶ διαίτας καταμανθάνουσιν
οὐ παρέργως, φοβεροὶ μὲν ὄντες τοῖς
ἁμαρτάνουσιν αἰδεστοὶ δὲ τοῖς ἀγαθοῖς καὶ
ποθεινοί· θεραπεύουσι γὰρ ἀεὶ καὶ διώκουσιν

athletes at games cannot themselves enter the competitions, but the one who trains young people for public affairs and civic contests, making them "to be a speaker of words and doer of deeds"[52] for their native cities, plays no small or trivial role in politics. Indeed, this person contributes towards that element to which Lycurgus turned his attention first and foremost: habituating the youth continually to obey all elders as though they were lawgivers.[53] And when Lysander said that people grow old most honorably in Lacedaemon, what was he thinking about? Was it that in Lacedaemon elders can most easily be idle and lend money, or sit together playing dice, or gather early to drink? Of course not. But he said this because all of the elders there, who in effect hold the rank of civic leaders or councilors or teachers, not only oversee

αὐτοὺς οἱ νέοι, τὸ κόσμιον καὶ τὸ γενναῖον
αὔξοντας καὶ συνεπιγαυροῦντας ἄνευ φθόνου.

25. Τοῦτο γὰρ τὸ πάθος οὐδενὶ χρόνῳ πρέπον
ἡλικίας, ὅμως ἐν νέοις εὐπορεῖ χρηστῶν
ὀνομάτων, ἅμιλλα καὶ ζῆλος καὶ φιλοτιμία
προσαγορευόμενον, ἐν δὲ πρεσβύταις
παντελῶς ἄωρόν ἐστι καὶ ἄγριον καὶ ἀγεννές.
διὸ δεῖ πορρωτάτω τοῦ φθονεῖν ὄντα τὸν
πολιτικὸν γέροντα μὴ καθάπερ τὰ βάσκανα
γεράνδρυα τῶν παραβλαστανόντων καὶ

public affairs, but they also continuously examine with great care everything that is related to the training, education, and daily regimen of the young people. This duty makes the elders fearsome to those who go wrong, and revered and beloved to those who are good. For the young people constantly minister to their elders and seek them out, while the elders increase and encourage the decorum and nobility of the young without provoking envy.

25. Now this emotion, envy, is inappropriate to any stage of life. Nonetheless, among the young it has many positive names, being called "competition," "zeal," and "ambition," while among elders it is completely out of season, uncivilized, and ignoble. And so, elder politicians, being well past feeling envy, must not, like malicious old

ὑποφυομένων σαφῶς ἀφαιρεῖσθαι καὶ
κολούειν τὴν βλάστην καὶ τὴν αὔξησιν, ἀλλ᾽
εὐμενῶς προσδέχεσθαι καὶ παρέχειν τοῖς
ἀντιλαμβανομένοις καὶ προσπλεκομένοις
ἑαυτὸν ὀρθοῦντα καὶ χειραγωγοῦντα
καὶ τρέφοντα μὴ μόνον ὑφηγήσεσι καὶ
συμβουλίαις ἀγαθαῖς, ἀλλὰ καὶ παραχωρήσεσι
πολιτευμάτων τιμὴν ἐχόντων καὶ δόξαν ἤ
τινας ὑπουργίας ἀβλαβεῖς μὲν ἡδείας δὲ τοῖς
πολλοῖς καὶ πρὸς χάριν ἐσομένας· ὅσα δ᾽
ἐστὶν ἀντίτυπα καὶ προσάντη καὶ καθάπερ
τὰ φάρμακα δάκνει παραχρῆμα καὶ λυπεῖ τὸ
δὲ καλὸν καὶ λυσιτελὲς ὕστερον ἀποδίδωσι,
μὴ τοὺς νέους ἐπὶ ταῦτα προσάγοντα
μηδ᾽ ὑποβάλλοντα θορύβοις, ὄχλων
ἀγνωμονούντων ἀήθεις ὄντας, ἀλλ᾽ αὐτὸν
ἐκδεχόμενον τὰς ὑπὲρ τῶν συμφερόντων
ἀπεχθείας· τούτῳ γὰρ εὐνουστέρους τε
ποιήσει τοὺς νέους καὶ προθυμοτέρους ἐν ταῖς
ἄλλαις ὑπηρεσίαις.

trees, prevent and obstruct the blossoming and the growth of the young politicians that are conspicuously blooming near them and growing underneath them. Instead, they must receive them kindly and make themselves available to the young people who reach out and make connections. Elder politicians must correct them, guide them, and help them grow, not only by offering leadership and good advice, but also by yielding to them public duties that bring honor and reputation, or certain tasks that cause no harm to the people but will in fact please them and earn their gratitude. But as for public duties that provoke resistance and adversity, just like drugs that sting and cause pain when first taken but later provide what is good and beneficial, elders must steer young people away from these sorts of duties and avoid subjecting them

26. Παρὰ πάντα δὲ ταῦτα χρὴ μνημονεύειν,
ὡς οὐκ ἔστι πολιτεύεσθαι μόνον τὸ ἄρχειν
καὶ πρεσβεύειν καὶ μέγα βοᾶν ἐν ἐκκλησίᾳ
καὶ περὶ τὸ βῆμα βακχεύειν λέγοντας ἢ
γράφοντας, ἃ οἱ πολλοὶ τοῦ πολιτεύεσθαι
νομίζουσιν, ὥσπερ ἀμέλει καὶ φιλοσοφεῖν τοὺς
ἀπὸ τοῦ δίφρου διαλεγομένους καὶ σχολὰς ἐπὶ
βιβλίοις περαίνοντας· ἡ δὲ συνεχὴς ἐν ἔργοις
καὶ πράξεσιν ὁρωμένη καθ᾽ ἡμέραν ὁμαλῶς
πολιτεία καὶ φιλοσοφία λέληθεν αὐτούς.
καὶ γὰρ τοὺς ἐν ταῖς στοαῖς ἀνακάμπτοντας
περιπατεῖν φασιν, ὡς ἔλεγε Δικαίαρχος, οὐκέτι

to public uproar, since they are not ready for the mobs that treat politicians unfairly. Rather, the elders themselves must bear the enmity that comes with doing what is good for the people, for thus they will make the young better disposed and more eager in the rest of their service.

26. In addition to stating all these things, we must mention that practicing politics does not consist only in holding office, leading embassies, shouting loudly in the assembly, and raging around the speaker's platform while giving a speech or proposing a law. Most people think that those activities are the sum of politics, however, just as they doubtless think that practicing philosophy is only a matter of conducting dialogues from a chair and reciting lectures from books. But the continuous practice of

δὲ τοὺς εἰς ἀγρὸν ἢ πρὸς φίλον βαδίζοντας.
ὅμοιον δ᾽ ἐστὶ τῷ φιλοσοφεῖν τὸ πολιτεύεσθαι.
Σωκράτης γοῦν οὔτε βάθρα θεὶς οὔτ᾽ εἰς θρόνον
καθίσας οὔθ᾽ ὥραν διατριβῆς ἢ περιπάτου
τοῖς γνωρίμοις τεταγμένην φυλάττων, ἀλλὰ
καὶ συμπαίζων, ὅτε τύχοι, καὶ συμπίνων καὶ
συστρατευόμενος ἐνίοις καὶ συναγοράζων,
τέλος δὲ καὶ δεδεμένος καὶ πίνων τὸ φάρμακον,
ἐφιλοσόφει· πρῶτος ἀποδείξας τὸν βίον ἄπαντι
χρόνῳ καὶ μέρει καὶ πάθεσι καὶ πράγμασιν
ἁπλῶς ἅπασι φιλοσοφίαν δεχόμενον.
  Οὕτω δὴ διανοητέον καὶ περὶ πολιτείας, ὡς
τοὺς μὲν ἀνοήτους, οὐδ᾽ ὅταν στρατηγῶσιν ἢ
γραμματεύωσιν ἢ δημηγορῶσι, πολιτευομένους
ἀλλ᾽ ὀχλοκοποῦντας ἢ πανηγυρίζοντας ἢ
στασιάζοντας ἢ λειτουργοῦντας ἀναγκαίως·
τὸν δὲ κοινωνικὸν καὶ φιλάνθρωπον καὶ
φιλόπολιν καὶ κηδεμονικὸν καὶ πολιτικὸν
ἀληθῶς, κἂν μηδέποτε τὴν χλαμύδα
περίθηται, πολιτευόμενον ἀεὶ τῷ παρορμᾶν

both politics and philosophy, which may be observed on a daily basis in deeds and in actions, escapes those people. For they claim that those who walk back and forth in the porticoes are "peripatetic,"[54] as Dicaearchus used to say, while that those who walk to the countryside or to a friend's house are not. But practicing politics is just like practicing philosophy. Socrates, for instance, did not set up desks for his students, sit in a teacher's chair, or reserve a prearranged time for lecturing and walking with his pupils. No, he practiced philosophy while joking around (when the chance arose) and drinking and serving on military campaigns and hanging around the marketplace with some of his students, and finally, even while under arrest and drinking the hemlock. He was the first to demonstrate that our lives are open to philosophy at all

τοὺς δυναμένους, ὑφηγεῖσθαι τοῖς δεομένοις,
συμπαρεῖναι τοῖς βουλευομένοις, διατρέπειν
τοὺς κακοπραγμονοῦντας, ἐπιρρωννύναι τοὺς
εὐγνώμονας, φανερὸν εἶναι μὴ παρέργως
προσέχοντα τοῖς κοινοῖς μηδ᾽ ὅπου σπουδή
τις ἢ παράκλησις διὰ τὸ πρωτεῖον εἰς τὸ
θέατρον βαδίζοντα καὶ τὸ βουλευτήριον, ἄλλως
δὲ διαγωγῆς χάριν ὡς ἐπὶ θέαν ἢ ἀκρόασιν,
ὅταν ἐπέλθῃ, παραγιγνόμενον, ἀλλά, κἂν μὴ
παραγένηται τῷ σώματι, παρόντα τῇ γνώμῃ
καὶ τῷ πυνθάνεσθαι τὰ μὲν ἀποδεχόμενον τοῖς
δὲ δυσκολαίνοντα τῶν πραττομένων.

times and in every aspect, while experiencing every emotion, and in each and every activity.

This, then, is how we must also conceive of the political life. Foolish people practice politics, not by serving as generals, secretaries, or popular leaders, but by inciting the mob, giving public speeches, fostering discord, or performing public service out of obligation; and, conversely, those who are civic-minded, philanthropic, devoted to the city, attentive, and truly political are always practicing politics by the promotion of those in power, the guidance of those needing direction, the support of those deliberating, the correction of those causing harm, and the reinforcement of those who are sensible. It is clear that these people attend to public business not only as a sideline; that they go to the theater[55] and the

27. Οὐδὲ γὰρ Ἀθηναίων Ἀριστείδης οὐδὲ
Ῥωμαίων Κάτων ἦρξε πολλάκις, ἀλλὰ πάντα
τὸν αὑτῶν βίον ἐνεργὸν ἀεὶ ταῖς πατρίσι
παρέσχον. Ἐπαμεινώνδας δὲ πολλὰ μὲν καὶ
μεγάλα κατώρθωσε στρατηγῶν, οὐκ ἔλαττον
δ᾽ αὑτοῦ μνημονεύεται μηδὲ στρατηγοῦντος
μηδ᾽ ἄρχοντος ἔργον περὶ Θετταλίαν, ὅτε τῶν

330

council chamber not merely to take pride of place when there is important business at hand or they are summoned there; that when they come to meetings, moreover, they attend not simply for their amusement as though they were attending a show or a lecture; and that even when they are not physically present, they nonetheless participate by thinking about the business at hand and inquiring about what occurred, approving of some of the actions taken, and expressing dissatisfaction with others.

27. For Aristides at Athens and Cato the Elder at Rome did not hold office very many times, but they did constantly dedicate their whole lives to serving their cities. Epaminondas had many great accomplishments as general, but no less worthy of memory is what he accomplished in

στρατηγῶν εἰς τόπους χαλεποὺς ἐμβαλόντων
τὴν φάλαγγα καὶ θορυβουμένων (ἐπέκειντο
γὰρ οἱ πολέμιοι βάλλοντες), ἀνακληθεὶς ἐκ
τῶν ὁπλιτῶν πρῶτον μὲν ἔπαυσε θαρρύνας τὸν
τοῦ στρατεύματος τάραχον καὶ φόβον, ἔπειτα
διατάξας καὶ διαρμοσάμενος τὴν φάλαγγα
συγκεχυμένην ἐξήγαγε ῥαδίως καὶ κατέστησεν
ἐναντίαν τοῖς πολεμίοις, ὥστ' ἀπελθεῖν ἐκείνους
μεταβαλομένους. Ἄγιδος δὲ τοῦ βασιλέως
ἐν Ἀρκαδίᾳ τοῖς πολεμίοις ἐπάγοντος ἤδη
τὸ στράτευμα συντεταγμένον εἰς μάχην, τῶν
πρεσβυτέρων τις Σπαρτιατῶν ἐπεβόησεν, ὅτι
διανοεῖται κακὸν κακῷ ἰᾶσθαι, δηλῶν τῆς ἐξ
Ἄργους ἐπαιτίου ἀναχωρήσεως τὴν παροῦσαν
ἄκαιρον προθυμίαν ἀνάληψιν βουλομένην εἶναι,
ὡς ὁ Θουκυδίδης φησίν· ὁ δ' Ἆγις ἀκούσας
ἐπείσθη καὶ ἀνεχώρησε. Μενεκράτει δὲ καὶ
δίφρος ἔκειτο καθ' ἡμέραν παρὰ ταῖς θύραις τοῦ
ἀρχείου, καὶ πολλάκις ἀνιστάμενοι πρὸς αὐτὸν οἱ
Ἔφοροι διεπυνθάνοντο καὶ συνεβουλεύοντο περὶ

Thessaly while serving neither as general nor elected leader. When the actual generals had led the army into a difficult position and were in disorder, for the enemy was pressing them and hurling weapons, they recalled Epaminondas from among the troops. First, he encouraged the army and so put a stop to its distress and fear. Then, having reordered and rearranged the battle formation, which had become jumbled, he easily led it out and confronted the enemy, so that they turned and marched away. And when King Agis had led his army against the enemy in Arcadia and had arrayed it for battle, one of the elder Spartan citizens called out to him, saying that he was intending to cure one evil with another. Thus, he showed Agis that his present ill-timed enthusiasm was a hopeful attempt to make amends for his blameworthy retreat

τῶν μεγίστων. ἐδόκει γὰρ ἔμφρων ἀνὴρ εἶναι καὶ
συνετὸς ἱστορεῖσθαι· διὸ καὶ παντάπασιν ἤδη
τὴν τοῦ σώματος ἐξημαυρωμένος δύναμιν καὶ τὰ
πολλὰ κλινήρης διημερεύων, μεταπεμπομένων
εἰς ἀγορὰν τῶν Ἐφόρων, ὥρμησε μὲν ἐξαναστὰς
βαδίζειν, μόλις δὲ καὶ χαλεπῶς προερχόμενος,
εἶτα παιδαρίοις ἐντυχὼν καθ᾽ ὁδόν, ἠρώτησεν,
εἴ τι γινώσκουσιν ἀναγκαιότερον ὂν τοῦ
πείθεσθαι δεσπότῃ· τῶν δὲ φησάντων "τὸ μὴ
δύνασθαι," τοῦτο τῆς ὑπουργίας λογισάμενος
πέρας ἀνέστρεψεν οἴκαδε. δεῖ γὰρ μὴ
προαπολείπειν τὴν προθυμίαν τῆς δυνάμεως,
ἐγκαταλειφθεῖσαν δὲ μὴ βιάζεσθαι. καὶ μὴν Γαΐῳ
Λαιλίῳ Σκιπίων ἐχρῆτο συμβούλῳ στρατηγῶν
ἀεὶ καὶ πολιτευόμενος, ὥστε καὶ λέγειν ἐνίους
ὑποκριτὴν τῶν πράξεων Σκιπίωνα ποιητὴν δὲ
τὸν Γάιον εἶναι. Κικέρων δ᾽ αὐτὸς ὁμολογεῖ τὰ
κάλλιστα καὶ μέγιστα τῶν συμβουλευμάτων, οἷς
ὥρθωσεν ὑπατεύων τὴν πατρίδα, μετὰ Ποπλίου
Νιγιδίου τοῦ φιλοσόφου συνθεῖναι.

from Argos. When Agis heard the elder, he obeyed and withdrew his army.[56] And every day the ephors used to reserve a chair near the doors of the town hall for Menecrates. They would often get up and go out to him, to ask him questions and get his advice on the most important matters, for they found him wise and intelligent whenever they consulted him. And once, after he had lost his physical strength entirely and was spending his days for the most part bedridden, the ephors summoned him to the marketplace. He arose and started to walk, barely and with great difficulty making his way forward. Along the way to the town hall, he met some young boys and asked them if they knew of anything that imposed a greater obligation than obeying one's master, to which they answered, "The inability to obey." Menecrates reasoned,

28. Οὕτω διὰ πολλῶν τρόπων τῆς πολιτείας οὐδὲν ἀποκωλύει τοὺς γέροντας ὠφελεῖν τὸ κοινὸν ἀπὸ τῶν βελτίστων, λόγου καὶ γνώμης

then, that he had reached the limit of his useful service, and he returned home. Our willingness to obey, therefore, should not give out before our ability, but once our willingness has been abandoned by our ability, we should not force ourselves to serve. Indeed, Scipio Aemilianus employed Gaius Laelius as his advisor whenever he was on campaign or holding office, so that some even claim that Scipio was an actor and Laelius had written his script. And Cicero himself confesses that the finest and greatest of his recommendations to the senate, by which he set the state aright while he was consul, were devised in cooperation with the philosopher Publius Nigidius.

28. Thus, through many forms of political activity, there is nothing that prevents older people from benefiting the public by means

καὶ παρρησίας καὶ φροντίδος πινυτῆς, ὡς δὴ
ποιηταὶ λέγουσιν. οὐ γὰρ αἱ χεῖρες ἡμῶν οὐδ᾽
οἱ πόδες, οὐδ᾽ ἡ τοῦ σώματος ῥώμη κτῆμα καὶ
μέρος ἐστὶ τῆς πόλεως μόνον, ἀλλὰ πρῶτον ἡ
ψυχὴ καὶ τὰ τῆς ψυχῆς κάλλη, δικαιοσύνη καὶ
σωφροσύνη καὶ φρόνησις· ὧν ὀψὲ καὶ βραδέως
τὸ οἰκεῖον ἀπολαμβανόντων, ἄτοπόν ἐστι
τὴν μὲν οἰκίαν καὶ τὸν ἀγρὸν ἀπολαύειν καὶ
τὰ λοιπὰ χρήματα καὶ κτήματα, κοινῇ δὲ τῇ
πατρίδι καὶ τοῖς πολίταις μηκέτι χρησίμους
εἶναι διὰ τὸν χρόνον, οὐ τοσοῦτον τῶν
ὑπηρετικῶν παραιρούμενον δυνάμεων, ὅσον
ταῖς ἡγεμονικαῖς καὶ πολιτικαῖς προστίθησι.

of their gifts: speech, judgment, frankness, and "wisdom of the mind," as the poets say. For not only does our city lay claim to our hands, feet, and bodily vigor, but above all it possesses our souls and the beauty that our souls contain, namely justice, self-control, and practical wisdom. These qualities develop late and slowly, and so it makes no sense that they should benefit our houses, fields, and other property and possessions, but no longer be of service to our country and fellow citizens merely on account of our age. For advanced age does not deprive us of the ability to serve so much as it augments our ability to lead and to practice politics.

IMPORTANT PERSONS AND TERMS

Unless indicated otherwise, all dates are BCE. An asterisk next to a name indicates that Plutarch included the person's full biography in the *Parallel Lives*.

aedile A Roman elected official responsible for the maintenance of the city, the stability of the grain supply, and the sponsorship of games and festivals. Less prestigious than other elected positions in Rome, this office was typically held early in a person's political career.

*Agesilaus King of Sparta (c. 445–359). He came to the throne with the support of Lysander and led military campaigns against both Persians and Greeks. His reign coincided with the decline of Sparta's military dominance of Greece.

*Alcibiades** Athenian politician (451–404). As an example in Plutarch's essays, he is known for being politically talented but reckless. Twice in his career he was forced out of Athens and took refuge with the Persians or in Sparta, both enemies of his native city.

*Alexander the Great** King of Macedon (356–323). He ascended the throne upon the death of his father Philip and subsequently led a combined Macedonian and Greek army into Asia to attack the Persian Empire. His conquest of Persia led to a fundamental realignment of power in the Greek world and beyond.

Amphictyonic Council A board that managed a religious sanctuary. The most famous council managed the oracle of Apollo at Delphi and included members from many Greek cities.

Antigonus   Macedonian noble and general under both Philip and Alexander (c. 382–301). He governed Phrygia in Asia Minor for Alexander, after whose death he fought against other former generals to gain control over a larger territory. He died in battle at an advanced age.

Areopagus   A prestigious council at Athens comprised of politicians who had been elected to the office of *archon*. It may have begun as an advisory body to kings and later to elected leaders, similar to the Roman senate. For most of its existence it was responsible for conducting trials, especially for cases of homicide.

*****Aristides**   Athenian politician (fifth century). He had a reputation for being just and was often represented as the chief political rival of Themistocles. Banished as a result of political fighting but soon recalled, he took a leading role in the second Persian War (480–479).

Arrhidaeus Son of Philip and half-brother of Alexander the Great (c. 357–317). He was proclaimed king upon Alexander's death but served mainly as a pawn for more powerful leaders. Alexander's mother, Olympias, had him murdered.

Augustus Gaius Julius Caesar Octavianus (63 BCE—14 CE). As the adopted son of Julius Caesar, he is referred to simply as Caesar in Plutarch's essays. To differentiate him from Julius, historians call him Octavian or Augustus, the title he assumed in 27 BCE when he became in essence the first Roman emperor.

Boeotia A region in central Greece, of which Thebes was the leading city.

Caesar Originally the family name of Julius Caesar, it came to be the general term for the Roman emperor.

*Cato the Elder Marcus Porcius Cato, Roman politician (234–149). Known for his rigid promotion of traditional Roman values and his strict self-discipline, he opposed the adoption of Greek customs, which he viewed as soft and morally corrupting. He is known as "the Censor" for the aggressive enforcement of his beliefs while holding that office, and as "the Elder" to distinguish him from his great-grandson of the same name.

*Cato the Younger Marcus Porcius Cato, Roman politician (95–46). Great-grandson of Cato the Elder, he was similarly known for his self-discipline and high moral standards. During the Roman civil war of the 40s, Cato opposed Julius Caesar and stood with the senate. He died by suicide while governor of Utica in North Africa.

censor A Roman elected official charged with conducting the official census in cooperation with a colleague. Censors were also charged with reviewing behavior and could exclude a citizen from political life on moral grounds.

Chabrias Athenian soldier and general (c. 420–357). Known for his invention of military tactics, he also served under foreign leaders, including Agesilaus of Sparta while on a campaign in Egypt.

*Cimon Athenian politician (fifth century). Often represented as the chief rival of Pericles during a period marked by heated factional fighting, in the course of which he was banished. His political enemies accused him of sympathizing with Sparta, having an incestuous relationship with his sister, and excessive drinking and sleeping.

Cleisthenes Athenian politician (late sixth and early fifth century). He played a role in ejecting the tyrants who were governing Athens during much of the sixth century. Many Athenians equated his political reforms with the foundation of the democracy at Athens.

Cleon Athenian politician (fifth century). Known as a demagogue, he became an example of earning political power through popular and aggressive policies, rather than stable political or military leadership.

consul The highest elected office in the Roman Republic. Consuls were elected in pairs and served for one year.

Demosthenes **Demosthenes** Athenian orator and politician (384–322). He was a gifted speaker who took a leading role in Athenian government, especially foreign policy. His most famous set of orations, the *Philippics*, were written in opposition to Philip of Macedon's increasing influence in Greek affairs.

dictator A formal but irregularly filled and temporary office of the Roman Republic. A dictator would be elected or appointed during a time of crisis and charged with fulfilling a particular task.

Diogenes Cynic philosopher (c. 412–c. 321). Originally from Sinope in Asia Minor, he spent most of his adult life in Athens and Corinth. He is typically represented as flouting conventions of society and living with a minimum of material possessions.

Dionysius The name of two tyrants, father and son, of Syracuse. Dionysius I ruled 405–367 and passed control to Dionysius II, who was forced from the city in 344 and lived the remainder of his life in Corinth.

Epaminondas Theban general (died 362). Under his leadership the Thebans achieved their greatest military victories, defeating Sparta at the battle of Leuctra (371) and invading Spartan territory in the years that followed. Though he led the Thebans to victory at the battle of Mantinea, he died in the fighting.

ephors These Spartan magistrates were five in total, each of whom was elected from among the citizens and held office for one year. Together with the kings, the ephors formed the executive element of the Spartan government, the other elements being the *gerousia* (council of elders) and the citizen assembly.

Epimenides Legendary holy man from Crete. As a boy he is said to have fallen asleep in a cave and awoken fifty-seven years later. He is also said to have been summoned to Athens to purify the city from a plague.

Euripides Athenian writer of tragedy (c. 480—c. 406). He wrote nearly ninety plays, eighteen of which survive. Plutarch quotes from both extant and non-extant works.

*Fabius Maximus Quintus Fabius Maximus Verrucosus, Roman politician (third century). He held the consulship five times and was dictator twice. During the Second Punic War (218–201) when the Carthaginians brought the war to Italy, he followed a strategy of non-engagement, which earned him the epithet "the Delayer."

Hannibal Carthaginian general (247–182). Acknowledged in ancient times as an excellent military leader, he led Carthage's invasion of Italy during the Second Punic War, but he was eventually defeated by the Romans at Zama in Africa.

Hesiod Greek epic poet (c. 700). His two major works are the *Theogony*, the story of the generations of the gods, and *Works and Days*, an instructional poem that argues for ethical behavior and respect for the gods.

Homer Greek epic poet (eighth century). Two of the poems attributed to Homer, the *Iliad* and the *Odyssey*, were the most widely read and highly regarded literary works of antiquity.

Lacedaemon   Another name for the Greek city of Sparta.

Laelius   Gaius Laelius, Roman politician and intellectual (c. 190–c. 129). A close associate of Scipio Aemilianus, he held the consulship among other offices and served with Scipio on campaign in Africa. He promoted the dissemination of Greek philosophy in Rome.

***Lucullus**   Lucius Licinius Lucullus, Roman politician (died 56). Following his consulship in 74, he led the campaign against Mithridates, king of Pontus. Replaced in this command by Pompey the Great, he returned to Rome to live a quiet life, for which he was accused of neglecting his civic duty and luxurious living.

***Lycurgus**   Spartan lawgiver. This legendary figure was credited in antiquity with establishing Sparta's laws and strict educational system.

*Lysander Spartan general (died 395). He was responsible for the final Spartan victory in the Peloponnesian War. When Agesilaus was contending for the Spartan throne, Lysander supported him and secured his ascent, though later Agesilaus found him controlling and sought to diminish his influence.

*Marius Gaius Marius, Roman politician (c. 157–86). Having worked his way up the ladder of Republican offices, Marius eventually attained the consulship, which he held seven times. After great military success in Numidia and Gaul, he became involved in civil conflict with the supporters of Sulla.

Masinissa King of Numidia (238–148). At times both an ally and an enemy of

Rome, he was known as a skilled warrior who remained in power well into old age. Plutarch refers to him as Libyan, which was the general designation for North Africa.

Menander   Athenian writer of comedies (c. 344–292). He wrote in the style called "new comedy," which is comparable to the modern situation comedy. His plays influenced the Roman comic writers Plautus and Terence.

military tribune   A junior officer attached to a Roman army.

Nestor   A character in both the *Iliad* and *Odyssey*, he was king of Pylos and famed for being older and wiser than the other leaders who took part in the Trojan War.

*Nicias   Athenian politician (c. 470–413). A moderate politician who was frequently at odds with other leaders, he led the campaign in Sicily against his will. He died amidst the Athenians' defeat.

Pammenes Theban general (fourth century). Guardian of Philip when the future king of Macedon lived in Thebes as a hostage, he was a successful military leader, first under the direction of Epaminondas, then in his own right.

Panaetius Stoic philosopher (c. 185–109). A native of Rhodes, he joined the entourage of Scipio Aemilianus in Rome.

Peloponnese The southern region of Greece, which before the ascent of the Roman Empire was dominated by Sparta.

Peloponnesian War The major war of the Greek classical period between alliances led by Athens and Sparta. Fought with varying levels of intensity between 431 and 404, it culminated with the surrender of Athens.

*__Pericles__ Athenian politician (c. 495–429).
Plutarch presents him as a persuasive
orator and a powerful statesman. He was
largely responsible for the building program that created Athens' most famous
monuments, such as the Parthenon. He
died of plague in the second year of the
Peloponnesian War.

__Philip__ King of Macedon (382–336). Responsible for establishing Macedonian
dominance over Greek affairs, he defeated the united Greek cities at Chaeronea (338) and formed an alliance, which
he intended to lead in a campaign against
the Persian Empire. He died by assassination, after which his son Alexander
ascended the throne.

*__Philopoemen__ Greek general (c. 253–182).
From the city of Megalopolis, he served in
the confederacy of Greek cities that broke

Spartan dominance in the Peloponnese and opposed the imposition of Roman control.

***Phocion** Athenian politician (402–318). Elected general forty-five times over his long career, he was a respected political and military leader known as "the Good." He supported Macedonian control over Athens, however, and this led him into conflict with supporters of democracy. He died after being condemned to drink poison.

Pindar Greek lyric poet (c. 518 – c. 446). His most famous compositions are odes commissioned by victors in the Pan-Hellenic games; that is, in the games at Olympia, Delphi (called the Pythian games), Nemea, and Isthmia (on the isthmus of Corinth).

Plato Athenian philosopher (c. 429–347). Plato's philosophy, in its so-called middle form, was the basis for Plutarch's own philosophical ideas. In the political essays, Plutarch draws in particular on the Platonic notion of "the good," which is the true essence of beauty or goodness, and which for the politician represents the highest standard of moral excellence.

Polybius Greek historian (c. 200 – c. 118). His father was an associate of Philopoemen in the resistance to Roman control over southern Greece. Polybius was eventually taken to Rome as a political hostage, where he became friends with Scipio Aemilianus. He wrote a biography of Philopoemen (now lost) and a history of Roman expansion, much of which survives.

*Pompey the Great Gnaeus Pompeius Magnus, Roman general and politician

(106–48). Having come to prominence in support of Sulla, he went on to hold the consulship three times and to experience extraordinary military success in Europe, Africa, and Asia. He became leader of the senate's resistance to Julius Caesar in the civil war of the 40s, but he died by assassination in Egypt after suffering defeat at the Battle of Pharsalus.

proconsul A Roman official who was granted the power of a consul over a specified geographical area, typically in the capacity of governor.

pythia The priestess of Apollo at Delphi who spoke the oracles believed to have come from the god. Apollo himself was referred to as the Pythian god, and the athletic contests held at Delphi were known as the Pythian Games.

quaestor The lowest of the elected offices in the Roman Republic. Several quaestors were elected each year (the number varied over the history of the Republic) and were responsible for accounting at the treasury and other administrative duties.

Scipio Aemilianus Publius Cornelius Scipio Aemilianus Africanus, Roman politician (185–129). Natural son of Lucius Aemilius Paullus, he was the grandson by adoption of Scipio Africanus, who defeated Hannibal to end the Second Punic War. Scipio Aemilianus had a long and illustrious military career, including the defeat of Carthage in the Third Punic War (146). His intellectual pursuits brought him into contact with both Romans, such as Gaius Laelius, and Greeks, such as Polybius.

Simonides Greek lyric poet (c. 556—c. 466). Simonides wrote poetry in a wide variety of genres. His best-known works are short elegies and epigrams about historical events.

*Solon Athenian politician (late seventh—early sixth century). Famed as a lawgiver, Solon reformed Athens' political system during a crisis caused by the unmanageable debt burdens taken on by small landowners. He was also a poet who wrote about his reforms, among other topics. Many of his poems survive.

sophist A teacher of rhetoric, grammar, and other subjects.

Sophocles Athenian writer of tragedy (died 406). He famously lived a very long life and wrote more than 120 plays, seven of which survive. Plutarch quotes from both extant and non-extant works.

*Sulla Lucius Cornelius Sulla, Roman politician (c. 138–78). Sulla came to prominence while serving under Marius in Africa. When Marius and his supporters later denied him a prestigious military command, he marched his army against Rome to assert his right. Later he used his army to defeat his political opponents and, as dictator, reformed many Republican institutions.

*Themistocles Athenian politician (c. 524–459). He played a leading role in the Greek victory in the Second Persian War (480–479), especially at the Battle of Salamis. Later he worked to reassert Athenian power, through the rebuilding of the city's walls among other actions. He is traditionally represented as the political rival of Aristides.

IMPORTANT PERSONS AND TERMS

Theopompus King of Sparta (c. 720–675). He is sometimes credited with constitutional reforms, including the establishment of the ephors.

Thucydides Athenian politician and historian (c. 460—c. 400). As a general during the Peloponnesian War, he lost an important battle to the Spartans in 424, after which he was banished from Athens. He wrote the history of the war, from the beginning (including the prelude to war) down to the year 411.

tribune of the plebs An elected office in the Roman Republic charged with representing the interests of the people. A board of ten was elected on an annual basis.

Xenophon Athenian soldier and author (born c. 430). Though raised in Athens, his most famous military adventure was as a mercenary in Persia, which is the subject of his book *Anabasis*. He fell out of favor with Athens when he fought with Sparta at the Battle of Coronea (394) and later settled in Spartan territory. He wrote books in a wide variety of genres, including history, philosophy, and the novel.

NOTES

TO AN UNEDUCATED LEADER

1. Plutarch is quoting from a lost tragedy by Euripides.
2. Plutarch is referring to bronze statues, which were cast over a clay core. Part or all of this core often remained inside the finished statue.
3. For the kings of Persia, Ahuramazda was the god of justice and their patron deity. The Greeks equated him with their Zeus.
4. From a lost tragedy of unknown title by Euripides.
5. Plutarch names three famous sculptors: Phidias created large-scale statues of Athena at Athens and Zeus at Olympia; Polyclitus of Argos created the *Doryphorus*, or Spearbearer; Myron of Eleutherae created the *Discobolus*, or Discus Thrower.
6. Excerpted from Homer, *Odyssey* 19.109, 111.

7. Cleitus was one of Alexander's officers. While both men were drunk at a celebration, Cleitus criticized Alexander for disrespecting Macedonians and favoring Persians. Enraged, Alexander killed him.

8. Zeus as king of the gods stands as a model for kings in general. Anaxarchus argues that Justice and Right do a king's bidding.

9. *Works and Days* 256.

10. Homer, *Iliad* 10.183–184.

11. After the victory of Julius Caesar's forces at the Battle of Thapsus, near Utica, Cato committed suicide rather than allow himself to be captured and then pardoned by Caesar.

12. In his *Life of Aratus* (26), Plutarch tells the same anecdote about Aristippus, who was tyrant of Argos during the third century BCE. He even adds the detail that Aristippus slept "in a state of agitation and fear" despite having secured the door to his upper room. Perhaps Plutarch intended to write Aristippus here for Aristodemus, who is otherwise unknown.

13. The contrast between the philosophically educated, benevolent king and the self-serving tyrant

was a commonplace of Greek political thought. The most famous exposition is Plato's argument in the *Republic* for the philosopher-king as the ideal ruler.

14. The notion of the pedestal is inspired by the famous passage in Plato's *Phaedrus* (253d–254e), where Plato compares the human soul to a chariot pulled by two horses. The charioteer represents Reason, while the horses are the Spirit, which responds to commands from Reason, and the Appetites, which are very hard to control. Plato writes that when the charioteer sees someone who is beautiful, he desires not that particular instance of beauty but instead is reminded of "the real essence of beauty," which he then observes "standing alongside self-control upon a holy pedestal."

15. From *Laws* (716a), where Plato is suggesting that the deity is the beginning and the end of all things.

16. Plutarch is referring again to the Platonic notion of an absolute beauty, which is in its essence beautiful, rather than merely possessing a beautiful appearance. Following Plato, Plutarch is conceiving of beauty in ethical terms and so I have translated

Plutarch's phrase "the most beautiful of things" as "the absolute standard of goodness."

17. Specifically, the *sarissa*, an especially long Macedonian spear.

18. Homer, *Iliad* 19.242.

19. In this third example, Plutarch brings the discussion back to the problem of political leadership, since confiscation of property was a penalty imposed upon criminals, and one which might be abused by a tyrannical leader.

20. Plutarch's comparison between sight and hearing is based on the theory of extramission, which held that seeing occurs when a ray of light emitted from the eye encounters an external object.

21. Plutarch is probably referring to Scipio Aemilianus, whom he uses as an example several times in his political essays.

HOW TO BE A GOOD LEADER

1. Homer, *Iliad* 9.55–56. Homer regularly refers to the Greeks as Achaeans.

2. Homer, *Iliad* 9.443.

3. Plutarch is quoting lines from an unknown poem. The Greek text is uncertain and the meaning obscure.

4. The speaker's platform, from which politicians addressed the citizen-assembly, was viewed by Plutarch as the focus of political life.

5. When Tiberius Gracchus was tribune of the plebs in Rome (133 BCE), his popular legislation led to conflict with the senate and eventually to his death by mob violence. His brother Gaius later carried on his program (also as tribune of the plebs 123–122 BCE), pursuing an even more aggressive agenda. When he failed to enact his full program and lost political office, he resorted to armed conflict and was killed.

6. As in his essay *To an Uneducated Leader*, Plutarch makes "absolute goodness" the basis of wise political leadership.

7. According to Plutarch's *Lives* of Cleon and Alcibiades, the Athenians in fact tolerated these antics.

8. After winning an important victory against the Spartans, Epaminondas was attacked in court back home in Thebes by rivals jealous of his success.

9. Miltiades was often given credit for winning the Battle of Marathon, where the Athenians defeated the Persians in 490 BCE. Plutarch's point is that Themistocles vowed not to rest until he had done something equally significant.

10. Considered by the Romans to be a gesture that undermined a man's masculinity.

11. The talent was a large sum of money.

12. Homer, *Iliad* 9.441.

13. Hesiod, *Theogony* 80. Calliope, whose name means "beautiful-voiced," was the muse of epic poetry.

14. Thucydides 2.65.

15. Not Thucydides the historian, but like Cimon and Ephialtes, a politician contemporary with Pericles.

16. Pericles promoted a policy of non-engagement at the outbreak of the Peloponnesian War, which ensured that Athens did not suffer a military defeat. Following his death just after the war started, other politicians pursued a more aggressive and expansionist policy, including the ill-fated campaign in Sicily.

17. Aristophanes, *Knights* 137. The Cycloborus was a loud, rushing river near Athens.

18. Pindar, *Olympian* 6.4.
19. Adapted from Homer, *Odyssey* 10.495.
20. Since the consuls in Rome were elected annually and typically could not run for reelection, Afranius had to wait only one year for the next election cycle, when Pompey's preferred candidates would not be running.
21. Plutarch returns again to his theme that the best politician is a lover of absolute goodness.
22. That is, Sulla was showing young Pompey the respect typically reserved for more senior men.
23. The "Eagle and the Wren" is presumably one of Aesop's fables but is unknown except for this reference.
24. Plato, *Laws* 762e.
25. This verse appears twice in the comedies of Aristophanes, *Wasps* 1033 and *Peace* 756.
26. Probably a reference to Cato the Younger, whom Plutarch pairs with Phocion in one book of his *Parallel Lives*.
27. All three men were considered enemies of Rome and were killed in battle or executed.
28. Homer, *Iliad* 17.171.
29. Homer, *Iliad* 7.358.

30. As a person of means, Antisthenes would normally have had a servant do his shopping.
31. That is, the festivals at Olympia, Delphi, Nemea, and the Isthmus of Corinth.
32. A mix of boxing and wrestling.
33. We would say "suit up," but the Greeks competed naked in athletic contests, and so they stripped for action.
34. The so-called sacred anchor was the largest of a ship's several anchors and was held in reserve, to be used only in extreme circumstances. Proverbially, to cast the sacred anchor meant to exercise one's last hope in a difficult situation.
35. Sophocles, *Women of Trachis* 1058.
36. Menemachus, the addressee of this essay, was likely a citizen of Sardis, which in ancient times was the capital of the independent kingdom of Lydia and dominated many Greek cities.
37. In the Greek theater, the actors' lines were written in various poetic meters.
38. For a year following the Peloponnesian War, the democracy at Athens was replaced by thirty tyrants who ruled jointly and persecuted their

political opponents. When the democracy was restored, an amnesty was declared for those who had supported the tyrants' government.

39. Athens was supporting the city of Miletus (in modern Turkey) when it was captured by the Persians in 494 BCE. Phrynichus produced his play soon after, and the Athenians fined him for reminding them of such a troubling event.

40. Alexander destroyed Thebes in 335 BCE, after it revolted against Macedonian control. Cassander, who ruled in Macedonia following Alexander's death, rebuilt the citadel in 316 BCE.

41. Harpalus was Alexander's treasurer. After misspending funds, he took refuge in Athens (in 324 BCE), where he was arrested but later escaped, raising the suspicion that some Athenians had accepted bribes from him.

42. Augustus captured Alexandria in Egypt in 30 BCE, during his war with Mark Antony. Arius Didymus of Alexandria was a philosopher who became his adviser.

43. This refers to the Roman practice of greeting powerful people at their houses in the hope of receiving political and other favors.

44. Plutarch is adapting Euripides, *Phoenician Women* 524–525.

45. In many Greek cities, citizens were divided into political units called tribes.

46. Adapted from Homer, *Iliad* 17.156–158.

47. Scipio Aemilianus and Lucius Mummius both served as censor in 142 BCE.

48. When Diomedes is sent to spy on the Trojans (Homer, *Iliad* 10.227–253), he selects as his partner Odysseus, who is known for the agility of his mind, and passes over other Greek heroes who were great fighters like himself.

49. Geryon was a mythological giant who possessed a triple body.

50. In the myth of Jason and the Golden Fleece, Hercules is left behind and so Jason and his men, the Argonauts, lack the physical strength necessary to steal the fleece. Medea, a witch and the daughter of the king who possesses the fleece, falls in love with Jason and uses her magical powers to help him accomplish his mission.

51. Homer, *Odyssey* 5.350.

52. Plato, *Republic* 416e.

53. Two famous statues. Plutarch is returning to a point he made in *To an Uneducated Leader*.
54. Two gulfs on the coast of Libya were named Syrtis.
55. Plutarch's point is that honors should not be awarded too early in a politician's career for doing well in minor offices.
56. Athletes who competed in sporting events sponsored by religious sites in Greece won crowns.

SHOULD AN OLD MAN ENGAGE IN POLITICS?

1. That is, people look for an excuse not to compete.
2. In an ancient board game similar to checkers, there was a set of pieces called sacred, and these pieces would be moved last. To make the sacred move, which meant to do something last, was proverbial in Plutarch's day.
3. As Plutarch conceives of the soul, the practical and divine elements were more beneficial than the emotions and the physical impulses and could lead to an enlightened way of living, but they were also harder to develop and preserve.

4. In his history of the Peloponnesian War, Thucydides reports the oration spoken by Pericles to memorialize the fallen Athenian soldiers after the first year of the war (2.35–46). That speech includes the statement quoted here.

5. From Euripides's play *Phoenician Women* (1688). Antigone asks this question of her father Oedipus after he has blinded himself and so become powerless as a leader. Oedipus answers, "He has been destroyed."

6. Here Plutarch refers to learning through on the job training in politics, a theme that he addresses more fully below and in the essay *How to Be a Good Leader*.

7. Alcibiades and Pytheas were Athenian politicians known for being active and influential while still relatively young.

8. That is, the Peloponnesian War against Sparta.

9. This passage comes from Xenophon's encomium of the Spartan king (*Agesilaus* 11.15).

10. *Oedipus at Colonus* 668–673. Sophocles wrote this play near the end of his life; it was produced posthumously by his grandson.

11. Plutarch continues the comparison between actors, who competed in performances at religious festivals, and politicians, who compete in public service. There was a religious component to public life, which allows Plutarch to consider the politicians' work sacred.

12. The *Paralus* was a state vessel used by the Athenians for official business. Demosthenes wrote a speech against his political opponent Meidias for assaulting him during a festival.

13. As punishment for killing a man unjustly, Zeus sentenced Hercules to spend one year as a slave to Omphale, Queen of Lydia. Plutarch here describes life in her court as luxurious and soft, in contrast to the more focused and hard life that Hercules had lived while performing his twelve labors. One of those labors was to kill the Nemean lion, and afterward Hercules wore the lion's skin as a sign of his triumph. The *aulos*, an ancient wind instrument often compared to the oboe, is also a symbol of softness: the Athenians thought that its music relaxed self-control, and for this reason Plato banned it from his Republic.

NOTES

14. Plutarch here refers to the three basic appetites for food, drink, and sex (that is, Aphrodite) which humans experience because our souls exist in physical bodies. He often contrasts those appetites with Reason, which in a philosophically trained person gains control over them.
15. As one method of bathing, the Greeks would apply oil to their bodies and then scrape them clean.
16. At *Phaedrus* 246b, Plato introduces the charioteer that drives a pair of winged horses as a metaphor for the human soul. Euripides mentions golden wings attached to the back of one of his characters in a lost play.
17. Plutarch refers to the ship believed to have been used by the mythological Athenian king Theseus when he sailed to Crete to kill the Minotaur. The Athenians are said to have used it for sacred voyages to the island of Delos, and to have preserved it into the fourth century BCE by constantly replacing rotted wood. "The Ship of Theseus" has become a philosophical problem about identity: how much wood can

be replaced before the ship is no longer the same one that belonged to Theseus?

18. Plutarch is quoting a fragment from a poem of Pindar. Aglaea is one of the Graces.

19. The things listed here are all responsibilities performed by civic leaders.

20. That is, after sailing through rough seas, not taking advantage of the calm seas.

21. That is, in a public space, like the modern café.

22. The fathers of Achilles and Odysseus.

23. Plutarch is quoting from a lost play by Sophocles.

24. Euripides, *Orestes* 258.

25. The joke seems to be that the old man, because he lived alone, was depending on his neighbors for help, and so his getting married will relieve them of the burden. But the saying may also imply that an old man's wedding becomes a source of amusement for his neighbors.

26. That is, the Epicureans. Plutarch wrote essays critical of Epicurean doctrine, including what he called their "apolitical life."

27. Homer, *Iliad* 8.453.

28. Homer, *Iliad* 19.165.

29. Homer, *Iliad* 2.53.
30. Plutarch actually writes *gerousia*, or "council of old men," the Greek equivalent of the Latin *senatus*, which is derived from the word *senex*, or "old man."
31. A *geras* ("gift of honor") would normally be granted by a king.
32. That is, Agamemnon, leader of the Greeks at Troy. The quotation that follows is from Homer, *Iliad* 2.372.
33. From the lost play *Antiope* by Euripides.
34. All these men were noted for the longevity of their careers.
35. Elsewhere Plutarch criticizes men who marry only for the sake of acquiring a dowry or producing children and then dissolve the marriage once it has served its purpose.
36. The sons of Tyndareus were Castor and Polydeuces (or Pollux), also known as the Dioscuri. They were thought to be present in the glowing light that is caused by electrical discharge and appears in the rigging of ships during thunderstorms. Now known as St. Elmo's fire, to the

ancients this light was a sign of divine protection and the end of rough weather.

37. The raging god is Dionysus, god of wine, and the sober god is Poseidon, god of the sea, or in this case, water.

38. In his treatise on politics, Aristotle famously claimed that human beings are by nature political animals (*Politics* 1253a).

39. Plutarch relates this anecdote in his *Life of Phocion* (24), with the added remark that the idea of men up to sixty years old being led into war by an eighty-year-old general cooled the Athenians' enthusiasm for battle. Plutarch's point here is that the elderly Phocion was still holding the generalship, but that he relied on wisdom rather than physical strength to lead the city.

40. Attalus II was king of Pergamum in Asia Minor. The Philopoemen mentioned here was one of his court officials, not the Greek general that Plutarch uses as an example elsewhere in this essay.

41. In Rome, a freedman was a former slave, who often remained in service after being granted freedom.

42. A character in Greek myth, Tithonus was granted the gift of immortality but not agelessness, and so he lived forever but nonetheless grew old.
43. Homer, *Iliad* 16.9.
44. Plutarch served as a priest of Pythian Apollo at Delphi. The Pythiad was the four-year interval between festivals at Delphi, as the Olympiad was the four-year interval at Olympia.
45. Greeks would sing to the accompaniment of the lyre, and so the idea is that an older person who can no longer reach the high notes will set the high-pitched lyre aside.
46. Euripides, *Hercules* 268–269.
47. Homer, *Iliad* 22.71.
48. Euripides, *Bacchae* 66.
49. Plutarch refers again to the *geras* ("gift of honor") that he claimed was etymologically related to *gerontes* ("old men") in section 10.
50. Homer, *Iliad* 9.55–57. In this part of the story, the Greek army is being pressed by the Trojans and the Greek leader, Agamemnon, proposes retreat. Diomedes responds with a rousing call to fight on. In the quotation, Nestor compliments

Diomedes but says, in a polite way, that his courageous enthusiasm has not solved the problem. As Plutarch's readers would have remembered, Nestor goes on to say, "But come, I, who claim to be older than you, will declare and explain everything."

51. This Timotheus was a lyre player and poet, while the Timotheus mentioned above was an Athenian general.

52. Homer, *Iliad* 9.443.

53. Lawgivers, such as Lycurgus in Sparta or Solon in Athens, were held in especially high regard, and the laws and customs attributed to them were sometimes treated with the authority of a constitution in a modern state.

54. Literally, "walking around" and by extension, to "walk and conduct discourse." The Greek verb is *peripatein*, which gives us the adjective "peripatetic," a common epithet of Aristotle's school of philosophy.

55. The popular assembly would sometimes meet in a city's theater.

56. During the Peloponnesian War, the Spartans criticized their king Agis for not subduing the

city of Argos and threatened to raze his house and fine him unless he produced some major success to compensate. Agis's attempt to avoid punishment was the impetus for his rash military action in Arcadia.